BOUTROS BOUTROS-GHALI

SECRETARY-GENERAL OF THE UNITED NATIONS

CONFRONTING
NEW
CHALLENGES

1995

REPORT ON THE WORK OF THE ORGANIZATION
FROM THE FORTY-NINTH TO THE FIFTIETH SESSION
OF THE GENERAL ASSEMBLY

D0911752

UNITED NATIONS · NEW YORK, 1995

96-41

Department of Public Information

Office of Conference and Support Services
Department of Administration and Management

Published by the United Nations
Department of Public Information
New York, NY 10017

United Nations Sales No. E.95.I.47
ISBN 92-1-100595-7
Litho in United Nations, New York

CONTENTS

FIGURES

TABLES

I. Introduction

F EW EVENTS in recent history have generated as much *1*
confidence in the future and such high hopes for a better
world as the fall of the Berlin Wall some five years ago,
symbolizing as it did the end of the cold war. The spectre of
global nuclear cataclysm, which has haunted humanity since
the dawn of the nuclear age, has receded, and in its place has
emerged the promise of an era of international peace freeing the
energies of nations to work together towards economic and
social progress for the whole of humankind.

At the time, there was a widespread belief that when no *2*
longer fuelled by military assistance provided by rival major
Powers, the many regional conflicts flaring in different parts of
the world could be quickly extinguished. The global economy
was expected to derive significant benefit from a huge "peace
dividend" accruing as a result of the abandonment of the costly
arms race. It was hoped that an important share of those resources would be invested in poor countries starved of capital
and skills and thus help to accelerate economic growth and
development worldwide.

Sadly, the record of world affairs over the past few years *3*
has largely belied those optimistic expectations. Many old conflicts continue to defy the efforts of the international community to bring about a settlement and new wars have continued to
erupt, almost all of them within States. Most disappointingly,
the total volume of assistance to developing countries has
not only failed to show growth but has, in fact, declined.

The fiftieth anniversary of the United Nations is therefore *4*
not only a time to review the Organization's first half century
and prepare it for its second: it is also an occasion to address

ways to regain the momentum in world affairs that appeared so dramatically at the outset of this decade.

5   In the same manner as my first three annual reports to the General Assembly, my fourth report endeavours to place in focus the efforts of the Organization to respond effectively to the multitude of new demands and problems resulting from the dramatic changes engendered by the end of the cold war. Those efforts relate both to the long-term goals embodied in the Charter of the United Nations — now apparently more accessible as a result of the sea change in international relations — and to the immediate tasks arising from the outbreak of new conflicts in different parts of the world and the resulting increase in demand for the Organization's preventive, peacemaking, peace-keeping and peace-building services.

6   Addressing the implications for the Organization of the massive increase in the number and complexity of peace-keeping operations, and their profoundly changed nature, I pointed, in my previous annual report, to the widespread misperception of the United Nations as an organization dedicated primarily to peace-keeping. I underscored that, in the midst of its efforts to contain and resolve immediate conflicts by peace-keeping and other means, the United Nations remained determined to pay more attention to the foundations of peace, not least those lying in the realm of economic and social development.

7   During the past year acute armed conflicts have continued to place heavy demands on the Organization's financial and human resources and to dominate public perception of the United Nations role and effectiveness. The problems presented by conflicts such as those in the former Yugoslavia, Afghanistan, Liberia, Rwanda, Burundi and Somalia are in many ways unprecedented. More often than not the mandates and resources provided to the Organization to deal with them have proved to be inadequate to address effectively the complex

tasks at hand. When journeying into uncharted territory with less-than-adequate means, set-backs are unavoidable. But these must not be allowed to become a source of disillusionment or to overshadow the successes that, notwithstanding formidable challenges, have been achieved by peace operations in various parts of the world, from Cambodia to Mozambique to El Salvador to Angola. Nor must adversity be allowed to weaken our resolve to carry forward efforts to save human lives and prevent larger conflicts, for which the United Nations remains an irreplaceable instrument. On the contrary, the set-backs suffered in the quest for peace and security must reinforce our determination to take the hard decisions required and seek continuously to develop improved approaches as a means of enhancing our capacity and effectiveness. With these objectives in mind, I issued, in January 1995, a Supplement to "An Agenda for Peace" (A/50/60-S/1995/1), which has been the subject of a presidential statement in the Security Council and is now being studied by the General Assembly. The experience of the past several months has given added force to the recommendations in the Supplement.

While the issues before the international community in   *8* this regard require careful and urgent attention, it is also extremely important that the difficulties encountered in peace-keeping operations, significant and disturbing as they may be, should not divert attention from other dimensions of the work of the Organization, which, though less visible, are equally essential and serve to lay the economic and social foundation for lasting peace.

In the domain of economic and social development, as in   *9* the area of peace-keeping, the international context within which the United Nations operates and the challenges that it faces have greatly changed. In the economic and social fields, as in the political, many areas of great concern remain where the United Nations has not, as yet, proved equal to the challenge. The situation of the least developed countries and of many parts of Africa remains critical. At the same time, the effort of the United Nations in support of development is vast and rich with distinct accomplishments. As such, it deserves better recognition and enhanced political and public support.

10   At both the practical and the conceptual levels, the period covered by the present report has been marked by notable advances in the Organization's capacity to guide the response of the international community to global change and to the new forms of economic and social problems facing the world.

11   I attach great importance, in this regard, to the ongoing discussions within the framework of the General Assembly on "An Agenda for Development". The first report on the subject, which I presented to the Assembly in May 1994 (A/48/935), was followed by hearings and submissions by a variety of sources and was then drawn upon in a large number of statements made during the general debate at the forty-ninth session of the General Assembly. In that light, I submitted to the Assembly, in November 1994, a set of recommendations aimed at giving practical force to the emerging consensus on the priorities and dimensions of development (A/49/665). Such consensus is being further advanced through the working group that is preparing the further consideration of the matter at the fiftieth session of the General Assembly.

12   In the same context, I have been particularly encouraged by the support that the role of the United Nations in the economic and social fields and the current work on the elaboration of "An Agenda for Development" have received at the annual summit meeting of Heads of State and Government of the seven major industrialized nations. The communiqué issued at Halifax in June 1995 (A/50/254-S/1995/501, annex I) specifically declared the readiness of the Group of Seven to work

with others in order to set out a fresh approach to international cooperation and to define the particular contribution expected of United Nations bodies.

At the same time, the ongoing series of global conferences *13* on key issues of development was carried forward with the World Summit for Social Development, held in March 1995, at Copenhagen. On that occasion a start was made towards combined and effective action across borders to address poverty, unemployment and social disintegration. In Beijing, where the Fourth World Conference on Women will be held this September, the world will act upon the newly achieved recognition that the advancement of women is fundamentally critical to the solution of many of the world's most pressing social, economic and political problems. These conferences will be followed next year by the United Nations Conference on Human Settlements (Habitat II) and the ninth session of the United Nations Conference on Trade and Development (UNCTAD).

A sustained, coordinated follow-up to those conferences, *14* together with a renewed effort in support of African development, has been the main focus of extensive consultations I have held during the year with the heads of the Bretton Woods institutions and the executive heads of the other agencies represented in the Administrative Committee on Coordination. These are covered in the section of the report dealing with the work of the Secretariat, as well as in the chapter of the report dealing with development, humanitarian action and human rights as the foundations of peace, chapter III.

During the period covered by the present report, I have *15* continued to emphasize the essential linkages between the political and development missions of the United Nations and to advance a comprehensive vision of the role of the Organization where the advancement of human rights and democracy are essential elements of both of those missions.

16   In parallel with the efforts to enhance the Organization's capacity in the field of peace and security and to introduce an improved conceptual framework for pursuing the Organization's development mission, reforms in the structures and methods of work of the Organization are gaining momentum.

17   To this end, I have put forward a management plan designed to create a mission-driven and result-oriented organization. In carrying out the plan, the achievement of five objectives is fundamental:

(*a*)   Better management of human resources, together with improvement in staff member capabilities and accomplishments;

(*b*)   Better management of the Organization's programme, from the identification of strategic priorities, through the budgetary process by which resources are allocated to achieve those priorities and finally through a performance measurement system by which programme managers are held accountable for achieving the strategic priorities;

(*c*)   Better information with which to manage, and its timely availability;

(*d*)   Better management of technology and extension of its availability throughout the Organization;

(*e*)   Better management of the Organization's cost structure and an enhanced programme for promoting efficiency and cost-effectiveness.

18   Reforming the United Nations into a simpler, more focused and more integrated organization, capable of pursuing the different aspects of its mission in a mutually reinforcing way and in the most efficient manner possible, has continued to be a key objective of my efforts during the past year, as it has been since I took office in January 1992. As described in the report, the past 12 months have seen further tangible progress towards streamlining operations, strengthening accountability,

tightening personnel and management standards, and eliminating waste and redundancy. I am, in this context, deeply committed to continuing to reduce the budget further while improving the quality of service to Member States.

In pursuing those efforts, I am keenly aware that Secreta-   *19*
riat reform, to be truly effective, must be part of a larger restructuring effort including the intergovernmental machinery to
adapt the Organization as a whole to the demands of the post-
cold-war era. Such a process requires the determination and full
commitment of all Member States.

A crucial component of that larger reform process should   *20*
be the achievement of a more dynamic relationship among the
main intergovernmental organs — the General Assembly, the
Security Council and the Economic and Social Council. I hope
that the account of developments in the work of those organs in
chapter II of the present report will prove helpful in considering
what adjustments and further improvements can be introduced
in this regard.

Within the realm of activities covered by the Economic and   *21*
Social Council, further steps to ensure more coherent management of operational activities carried out under the aegis of the
various programmes and funds of the United Nations, as well as
improved coordination of the humanitarian activities carried
out by various parts of the Organization, are other essential elements of reform requiring renewed attention at the intergovernmental level.

In the same context, I am firmly convinced that no reform   *22*
effort can succeed without addressing the basic issue of providing the Organization with a more adequate and reliable financial base. This issue is developed in chapter II of the present
report, where I endeavour to highlight the seriousness of the
financial crisis facing the Organization. The difficult financial
situation is compounded by the continuing late payment of

contributions by many Governments. It is increasingly proving to be the most serious obstacle to the effective management of the Organization. I therefore particularly appreciate the serious effort under way in the High-level Open-ended Working Group on the Financial Situation of the Organization, established during the forty-ninth session of the General Assembly, to devise constructive and long-lasting solutions in this crucial area.

23   Two other, related dimensions of the ongoing reform effort need to be highlighted and are given prominence in the present report.

24   One relates to the expansion in the depth and coverage of the assistance provided by the Organization to Member States in the process of democratization. Requests for electoral assistance continue to grow. Beyond this type of assistance, there is a growing demand for United Nations support in preparing the social, as well as institutional, ground in which democracy can take root. I hope that the development of a comprehensive approach to the role of the United Nations in these areas will be further advanced at the fiftieth session of the General Assembly, in the light of the report on the subject I have submitted pursuant to General Assembly resolution 49/30 of 7 December 1994 (A/50/332).

25   The past year has also deepened awareness that the efforts of States to democratize will have an increased likelihood of success when democratization extends to the international arena. The progressive opening of the United Nations to civil society is an important part of this process. Also in this respect, the global conferences held by the United Nations in recent years are making a crucial contribution. By bringing together State as well as non-State actors they are serving to create strong, worldwide issue-based constituencies around key dimensions of development. The democratic nature of this conference series

contributes immensely to the legitimacy and effectiveness of the programmes of action being adopted.

Indeed, the new world environment clearly demands more *26* systematic cooperation between the United Nations and all other actors engaged in promoting political and economic security at all levels, whether they be regional or subregional organizations (progress in cooperation with these entities is covered in chapter IV of the present report), or non-State actors such as citizen groups, grass-roots movements and non-governmental organizations of all types. The strengthening of coordination and cooperation between these actors and the various elements of the United Nations system can serve only to enhance effectiveness in fulfilling the goals of the Charter. It also serves to reinforce democratic principles in world affairs and in the emerging international system.

I have sought in this report to provide a clear and compre- *27* hensive account of the work of the Organization as it helps Member States to make the transition to a new international era. I firmly believe that success in this great task requires nothing less than the full participation of all concerned — not only the United Nations and its Member States, but individuals, the private sector, the academic community and non-governmental, regional and international organizations. It is to inspire the widest reflection upon and assessment of the only world Organization at our disposal, and in accordance with Article 98 of the Charter of the United Nations, that I submit the present annual report.

II. Coordinating a comprehensive strategy

A. ORGANS OF THE UNITED NATIONS

W HILE PURSUING an extremely heavy work schedule, *28*
the organs of the United Nations have consolidated reforms in their work programmes during
this year, allowing for greater gains in efficiency.

1. *General Assembly*

During its forty-ninth session, the General Assembly has con- *29*
tinued to focus on issues related to the maintenance of peace and
security, economic and social development and strengthening
and reform of the United Nations to enhance its ability to fulfil
the goals of the Charter in a world that has changed dramatically
since the Charter was drafted.

By comparison with 20 years ago, there has been a shift of *30*
emphasis. The Assembly now devotes somewhat less attention
than it did then to the main regional conflicts, several of which
have fortunately been resolved during the last decade, and devotes more time to economic and social matters and to a number
of generic questions of primordial importance for the effective
functioning of the Organization, notably a cluster of financial
issues. These arise from the failure of Member States to pay
their assessed contributions in full and on time and from the
enormous expansion in the cost of peace-keeping, which has
risen from about $626 million per annum in 1986 to about
$3.6 billion in 1995.

The Organization now faces a very serious financial situ- *31*
ation. In a statement to the Assembly on 12 October 1994, I
drew attention to this, emphasizing that it had become an urgent
political question. I was gratified by the Assembly's subsequent

decision to establish a high-level working group and to entrust to it the consideration of additional measures to ensure a sound and viable financial basis for the Organization. That working group has worked intensively during 1995. I addressed it on 22 June and sought its urgent assistance in averting a serious financial crisis. In parallel, the Assembly established another working group of experts on the principle of capacity to pay.

32   An index of the severity of the current problems is that the Organization as at January 1995 owed some $850 million to Governments who have contributed troops and equipment to peace-keeping operations. This debt represents an involuntary loan to the Organization by Member States who have in addition accepted the risk of exposing their young men and women to the perils of peace-keeping. This is manifestly unjust.

33   Another index is the number of Member States whose arrears exceed the contributions due for the last two years and who are therefore, under Article 19 of the Charter, unable to vote in the General Assembly. As at mid-August, they numbered 17, nearly 10 per cent of the membership. A number of other Member States have indicated to the President of the Assembly that they are not able to meet their obligations under Article 17 and will therefore also soon lose their right to vote.

34   As regards the financing of peace-keeping, the General Assembly reaffirmed at its forty-ninth session that the costs of peace-keeping are the collective responsibility of all Member States in accordance with Article 17 of the Charter. The Assembly also adopted procedures to strengthen the administrative and budgetary aspects of peace-keeping, including the establishment of a financial year for each peace-keeping operation starting on 1 July and a request to the Secretary-General to submit twice a year, for the Assembly's information, a table summarizing the proposed budgetary requirements of each operation.

Development continued to receive special attention from   *35*
the General Assembly, emphasizing that the importance of this
aspect of the Organization's activities should not be overshad-
owed by the intense public interest in its peace-keeping activities. The holding of three important United Nations conferences during a period of 12 months (on population and
development in Cairo in September 1994, on social development in Copenhagen in March 1995 and on women in Beijing in
September 1995) was evidence of the importance that Member
States attach to the Organization's role in the economic and
social fields.

On 6 May 1994, I published "An Agenda for Develop-   *36*
ment" (A/48/935). In response the General Assembly established an ad hoc open-ended working group to elaborate further
an action-oriented, comprehensive agenda that would take into
account reports and recommendations presented by the Secretary-
General, the work of the Economic and Social Council, views
expressed in the Assembly itself and a number of other views
and proposals.

The question of enlargement of the Security Council at-   *37*
tracted intense interest throughout the period under review, as a
possible means of making more efficient and democratic the
work of the Organization in the field of peace and security. In
September 1994 the General Assembly reviewed the progress
report of the Open-ended Working Group on the Question of
Equitable Representation on and Increase in the Membership of
the Security Council and other matters related to the Security
Council, and decided that the Working Group should continue
its work and submit a report before the end of the forty-ninth
session. The Working Group has held 21 meetings and a number of informal consultations and has addressed two clusters of
issues, the first covering the size and composition of the Council, including permanent, non-permanent and new categories of

membership, and the second the Council's working methods and procedures, its efficiency and effectiveness, and its relationship with other United Nations organs.

38   The Assembly has increasingly adopted the informal, open-ended working group as an effective instrument in seeking solutions to major problems relating to the efficient working of the Organization. These bodies, each comprising the entire membership, have been instrumental in allowing a concentrated and issue-specific exchange of views on Security Council reform, "An Agenda for Peace", "An Agenda for Development", the financial situation of the United Nations and, most recently, the strengthening of the United Nations system. The activities of these working groups, their interrelated mandates, the depth and complexity of their deliberations and the frequency of their meetings pose a challenge to the capacity of the Secretariat to provide the required substantive and technical support from within already scarce resources.

39   The agenda for the forty-ninth session comprised 164 items, a reduction from 180 items in the previous session (see fig. 1). This results from the consolidation of related items and the decision to discuss some of them only every second or third year. Further rationalization seems possible. Broadly worded agenda items allow flexibility to examine several topics or aspects of a question under a single item. Areas where this possibility could be explored are disarmament (18 items on the agenda of the forty-ninth session), cooperation between the United Nations and intergovernmental organizations (5), decolonization (5) and the financing of peace-keeping operations (19). There are also 10 items that have not been considered at all for several years.

40   An issue closely related to the number of items on the agenda is the number and periodicity of reports requested by the Assembly. In addition to the reports of principal organs and

FIGURE 1

**General Assembly resolutions
and agenda items, 1989-1995**

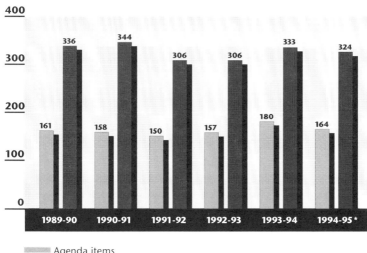

Agenda items
Resolutions
* As at 10 August 1995

their subsidiary bodies, over 200 reports of the Secretary-General were issued at the forty-ninth session, not including several reports of special rapporteurs and of the Office of Internal Oversight Services. The difficulties and expense involved in producing so many reports in a timely manner are evident, given the frequency with which the Assembly and other principal and subsidiary organs now meet. Streamlining and cost-cutting efforts cannot ultimately succeed unless the number of reports requested is significantly reduced.

During the forty-ninth session of the General Assembly, its General Committee and its Main Committees held 377 meetings, as compared with a total of 401 during the forty-eighth session and 426 during the forty-seventh session. The Main Committees held 237 informal meetings and consultations, a   *41*

FIGURE 2

**Participation of Heads of State and Government
in the general debate, 1989-1994**

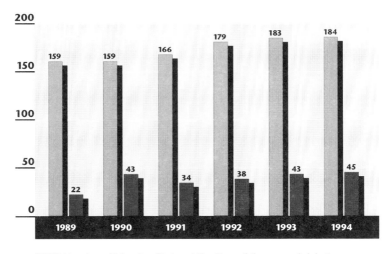

Number of Member States at the time of the general debate
Heads of State and Government

decrease from the 285 held during the forty-eighth session.
Meetings held by working groups increased to 141 from the
previous session's 86. The Assembly has so far adopted 324
resolutions during its forty-ninth session, compared with 333
during the forty-eighth session. Some 79 per cent were adopted
without a vote or by consensus, as compared with 81 per cent at
the previous session. The number of Heads of State and Government who participated in the general debate of the Assembly
rose from 43 (23 per cent) of the membership to 45 (24 per cent)
at the forty-ninth session (see fig. 2).

2.   *Security Council*

42   During the period under review, the Security Council has continued to meet, on an almost daily basis, to review the issues on

its agenda, to warn about the threats to peace around the world, to call on antagonists to restrain their ardour for combat, to take various types of action to control and resolve conflicts, and to muster regional and international support for those measures (see fig. 3). Towards these objectives, the Security Council has demonstrated a determination to unify its ranks in order to address more effectively the various complex issues that confront it today. One of the Council's greatest contributions has been its patient and deliberate search for consensus within its own ranks. This positive trend has enabled Council members to approach the issues on its agenda with a greater degree of harmony and cohesion (see figs. 4 and 5).

FIGURE 3

Security Council:
formal meetings and consultations of the whole,
1988-1995

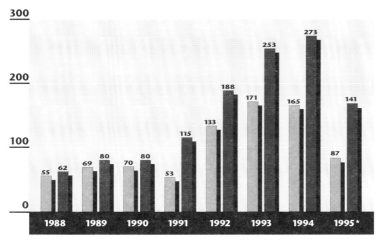

Meetings
Consultations

* As at 17 August 1995

43   The main focus of the Security Council's concern has been the former Yugoslavia and central Africa. In the former Yugoslavia the Council endeavoured to defuse the conflicts, prevent their further spread and mitigate their impact on civilian populations. To that end, it addressed many issues, including the changing peace-keeping role of the United Nations, humanitarian emergencies, mass violations of human rights and the difficult issues arising from the use of United Nations troops to protect humanitarian relief deliveries. The Council also offered active support to efforts by interested Member States, in particular those comprising the Contact Group, as well as the International Conference on the Former Yugoslavia, to bring about negotiated solutions to the conflicts in the region. The Council

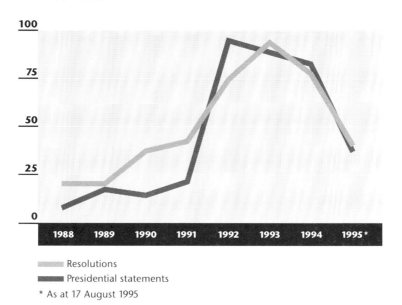

FIGURE 4

**Security Council:
resolutions and presidential statements,
1988-1995**

Resolutions
Presidential statements
* As at 17 August 1995

continued to make active use of mandatory sanctions as a
means of achieving the above purposes. The Council's determination to ensure the resolution of the crises in a comprehensive
way, as well as to strengthen cooperation between the United
Nations and relevant regional organizations, in particular the
European Union (EU) and the North Atlantic Treaty Organization (NATO), still offers the best hope of bringing to an
end the human tragedy in the former Yugoslavia.

At the beginning of the period under review, the Security   *44*
Council had authorized the deployment of six major peace-
keeping operations in Africa, more than in any other continent.

FIGURE 5

**Security Council:
resolutions adopted since 1946**

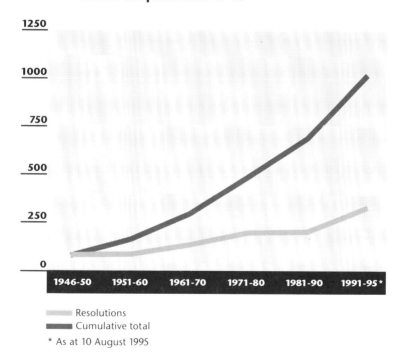

Resolutions
Cumulative total
* As at 10 August 1995

Four of them remain, the one in Mozambique having completed its mandate with conspicuous success and the one in Somalia having been withdrawn after it had succeeded in its humanitarian efforts but had been denied the necessary cooperation of the Somali parties with efforts to promote national reconciliation. In addition to the four remaining peace-keeping operations, in Angola, Liberia, Rwanda and Western Sahara, the Council has been concerned with peace-making efforts in other African countries, especially Burundi and Sierra Leone. During the period under review the Council dispatched an unprecedented number of missions, all of them to African destinations: Burundi (twice), Mozambique, Rwanda, Somalia and Western Sahara. The conflicts in Africa, like those in the former Yugoslavia, are primarily internal, but they have major implications for the security of the subregions concerned. As in the former Yugoslavia, they have disastrous humanitarian consequences, and the Council has had to devote as much attention to alleviating the misery of the civilian populations affected as to efforts to control and resolve the conflicts. Cooperation with the Organization of African Unity (OAU) and with subregional organizations in Africa has been an important feature of the Security Council's efforts.

45   Seven sanctions regimes remain in effect and generate much work for the Council. In order to ensure the adequate servicing of the various sanctions committees and the expeditious processing by the Secretariat of applications for humanitarian supplies, I have reinforced the unit responsible in the Department of Political Affairs. For their part, the sanctions committees, drawing on their own experience, have initiated measures to streamline their working procedures and to ensure greater transparency in the conduct of their work in conformity with a set of measures decided by the Security Council (see S/1995/234).

Cooperation on sanctions with regional organizations has *46* been important, with special reference to the contributions of the Organization of American States (OAS) in Haiti and of EU and the Organization for Security and Cooperation in Europe (OSCE) in the former Yugoslavia. The temporary assignment of liaison officers from the EU/OSCE Sanctions Assistance Missions Communications Centre has provided the Secretariat and the relevant committees with customs expertise and with advice on the practical implementation and monitoring of sanctions. Member States could further assist the efforts of the committees and the Secretariat by screening more effectively their nationals' applications to the committees and by cooperating in further streamlining of the committees' procedures.

In order to ensure that sanctions remain a credible instru- *47* ment for promoting international peace and security, Member States will need to address a range of problems encountered in the implementation of sanctions. Recommendations in this regard were put forward in my Supplement to "An Agenda for Peace" (A/50/60-S/1995/1).

The Security Council's methods of work received consid- *48* eration during an extensive debate on the annual report of the Council to the General Assembly at its forty-ninth session. Member States exchanged views on a broad range of issues related to the functioning of the Council. The Council made known its intention, as part of its efforts to improve the flow of information and the exchange of ideas between members of the Council and other Member States, to have increased recourse to open meetings, in particular at an early stage in its consideration of a subject, on a case-by-case basis. The Council has already initiated the holding of orientation debates. Briefings by the President of the Security Council for States non-members of the Council have become institutionalized.

49   In the face of persisting conflict in Africa, Europe and elsewhere, the Security Council has demonstrated that it remains committed to the goals of strengthening peaceful and cooperative relations between Member States and helping communities within States to live peacefully with one another, to rebuild and to work towards stable and productive societies.

50   It must be emphasized, however, that only if the decisions of the Security Council enjoy the full support of the international community, and only if the parties to the conflict carry out those decisions in full, can the Council fulfil its responsibilities under the Charter to maintain and consolidate international peace and security.

3.   *Economic and Social Council*

51   The Economic and Social Council held its substantive session from 26 June to 28 July 1995 in Geneva. The Council's high-level segment dealt with one of the most pressing issues on the international agenda: the development of Africa. A spirit of partnership prevailed during the debate in the Council and conclusions were reached on conflict prevention and resolution, natural disasters, external debt, resource flows, trade, capacity-building, agriculture and food security, and other areas. The segment was attended by a large number of ministers and other high-level representatives. One day was devoted to a policy dialogue with Mr. Michel Camdessus, Executive Director of the International Monetary Fund (IMF), Mr. James Wolfensohn, President of the World Bank, Mr. Renato Ruggiero, Director-General of the World Trade Organization, and Mr. Carlos Fortin, Officer-in-Charge of UNCTAD, on major issues in the world economy.

52   The Council's coordination segment addressed the coordinated follow-up and implementation of the results of major recent international conferences in the economic, social and

related fields. The agreed conclusions envisage the integrated consideration by the General Assembly of themes common to those conferences with a view to promoting better coherence and integrated policy guidance. This may involve measures to improve the coherence of the work of the relevant Main Committees of the Assembly. The Council, for its part, decided to carry out an annual review of cross-cutting themes common to major international conferences and to take action to ensure the necessary coordination of agendas and work programmes of the functional commissions involved in the follow-up to the various international conferences. Attention was also given to measures for the strengthening of inter-agency coordination at the regional and country levels, and to the role of the resident coordinators in facilitating national reporting on progress achieved in the follow-up to global conferences. The Council invited the Administrative Committee on Coordination to bring system-wide coordination issues to the attention of the Council and to make recommendations thereon. Implementation of the agreed conclusions will enhance complementarity and coherence between the Council and the General Assembly, including their subsidiary bodies, as well as interaction between the United Nations and the Bretton Woods institutions and the World Trade Organization. The complementary steps initiated by the Administrative Committee on Coordination to pursue conference agendas within a common framework will promote unity of purpose and action in the United Nations system as a whole.

The operational activities segment began to exercise its 53 new mandate to provide policy guidance to the United Nations funds and programmes. The guidance provided covers priorities in budget allocations, improved coherence in country programmes and improved cost-effectiveness of administrative services, including the possible use of common administrative services at the field level. The Council reaffirmed the need to increase substantially the availability of resources allocated to operational activities for development on a predictable, continuous and assured basis commensurate with the needs of developing countries.

54   In line with these conclusions and in accordance with General Assembly resolution 47/199 of 22 December 1992, I will submit to the Assembly a range of specific recommendations, in the context of the triennial comprehensive policy review of operational activities, on further steps to strengthen the role of the Economic and Social Council in this field and on important subjects such as improved substantive operational coordination at the country level, increasing the predictability and levels of resources, strengthening the resident coordinator system and a variety of programme tools such as the country strategy note, the programme approach and national execution.

55   The Council initiated a review of arrangements for consultations with non-governmental organizations. By its resolution 1993/80, the Council established the Open-ended Working Group on the Review of Arrangements for Consultations with Non-Governmental Organizations. A primary objective is to update and introduce coherence in the rules governing the participation of non-governmental organizations in international conferences convened by the United Nations. The Council requested the Working Group to examine ways and means of improving practical arrangements for the work of the Committee on Non-Governmental Organizations and the Non-Governmental Organizations Unit of the Secretariat.

56   The Working Group held its first substantive session from 20 to 24 June 1994. An inter-sessional meeting took place on 7 and 8 November 1994. Its second substantive session was held from 8 to 12, 26 and 31 May 1995. At its substantive session, the Economic and Social Council approved the recom-

mendation of the Working Group that its mandate be extended for one year and that its final report be presented to the Council at its substantive session of 1996.

In accordance with Economic and Social Council resolu- 57 tion 1994/24, a Committee of Co-Sponsoring Organizations was constituted by the heads of the six co-sponsors of the joint programme on HIV/AIDS (the United Nations Children's Fund (UNICEF), the United Nations Development Programme (UNDP), the United Nations Population Fund (UNFPA), the United Nations Educational, Scientific and Cultural Organization (UNESCO), the World Health Organization (WHO) and the World Bank), known as UNAIDS. As the United Nations system's main advocate for the global response to the HIV/AIDS epidemic, UNAIDS has three mutually reinforcing roles: to provide globally relevant policy on HIV/AIDS and promote international best practice and research; to provide technical support for an expanded response to HIV/AIDS, particularly in developing countries; and to advocate a comprehensive, multisectoral response to HIV/AIDS, well-resourced and strategically, ethically and technically sound.

At its second meeting, on 12 December 1994, the Commit- 58 tee of Co-Sponsoring Organizations unanimously recommended Dr. Peter Piot as director of the UNAIDS programme and the Secretary-General appointed Dr. Piot as Executive Director for a period of three years starting on 1 January 1995. On 5 May, the Economic and Social Council decided on the regional distribution of seats for 22 Member States to be represented on the Programme Coordinating Board of UNAIDS. It decided that each of the six co-sponsoring organizations, as well as five nongovernmental organizations, would participate in the work of the Board. The Board held its first meeting on 13 and 14 July at Geneva.

59   The Commission for Social Development began its consideration of arrangements for the follow-up to the World Summit for Social Development's Copenhagen Declaration on Social Development and Programme of Action at its 34th session, held in New York from 10 to 20 April 1995. The Economic and Social Council concluded that the scope and methods of work of the Commission should be adapted to enable it to play a more effective role in promoting an integrated approach to social development in the aftermath of the World Summit. It decided that the Commission should hold a special session in 1996 to review from this perspective its mandate, terms of reference and scope of work, elaborate a multi-year programme of work and make recommendations to the Council on the frequency of the Commission's meetings.

60   During its session the Commission also heard the first report of Mr. Bengt Lindqvist, the Special Rapporteur on the Monitoring of the Standard Rules for the Equalization of Opportunities for Persons with Disabilities. The Commission also started preparations for the International Year of Older Persons, to be observed in 1999, and advanced the preparations of a world programme of action for youth, to be adopted by the General Assembly during its fiftieth session.

61   The Commission on Sustainable Development held its third session, including its high-level segment, in New York from 11 to 28 April 1995. More than 40 ministers attended, holding portfolios such as the environment, forestry, agriculture, tourism, development and finance. Fifty-five Governments submitted national reports on their activities in support of sustainable development by the twenty-first century. The session included panel discussions between senior officials from Governments, international financial institutions, United Nations agencies and programmes, the business community and non-governmental organizations. Two days were dedicated to the sharing of national experiences in implementing Agenda 21, adopted by the United Nations Conference on Environment and Development in June 1992, and a "Day of Local Authorities" examined grass-roots efforts to achieve sustainable development. These initiatives received welcome support from the large number of non-governmental organizations attending the session, who see in the Commission a transparent and participatory mechanism for addressing sustainable development concerns, including those at the national and community levels. The Commission agreed to establish an intergovernmental panel to formulate by 1997 coordinated proposals for action with regard to the management, conservation and sustainable development of all types of forest. The Commission also endorsed work programmes on consumption and production patterns, the elaboration of sustainable development indicators and the transfer of environmentally sound technology.

The concluding high-level segment (26-28 April) of the Commission addressed challenges on the path towards the full implementation of Agenda 21. The Chairman's summary noted that the insufficiency of the financial resources available to support national efforts, particularly in developing countries and economies in transition, remains a continuing constraint to achieving sustainable development. *62*

The Committee on New and Renewable Sources of Energy and on Energy for Development, a subsidiary expert body of the Economic and Social Council, held a special session on rural development from 6 to 17 February. It proposed a strategy that would include development of national sustainable energy action programmes for agricultural and rural development; priority for rural energy development; capacity-building in rural energy development; new directions in management and institutional arrangements; new financial and investment arrangements; accelerated development and implementation of *63* new technologies; new international actions for rural energy development; and strengthening of sustainable energy activities within the United Nations system. The Commission on Sustainable Development agreed at its April 1995 session to encourage Governments to integrate renewable forms of energy into their national strategies for sustainable and rural development. It urged Governments to support efforts of interested developing countries towards the sustainable use of an appropriate mix of fossil and renewable sources of energy for rural communities.

64   The Fourth World Conference on Women: Action for Equality, Development and Peace is intended to coalesce reflection about the advancement of women and propose new directions into the twenty-first century. During the autumn of 1994 regional preparatory meetings were held in four regions, a number of expert group meetings on specific themes were organized and informal consultations were held with Member States on the draft of the platform for action. From 16 March to 7 April, the Commission on the Status of Women, acting as preparatory committee for the Conference, met and continued negotiations on the platform for action. Subsequent to the session, the focus shifted to promoting participation by Governments and non-governmental organizations in the Conference, ensuring public information about it and supporting the intergovernmental negotiation process. From 31 July to 4 August, informal consultations were convened by the chairperson of the Commission to continue negotiations. The Conference preparations have involved the largest number of non-governmental organizations ever accredited for a United Nations conference and a major effort has been made to facilitate their participation in the process.

65   The Division for the Advancement of Women completed, as conference documents, two major studies, one entitled

"Women in a Changing Global Economy: The 1994 World Survey on the Role of Women in Development", and the second a review and appraisal of the Nairobi Forward-looking Strategies for the Advancement of Women. In-depth studies of women and education and training, women in international decision-making and women in economic decision-making were also completed. Steps have been taken to ensure that the relevant human rights mechanisms of the United Nations regularly address violations of the rights of women, including gender-specific abuses, through provision of gender-based information to treaty bodies, work on the development of an optional protocol to the Convention on the Elimination of All Forms of Discrimination against Women and work on guidelines for integrating gender into human rights monitoring.

66 The issue of how best to ensure advancement of women in the work of the Secretariat and the United Nations system as a whole is one of the major areas central to the Conference and its follow-up. The institutional mechanisms for this are being reviewed internally and by Governments of Member States.

4. *Trusteeship Council*

67 In 1994, with the termination of the Trusteeship Agreement for the last Trust Territory of the Pacific Islands and Palau's admission as the 185th Member of the United Nations, the Trusteeship Council completed the task entrusted to it under the Charter with respect to the 11 Territories that had been placed under the Trusteeship System. The other 10, the majority of them in Africa and the Pacific, had already attained independence, either as separate States or by joining neighbouring States. The Trusteeship Council thereupon amended its rules of procedure and will in future meet only as and where occasion may require.

68 In a letter dated 2 June 1995 addressed to me (A/50/142), the Permanent Representative of Malta requested, on behalf of his Government, that the General Assembly include an item entitled "Review of the role of the Trusteeship Council" in the provisional agenda of its fiftieth session. The Government of Malta would like the Assembly to consider transforming the Council's role so that, in addition to its role under the Charter, the Council would hold in trust for humanity its common heritage and common concerns.

69   In my 1994 annual report on the work of the Organization, I recommended that the General Assembly proceed with steps to eliminate the organ, in accordance with Article 108 of the Charter. I regret that no decision to abolish the Trusteeship Council has been taken.

5. *International Court of Justice*

70   The International Court of Justice at The Hague is the principal judicial organ of the United Nations and, as such, holds important responsibilities in the settlement of disputes of a legal nature.

71   In 1994-1995, the Court continued to have a record number of 13 cases before it. Eleven were contentious cases in which the parties were States from different parts of the world. Two were requests for an advisory opinion, one submitted by the World Health Organization (WHO) and the other by the General Assembly.

72   In the period under review, judgments have been given in two cases, in one of which hearings were held. In a third case, hearings have been postponed. In other cases a great number of pleadings have been filed within the prescribed time-limits. One contentious case and one request for an advisory opinion were brought before the Court.

73   The hearings in the case concerning the *Aerial Incident of 3 July 1988 (Islamic Republic of Iran v. United States of America)*, scheduled to take place in September, were postponed *sine die* at the joint request of the two parties.

Written comments were filed by several States by 20 June 74
1995, the time-limit fixed by the President of the Court by an
Order of 20 June 1994 on written statements submitted in connection with the request by WHO for an advisory opinion on
the *Legality of the Use by a State of Nuclear Weapons in Armed
Conflict*. The written proceedings are thus closed.

In December 1994, the General Assembly laid before the 75
Court a request for an advisory opinion on the *Legality of the
Threat or Use of Nuclear Weapons*. In February 1995, an Order
was made fixing two time-limits, one within which written
statements relating to the question might be submitted to the
Court by States entitled to appear before the Court and by the
United Nations, and one within which States and organizations
having presented written statements might present written
comments on the other written statements. Written statements
have been filed by a number of States. Written comments are
expected by 20 September 1995.

Public sittings for the purpose of hearing oral statements or 76
comments will open on 30 October 1995. These oral proceedings will cover the requests for advisory opinion submitted
by WHO and the General Assembly.

As each of the parties in the case concerning the *Gabčíkovo-* 77
Nagymaros Project (Hungary/Slovakia) had filed a counter-
memorial within the prescribed time-limit of December 1994,
the President of the Court, also in December, made an Order
fixing the time-limit for the filing of a reply by each of the parties. Each party having filed its reply within the prescribed
time-limit, the written proceedings are now closed.

In the case concerning *Maritime Delimitation and Territo-* 78
rial Questions between Qatar and Bahrain (Qatar v. Bahrain),
the Court, in July 1994, had delivered a judgment in which it
found that the exchange of letters of December 1987 between
the King of Saudi Arabia and the Amirs of Qatar and Bahrain,

and the minutes signed at Doha on 25 December 1990, were international agreements creating rights and obligations for the parties, and that, by the terms of those agreements, the parties had undertaken to submit to it the whole of the dispute. The Court fixed 30 November 1994 as the time-limit within which the parties were jointly or separately to take action to that end and reserved any other matters for subsequent decision.

79   In February 1995, the Court delivered a judgment by which it found that it had jurisdiction to adjudicate upon the dispute between Qatar and Bahrain that had been submitted to it; that it was seized of the whole of the dispute; and that the application of Qatar as formulated on 30 November 1994 was admissible. In April the Court issued an Order fixing a time-limit for the filing by each of the parties of a memorial on the merits.

80   Hearings in the case concerning *East Timor (Portugal v. Australia)* were held in January and February 1995. On 30 June, the Court delivered its judgment, by which it found that it could not, in the absence of the consent of Indonesia, adjudicate upon the dispute referred to it by Portugal concerning a treaty of December 1989 between Australia and Indonesia on exploitation of the continental shelf of the so-called "Timor Gap".

81   In the case concerning *Application of the Convention on the Prevention and Punishment of the Crime of Genocide (Bosnia and Herzegovina v. Yugoslavia (Serbia and Montenegro))*, the President of the Court, in March, made an Order extending the time-limit for the filing of the counter-memorial of Yugoslavia (Serbia and Montenegro). Yugoslavia (Serbia and Montenegro) filed preliminary objections in June 1995 relating to admissibility and jurisdiction. In July 1995, the President of the Court made an Order fixing the time-limit for the filing by Bosnia and Herzegovina of observations on the preliminary objections, proceedings on the merits having been suspended by operation of the Rules of Court.

In the cases concerning *Questions of Interpretation and*   82
Application of the 1971 Montreal Convention arising from the
Aerial Incident at Lockerbie (Libyan Arab Jamahiriya v. *United*
Kingdom) and *Questions of Interpretation and Application of*
the 1971 Montreal Convention arising from the Aerial Incident
at Lockerbie (Libyan Arab Jamahiriya v. *United States of Amer-*
ica), the respondent States filed preliminary objections to the
jurisdiction of the Court on 16 and 20 June respectively.

On 28 March 1995, Spain instituted proceedings against   83
Canada with respect to a dispute relating to the Canadian
Coastal Fisheries Protection Act, as amended on 12 May 1994,
and to the rules of application of that Act, as well as to certain
measures taken on the basis of that legislation, more particularly the boarding on the high seas, on 9 March, of a fishing
boat, the *Estai,* sailing under the Spanish flag. Taking into account the agreement concerning the procedure reached between the parties at a meeting with the President of the Court,
held on 27 April, the President, by an Order of 2 May, decided
that the written proceedings should first be addressed to the
question of the jurisdiction of the Court to entertain the dispute
and fixed time-limits for the filing of the memorial of Spain and
the counter-memorial of Canada.

By a letter dated 9 August, the Government of New   84
Zealand gave the Court formal advance notice of its intention to
bring France before the Court in connection with the French
nuclear testing in the South Pacific.

Because of the new cases mentioned above, the Court's docket   85
has remained well-filled. Besides the cases referred to, the following were on the Court's list during the period under review:

(*a*)   *Maritime Delimitation between Guinea-Bissau and*
Senegal (Guinea-Bissau v. Senegal);

(*b*)   *Oil Platforms (Islamic Republic of Iran v. United*
States of America);

(*c*)   *Land and Maritime Boundary between Cameroon and Nigeria (Cameroon v. Nigeria).*

86   Following the death, on 28 September 1994, of Mr. Nikolai K. Tarassov (Russian Federation), Mr. Vladlen S. Vereshchetin (Russian Federation) was elected to fill the resulting vacancy on 26 January 1995. The vacancy created by the death, on 24 February, of Mr. Roberto Ago (Italy) was filled by the election, on 21 June, of Mr. Luigi Ferrari Bravo (Italy). The vacancy created by the resignation, as at 10 July, of Sir Robert Yewdall Jennings (United Kingdom of Great Britain and Northern Ireland) was filled by the election, on 12 July, of Mrs. Rosalyn Higgins (United Kingdom of Great Britain and Northern Ireland).

6.   *Secretariat*

87   The purpose of my management plan is to create a mission-driven and result-oriented Organization, with specific goals of enhanced performance, better productivity and increased cost-effectiveness. The foundation of the management plan is the new system of accountability and responsibility that I have established. The system is designed to create a new management culture, assisting and supporting programme managers in achieving the strategic objectives of the Organization and in executing legislative mandates. In effect, the new system of accountability and responsibility empowers managers with the freedom to manage — streamlining administrative procedures, introducing considerable decentralization and delegation, allowing greater flexibility in the management of resources and encouraging greater innovation and initiative.

88   The first of the five major objectives is better management of human resources, together with improvement in staff capabilities and accomplishments. An entirely new strategy for human resources was introduced in the Organization and

subsequently endorsed by the General Assembly at its forty-ninth session. The implementation of the system will modernize and reform the management of human resources. Among the components of this new system is a new work planning and performance appraisal system, which is based on staff/management-agreed work outputs and performance measurements.

The strategy is based on the need to access the continuously changing and evolving role of the Organization and the requirement to respond progressively to changing needs with a breadth and depth of skills. The strategy involves a concerted effort to provide career training that meets changing staff needs. There is also the need, as a management tool, for active implementation of an attrition programme. An early separation programme for staff at various levels in both the Professional and General Service categories will contribute to an adaptable staff with a varied skills mix, leading to greater effectiveness and efficiency in the context of constantly changing demands on the Secretariat. Lastly, a total remake of the adjudication process has begun, replacing litigation of staff/management issues with an informal dispute-reconciliation process or timely and time-saving arbitral disposition.   *89*

Vigorous efforts are being made by the Office of Human Resources Management to integrate goals and targets for improvement in the status of women into the overall strategy. The adoption of a proactive, more people-centred human resource strategy has been conducive to achieving this goal. The percentage of women in posts subject to geographical distribution is continually rising and at the end of July 1995 stood at 33.6 per cent, up from 32.6 per cent at the end of June 1994. During the same period 51.42 per cent of all promotions were those of women.   *90*

91   The second objective is better management of the Organization's programme from the identification of strategic priorities, through the budgetary process by which resources are allocated to achieve those priorities and through a performance measurement system by which programme managers are held accountable for achieving the strategic priorities. Clearer lines of responsibility and greater managerial accountability characterize the new format for the medium-term plan, the Organization's basic strategic document. The new format of the medium-term plan provides for clearly defined objectives and emphasizes full congruence between the identified programmes and the departments responsible for their implementation. The process of managerial responsibility and accountability has been considerably tightened through improved linkage between programmes, budgets and performance measurement. Financial congruence has been achieved at each step in planning and execution. Member States will now be able to tell what is to be done, who is responsible for doing it and what is accomplished.

92   Third is better information with which to manage and its timely availability. Work continued in 1994 and 1995 on the development of the Integrated Management Information System (IMIS), which aims at modernizing and enhancing the internal flow and use of management information in such areas as human resources, finance, accounts and procurement. The IMIS project represents an ambitious effort to make good, through one massive effort, 30 years of neglect in upgrading existing electronic data-processing systems. The system is a revolutionary step towards the electronic integration of all of the offices of the Organization performing administrative tasks regardless of location. The first two releases of the system, the human resource components, were fully and successfully implemented at Headquarters. The other releases — accounts, finance and procure-

ment — will be gradually phased in during the next year, with the whole system operational worldwide by the end of 1997.

Fourth is management of technology and extension of its   *93* availability throughout the Organization. Technology, with its potential for improved services and greater cost-effectiveness, will also facilitate the role of Conference Services. Technological advances in communication and networking, text-processing, desktop publishing, translation and document tracking have provided savings. Further expansion of the United Nations telecommunication network will produce additional savings for the United Nations system as a whole. The optical disk system, now being expanded to accommodate increasing user demand, offers easy, high-speed electronic access to United Nations documents. The development of remote translation and text-processing techniques has brought down the cost of holding meetings away from established headquarters by reducing the staff required on-site. As a result, the number of staff who travelled to the Cairo Conference was significantly reduced from that of previous conferences, and no translators will be going to the Beijing Conference.

The fifth objective is better management of the Organiza-   *94* tion's cost structure and an enhanced programme for cost-effectiveness. The budget process is being used to drive the Organization to a higher level of efficiency. The proposed 1996-1997 programme budget is smaller than the budget for the biennium 1994-1995. The proposals include the abolition of 201 posts, offset in part by the proposed creation of 66 new posts in priority areas of peace-keeping, international and regional cooperation for development, drug control, crime prevention, population, human rights and humanitarian affairs and internal oversight. The aggregate reduced spending will be achieved through more cost-effective ways of implementing mandates, rationalizing work programmes and technological innovations. The proposed reductions were achieved without curtailment of mandated activities. At the same time, efficiency gains of $35 million have been proposed throughout the Secretariat without compromising the quality of programme outputs.

95 Identifying efficiency gains is now a key component of management planning. The first phase of this programme has concentrated on the simplification of existing procedures: redefining work programmes, improving productivity, substituting lower cost alternatives, streamlining staff requirements and reducing overheads.

96 The next phase will concentrate on the elimination of duplication and overlap in programme delivery and the elimination of programmes without a mandate and programmes that do not return adequate value to Member States.

97 An Efficiency Board, chaired by the Under-Secretary-General for Administration and Management, Mr. Joseph Connor, will identify during the next biennium further significant opportunities for cost containment beyond those proposed in the 1996-1997 budget. These will include removing over-regulating procedures in the personnel, finance and purchasing areas, eliminating duplicate efforts between Headquarters and other duty stations, and studying "outsourcing" alternatives.

98 Procedures are being revised for better transparency and fairness of procurement efforts. Some steps already taken, or in the initial phase, include the extension of basic professional procurement training; revised delegation of procurement authority for peace-keeping missions; institution of global system/blanket contracts; review and updating of the vendor roster; and establishment of the office of ombudsman, to which all vendors may address complaints.

99 In its first year of operations, the Office of Internal Oversight Services, headed by Under-Secretary-General Mr. Karl-

Theodor Paschke, has provided the United Nations with oversight coverage, promoting effective and efficient programme
management. The Office also finds and reports on instances of
waste, fraud and mismanagement. I look forward to the findings and conclusions of the first annual report of the Office, to
be submitted to the General Assembly in September 1995.

The Office of Legal Affairs, headed by Mr. Hans Corell,   *100*
has been heavily involved in legal work related to the continued
expansion and diversification of the activities of the Security
Council, ranging from the establishment of a new international
criminal tribunal to establishing new peace-keeping missions
and winding down others.

During the period under review, the Office was involved in   *101*
current operations such as those in Angola, Georgia, Guatemala, Haiti, Mozambique, Rwanda, Somalia, Tajikistan, Western Sahara and the former Yugoslavia. Legal officers from the
Office have served as legal advisers in a number of those operations.

The Office of Legal Affairs is involved in the implementa-   *102*
tion of various aspects of Security Council decisions. It has
assisted in the drafting and interpretation of status-of-forces
agreements and status-of-mission agreements and given advice
to operational departments. The Office has developed modalities and instruments for the procurement of necessary systems,
facilities, equipment and services required for peace-keeping
and other activities. Particular attention was given to the rights
of contractors and to third-party claims arising out of Chapter
VII operations.

Novel issues of international humanitarian law have arisen   *103*
during the period under review. The Office has provided advice
and opinions in relation to the detention of United Nations personnel in Bosnia and the treatment of Bosnian prisoners by
United Nations forces. The progress towards a referendum in

Western Sahara has required legal assistance in the preparation of a code of conduct for the referendum campaign.

104   The Office of Legal Affairs advised on the question of setting up an international judicial commission to investigate the Burundi *coup d'état* of 1993 and on the proposed establishment of a commission of inquiry or truth in Burundi. The Office assisted in the drafting of the terms of reference of the International Commission of Inquiry to investigate the events at Kibeho, Rwanda.

105   The Office contributed to filling a gap in United Nations practice, highlighted following a United Nations inquiry into a 1993 massacre of civilians in Liberia, by preparing a set of guidelines for United Nations investigations into allegations of massacres. The Secretary-General has approved the guidelines for publication and circulation.

106   The establishment by the Security Council of international tribunals dealing with serious violations of international humanitarian law in the former Yugoslavia and Rwanda raises difficult and complex legal issues. The Office of Legal Affairs is providing legal and administrative support to the International Criminal Tribunal for the Former Yugoslavia. The Office played a central role in launching the International Criminal Tribunal for Rwanda by providing advice on the drafting of the statute and rules of procedure and evidence and by providing the initial budget for the administrative and financial support from Headquarters, coordinating a technical mission to the field in order to negotiate a headquarters and lease agreement for its premises and preparing reports on the seat of the Tribunal.

107   At its past session, the General Assembly established an ad hoc committee open to all States to review substantive and administrative issues arising out of the draft statute for an international criminal court elaborated by the International Law Com-

mission. The ad hoc committee held a first series of meetings in April 1995 focusing on the following subjects: establishment and composition of the Court, applicable law and jurisdiction, exercise of jurisdiction, methods of proceedings (due process), relationship between States parties and the Court, and budget and administration. While progress has been made in the consideration of these issues, the ad hoc committee agreed to hold a second series of meetings from 14 to 25 August. Its report will be before the General Assembly at its forthcoming fiftieth session.

The continuation of economic sanctions and other measures against Iraq, the Federal Republic of Yugoslavia (Serbia and Montenegro) and the Libyan Arab Jamahiriya requires monitoring and assistance by the Office and advice to the various sanctions committees. In the case of Iraq, the Office advises on the scope of mandates under relevant Security Council resolutions, such as those concerning compensation to Iraqi farmers relocated from Kuwait and the return of Kuwaiti property. The Office is supporting the work of the Compensation Commission, which has been carrying out an impressive amount of work in processing claims, and will soon examine the more complex and larger claims of corporations and Governments.   *108*

The Office of Legal Affairs is ensuring consistency in the implementation of General Assembly decisions on the participation of the Federal Republic of Yugoslavia (Serbia and Montenegro) and its status throughout the United Nations system. The question lies at the intersection between international law and United Nations political decisions on sensitive issues.   *109*

The Office of Legal Affairs was responsible for the organization and agenda of the United Nations Congress on Public International Law, held from 13 to 17 March in New York, under the general theme "Towards the Twenty-first Century: International Law as a Language for International Relations". Some   *110*

571 scholars and professionals from 126 countries attended the event, which marked the mid-point of the United Nations Decade of International Law. International lawyers exchanged views on such issues as the progressive development of international law and its codification; research, education and training in international law; and the challenges expected in the twenty-first century.

111   The Office of Legal Affairs provides advice relating to the technical aspects of treaties and treaty law. The information in the *Multilateral Treaties deposited with the Secretary-General* is electronically updated daily. Outdated and disparate laws governing international trade pose an obstacle to the maintenance and expansion of trade links. The success of economic and social reforms currently under way in many States depends on the adoption of adequate laws that facilitate international trade. The Office of Legal Affairs is assisting the United Nations Commission on International Trade Law (UNCITRAL) to elaborate modern and harmonized trade laws as well as non-legislative texts aimed at facilitating international trade. Issues recently addressed are the draft convention on independent bank guarantees and stand-by letters of credit, and the use of electronic data interchange in international trade.

112   The United Nations Convention on the Law of the Sea calls for the establishment of three new institutions subsequent to the entry into force of the Convention: the International Seabed Authority, the International Tribunal for the Law of the Sea and the Commission on the Limits of the Continental Shelf. The Office of Legal Affairs convened and serviced the first and second parts of the first session of the Assembly of the International Seabed Authority, held from 16 to 18 November 1994 and from 27 February to 17 March 1995, respectively, at Kingston. The third and final part of the Assembly was held also at Kingston from 7 to 18 August.

Pursuant to the mandate provided by the General Assembly in its resolution 49/28 of 6 December 1994, the Office of Legal Affairs convened the first part and serviced the first and second parts of the Meeting of States Parties to the United Nations Convention on the Law of the Sea, held in November 1994 and May 1995 in New York, relating to the organization of the International Tribunal for the Law of the Sea. The Meeting agreed on the approach to be taken in the establishment of the Tribunal and its initial functions. The Office is involved in the preparation of the draft budget, which will be submitted to the next Meeting of States Parties, to be held from 27 November to 1 December 1995 in New York. *113*

The Office of Legal Affairs is carrying out preparatory work regarding the Commission on the Limits of the Continental Shelf. Following the 1993 findings of an ad hoc group of experts that examined the relevant provisions of the Convention on the definition of the continental shelf, the Office prepared background notes, initiated cooperative arrangements with competent international organizations and is in the process of convening a group of experts to deal with the composition and work programme of the Commission, scheduled to meet from 11 to 14 September in New York. *114*

The United Nations Conference on Straddling Fish Stocks and Highly Migratory Fish Stocks concluded its substantive work on 4 August with the consensus adoption of an Agreement for the Implementation of the United Nations Convention on the Law of the Sea of 10 December 1982 relating to the Conservation and Management of Straddling Fish Stocks and Highly Migratory Fish Stocks. The Conference decided to hold a formal signature ceremony on 4 December. The Office of Legal Affairs convened and serviced the fifth and sixth sessions of the Conference, from 27 March to 12 April and from 24 July to 4 August, respectively, in New York. *115*

116   Pursuant to General Assembly resolution 49/28, the Office of Legal Affairs is strengthening the system for the collection, compilation and dissemination of information on the law of the sea and developing an integrated database on legislation and marine policy, as well as establishing a system for notifying Member States and relevant international organizations of information submitted by States and intergovernmental bodies.

117   The Department of Public Information, headed by Mr. Samir Sanbar, is seeking to surmount resource constraints by engaging in closer professional cooperation with other bodies of the United Nations system, especially UNDP, UNICEF and UNFPA.

118   A coordinated and unified public information strategy aimed at increasing public understanding and support for the United Nations has become of crucial importance for the Organization's peace-keeping and other political missions. The Department of Public Information has formed an interdepartmental working group consisting of those departments playing a leading role in such field operations with a view to developing practical proposals for informational projects.

119   To convey an accurately balanced view of United Nations activities, the Department has made a special effort to highlight economic and social development activities and issues, in particular the recent major United Nations conferences held in Cairo, Copenhagen and Beijing, and the forthcoming Habitat II Conference in Istanbul. Focal points have been established within the Department for each conference to design, in cooperation with the substantive departments concerned, public information strategies and programmes that are budgeted jointly. Assessment of post-conference feedback has shown the value of this multifaceted approach to the promotion of international conferences.

A major new activity of the Department's publishing *120* programme is the Secretary-General's Blue Books Series. The Series describes the role the United Nations has played in some of the pivotal peace operations and other international issues of our time. Each volume in the Series encapsulates — in an overview provided by the Secretary-General — how the United Nations marshalled international forces, opinion or consensus to achieve objectives in such areas as the struggle against apartheid, the drive to stop the proliferation of nuclear weapons and the promotion of human rights. Blue Books on peace operations in Cambodia, El Salvador and Mozambique have been published. *The United Nations and the Advancement of Women* was published in August 1995 and made available for the Fourth World Conference on Women in Beijing. Some 17 titles are currently planned for publication.

The Department's dissemination of information to direct *121* users and redisseminators has been enhanced by modern technology and techniques, including the use of several electronic networks. On the Internet, for example, can be found the Department's database containing important United Nations documentation and publications. These materials reach their audiences in electronic form at enormous speed and are accessed by an average of 16,000 users daily. On the occasion of the fiftieth anniversary of the signing of the Charter of the United Nations at San Francisco on 26 June 1995, the Department launched the "UN Home Page" on the World Wide Web. This pilot project provides instantaneous information to Internet users in a multimedia service format consisting of text, graphics and sound. Examples of its contents include basic information about the United Nations and its history, press releases, documents, publications and photos, as well as pictorial highlights of the guided tour of Headquarters. To make documentation accessible to a wider audience, the United

Nations Bibliographic Information System (UNBIS Plus) has been produced on CD-ROM.

122   Radio is one of the most cost-effective and penetrating media available to the Department, which is improving access by United Nations Radio to airwaves worldwide. Currently, 29 programmes in 15 languages are being sent to broadcasters in over 180 countries. The Department also operates an electronic radio news service in English, French and Spanish that facilitates access by broadcasters to news programmes updated twice daily and is accessible through regular telephone lines.

123   The Department continues with the help of new technologies to reach its goals to explore the huge potential represented by television audiences. For instance, the Department transmitted "Year in Review" via satellite to broadcasters around the world in the six official languages. The programme was received and retransmitted by major broadcasters in over 24 countries, representing a total potential audience of over 360 million television households. This satellite transmission proved to be an extremely quick and cost-effective distribution channel and represented the largest audience ever reached by the programme.

124   In connection with the fiftieth anniversary, the Department initiated a major campaign of television spots. A series of 40 "UN Minutes" were produced, charting the history and accomplishments of the Organization. In addition, a series of "Question and Answer" quiz announcements were made. These television spots have been aired on both domestic and international Cable News Network channels, and by Time Warner Cable Company on many channels in the New York area. The Department thus obtained several million dollars worth of free air time donated by these two companies alone.

Responsibility for the Department's global outreach activi- *125* ties is assumed in large part by the network of information centres and services located in 68 countries around the world. They perform both a passive information role in dealing with a mounting volume of inquiries and requests for information, and an active role in engaging in a wide variety of contacts in pursuance of their mandate. As an example of the latter role, the centres have been the catalyst for the creation of approximately 80 national committees for the observance of the fiftieth anniversary.

The United Nations Office at Geneva, under its Director- *126* General, Mr. Vladimir Petrovsky, continues to provide administrative and logistical support to Geneva-based United Nations programmes and activities in human rights, humanitarian operations, trade and development, as well as major environment, disarmament and security-related matters.

There is a growing demand from Member States to visit *127* the United Nations Office at Geneva to establish or explore further cooperation between their countries and Geneva-based specialized agencies and programmes. Seven official visits were organized for that purpose and included the Heads of State or Government of Guatemala, Italy, Kazakstan, Kyrgyzstan, Lithuania, Slovenia and Tunisia. These exchanges are a major factor in consolidating the Office's role in the region and beyond.

Activities with regional organizations increased through- *128* out the year. A number of tripartite meetings took place with the participation of the Council of Europe, OSCE and the United Nations, represented by the United Nations High Commissioner for Refugees and the Centre for Human Rights. During the course of the year, the International Committee of the Red Cross (ICRC) was also associated with the meetings, which dealt with humanitarian issues in Europe.

129   Dialogue with Member States of the region contributed to the organizing of national committees for the United Nations fiftieth anniversary, important activities at the national level and joint projects included in the Geneva programme for the fiftieth anniversary. In that respect, cooperation with the host country and Geneva authorities, including major building projects to meet the needs of the United Nations Office at Geneva, was particularly fruitful.

130   The United Nations Office at Geneva continues to host an increasingly large number of meetings. From September 1994 to March 1995, 1,775 meetings were serviced with interpretation (including 154 meetings outside Geneva) and 2,455 without interpretation (including 105 meetings outside Geneva). During the period from April to August 1995, 1,354 meetings were planned to be held with interpretation (including 148 meetings outside Geneva) and 1,760 without interpretation (including 68 meetings outside Geneva).

131   In addition to servicing the Office's established bodies, the Palais des Nations hosted a number of important political or peace-keeping-related meetings, such as the International Conference on the Former Yugoslavia, the Compensation Commission, the meetings of the Georgia/Abkhazia parties and the Commission of Experts on Rwanda. The United Nations Centre on Transnational Corporations and the Centre for Science and Technology for Development were transferred to Geneva in 1993/94, and the Commission on Transnational Corporations and the Commission on Science and Technology for Development held regular sessions producing important documentation. The increasing activities of the Centre for Human Rights will give rise to new committees and/or working groups, which will meet at the United Nations Office at Geneva. These developments will require careful management of the allocation of facilities.

The Office has been involved in United Nations work on   *132*
the International Conference on the Former Yugoslavia; the
Georgia/Abkhazia conflict; the meetings between Portugal and
Indonesia concerning East Timor under the good offices of the
Secretary-General; the talks on Yemen; and discussions on biological, conventional and nuclear weapons. The Office has also
been involved with the Economic Commission for Europe
(ECE), UNCTAD and the United Nations Compensation Commission, and has provided support for the Office of the High
Commissioner for Human Rights, the United Nations Assistance Mission in Rwanda (UNAMIR), round tables organized
by the Department for Humanitarian Affairs for a number of
countries in Africa and Asia, and working groups of the United
Nations Protection Force (UNPROFOR).

During this period the round table set up by the Director-   *133*
General, with the participation of senior and staff representatives of all Geneva-based organs and programmes, made
recommendations aimed at strengthening and simplifying security arrangements, as well as achieving a larger degree of
control over documentation, with the ultimate goal of sizeably
reducing its volume.

The Office has conducted two main studies aimed at iden-   *134*
tifying areas of duplication and overlap in the administrative
sector within the Office, as well as between the Office and various United Nations entities and programmes located at Geneva.
The first phase of a management study led to a greater delegation of authority between Headquarters and Geneva in the personnel and budget/finance fields. Such delegation will not only
sizeably reduce duplication and overlap, but will also allow for
more timely processing of administrative actions at Geneva.
The next phase of the management study will finalize administrative arrangements at Geneva and determine the relationship
between the various entities. The second study, a work-flow

analysis conducted in the context of the future introduction of IMIS at Geneva, has just been completed. By the end of the year, the reorganization will be almost completed, permitting the Office to respond more efficiently to the increasing demands placed upon it by Member States of the region and the Organization as a whole.

135   Also located at Geneva, the United Nations Institute for Training and Research (UNITAR) has completed its restructuring process as requested by the General Assembly in its resolution 47/227 of 8 April 1993. This year UNITAR completed a training programme in international affairs management, including peacemaking and preventive diplomacy, environmental law and policy, and a fellowship in international law. In addition, the UNITAR training programme for the management of economic and social development has been reorganized. The aim of the programme now is to upgrade the professional skills of human resources in specific fields and to put the UNITAR training initiative at the service of multilateral and bilateral cooperation agencies, in particular the secretariats of organizations in charge of facilitating the implementation of international legal instruments. The coming years are likely to see a consolidation of UNITAR training and capacity-building activities, while research programmes are progressively discontinued. It is hoped that Member States will ensure the long-term continuity of the Institute.

136   The United Nations Office at Vienna, headed by the Director-General, Mr. Giorgio Giacomelli, provides administrative support to the United Nations Fund for Drug Abuse Control and other United Nations activities based at Vienna, serves functions related to crime prevention and cooperation in space activities, and is an important meeting-place and support centre for peace-keeping operations. From 1 July 1994 to 1 July 1995, a total of 2,209 meetings were planned and serviced at Vienna.

Beginning 1 April 1995, after extensive negotiations, the *137*
United Nations Industrial Development Organization (UNIDO)
and the United Nations Office at Vienna merged conference
planning, coordinating and language and servicing capabilities
to form a Unified Conference Service under the Office's management. A number of seminars, training courses and technical
cooperation projects have taken place; others are being planned
or are being implemented.

The Crime Prevention and Criminal Justice Branch of the *138*
United Nations Office at Vienna has promoted international cooperation in crime prevention and criminal justice and provided
assistance to Member States on problems of both national and
transnational crime. The Office organized the International
Conference on Preventing and Controlling Money Laundering
and the Use of the Proceeds of Crime: A Global Approach
(Courmayeur, Italy, 18-20 June 1994), the World Ministerial
Conference on Organized Transnational Crime (Naples, Italy,
21-23 November 1994) and the Ninth United Nations Congress
on the Prevention of Crime and the Treatment of Offenders
(Cairo, 29 April–8 May 1995).

The World Ministerial Conference on Organized Trans- *139*
national Crime adopted the Naples Political Declaration and
Global Action Plan against Organized Transnational Crime,
approved by the General Assembly in its resolution 49/159 of
23 December 1994. In the Declaration, Heads of State and
Government, ministers responsible for criminal justice systems
and other high-level representatives of Governments expressed
their resolve to protect their societies from organized crime
through effective legislative measures and operational instruments. The Global Action Plan emphasized that the United
Nations should facilitate the provision of technical cooperation, including the systematic exchange of experience and expertise, by drafting legislation, providing special training for

criminal justice officials and gathering, analysing and exchanging information.

140   The Ninth United Nations Congress on the Prevention of Crime and the Treatment of Offenders found that new forms and dimensions of crime and the links among criminal organizations threatened the security and stability of States and made global action imperative. The Congress discussed four substantive topics and held six demonstration and research workshops that permitted a more technical consideration of priority issues of direct concern to Member States. The discussion on combating corruption involving public officials attracted considerable attention and a number of recommendations were proposed. The plenary meeting on technical cooperation assessed the progress achieved and problems encountered in operational activities. Member States, in particular developing countries and countries in transition, discussed their needs for assistance from the United Nations and the international community.

141   The work of the Crime Prevention and Criminal Justice Branch was oriented towards operational activities and technical assistance, in particular for developing countries and countries in transition. The Branch focused its efforts on the promotion of effective and fair criminal justice systems based on the rule of law, taking account of United Nations norms, standards and model treaties. It provided assistance to Member States, upon request, in legislative and criminal justice reform, the elaboration and implementation of criminal codes and international treaties, the planning and formulation of national criminal justice policies and strategies, and the establishment of information networks and databases. The programme also contributed to peace-keeping and peacemaking missions of the United Nations by assisting in building legal and criminal justice infrastructures, and providing support to the missions and countries concerned. Two interregional advisers provided advisory services to various countries, carried out needs assessment missions and developed project proposals.

The Commission on Crime Prevention and Criminal Justice, the body responsible for policy guidance in this field, meets annually at Vienna. At its fourth session, held from 30 May to 9 June 1995, the Commission addressed the conclusions and recommendations of the Ninth United Nations Congress on the Prevention of Crime and the Treatment of Offenders, as well as of the World Ministerial Conference on Organized Transnational Crime. It recommended follow-up measures to the conclusions of the Congress and to the Naples Political Declaration and Global Action Plan adopted by the Conference. All recommendations of the Commission were approved by the Economic and Social Council during its substantive session, held at Geneva from 26 June to 28 July 1995. *142*

The Crime Prevention and Criminal Justice Branch cooperated closely with the United Nations International Drug Control Programme and the Centre for Human Rights. The Branch also undertook cooperation and coordination activities with the interregional, regional and associated institutes in the field of crime prevention and criminal justice and with intergovernmental and non-governmental organizations in areas of mutual concern. *143*

The Office for Outer Space Affairs, which relocated to the United Nations Office at Vienna in October 1993, implemented its multisectoral programme with political, legal, scientific and technical assistance components. Through its Programme on Space Applications, the Office organized and conducted workshops, training courses and symposia on various aspects of space science and technology and their applications for economic and social development. The Office continued its service as the substantive secretariat for the General Assembly's Com- *144* mittee on the Peaceful Uses of Outer Space, its Scientific and Technical Subcommittee and its Legal Subcommittee, as well as their subsidiary bodies.

145   Further progress was made on the Office's initiative to establish regional centres for space science and technology education in the developing countries. Those centres will provide individuals from developing countries with education and training in space-related disciplines and applications. In 1994, the Office decided to establish a centre, which will be co-hosted by Brazil and Mexico, for the Latin American and Caribbean region, and to establish the first node of the centre for the Asia and Pacific region in India. It is expected that 1995 will yield firm agreements on the location of the centres in the Middle East and Africa. The Office in 1994 expanded its Space Information Service to include a limited computer database capability as well as a gateway, or "home page", on the Internet. The home page provides basic data on the space-related activities of the United Nations and is the first step in the development of the broad information system mandated by the General Assembly. The Office has initiated plans to provide support for the preparatory work in intergovernmental committees concerning the convening of a third United Nations Conference on the Exploration and Peaceful Uses of Outer Space.

146   The Administrative Committee on Coordination, comprising the executive heads of the specialized agencies, including the Bretton Woods institutions, as well as all United Nations programmes under the chairmanship of the Secretary-General, provides the main instrument to establish an effective system of inter-agency cooperation and coordination within the United Nations system. In line with the objectives that have guided the recent restructuring of its machinery, the Committee's capacity to identify the main policy issues facing the international community and to promote and organize joint initiatives and responses towards common objectives has been progressively strengthened. The improvements the Secretary-General seeks to introduce within the United Nations, at both the policy and management levels, must be pursued as an integral part of a broader effort to adapt priorities and methods of work to changing requirements at the level of the system as a whole. Thus, at its past two sessions, the Committee pursued its consideration of policies that could lead to a more effective division of labour and to greater complementarity of action within the United Nations system. The Committee devoted particular attention to building and strengthening cooperative arrangements between the Bretton Woods institutions and United Nations funds, programmes and other specialized agencies. In the same context, particular attention was given by the Committee to ways and means of enhancing the capacity of the resident coordinator system to promote effective coordination among all economic and social actors at the country level in support of national development efforts. The achievement of greater complementarity between the country strategy notes, launched by the General Assembly, and the policy framework papers, under the aegis of the Bretton Woods institutions, was viewed as a key objective to those ends.

At the global level, the Committee's efforts to promote a *147* coordinated follow-up to the results of major conferences on interrelated development issues are helping to promote a more effective division of labour within the system, drawing on the new policy insights, priorities and commitments generated by those conferences. The continuing discussions in the Committee on the follow-up to the United Nations Conference on Environment and Development and its consideration, at its session in February 1995, of issues relating to international drug abuse control have helped equally to promote a more effective distribution of responsibilities and mutually reinforcing activities by the organizations of the United Nations system in addressing emerging global priorities.

148   African economic recovery and development was a major focus of attention at the last two sessions of the Committee. While United Nations organizations individually and collectively have placed high priority on the development of Africa, the current level of effort does not match the scale of economic and social problems confronting the region. The Committee concluded that a much higher level of commitment and resources at all levels was necessary to overcome the crisis facing many countries of the continent. As Chairman of the Committee, the Secretary-General called for a renewed joint effort to develop further practical initiatives with clear targets. The Committee agreed to establish a high-level steering committee to present a set of concrete recommendations for approval at its next session. The broad programme areas identified for this purpose include availability and management of water; sustainable food security; human development and capacity-building; and the follow-up to the World Summit for Social Development, with special emphasis on poverty alleviation. The steering committee also focuses on the consideration of means to enhance political and financial support for African development. Its initial work was drawn upon in preparing for the high-level segment of the Economic and Social Council devoted to African development.

149   Regarding management issues, members of the Committee reaffirmed their strong commitment to ensuring the advancement of the status of women throughout the United Nations system. It was generally agreed that management commitment at the highest levels was crucial to the achievement of gender equality. The Committee identified specific measures to increase the flexibility with which the United Nations system deals with women candidates; to remove obstacles to their re-

cruitment, retention in service, promotion and mobility; and to create a supportive environment.

The Committee also addressed issues affecting the secu-   *150*
rity and safety of United Nations staff, as well as questions relating to improvements in conditions of service. A special meeting in June of the Consultative Committee on Administrative Questions, in which most senior agency officials responsible for administration and management participated, pursued ways to enhance management effectiveness throughout the system.

In February 1995, all Committee members, and a number   *151*
of distinguished personalities who have led independent reviews on ways to strengthen the United Nations system, met at Vienna at a Forum on the Future of the United Nations. The Forum addressed the changing requirements for global and regional governance arising from the emerging new political and economic framework and their implications for the Organization; new approaches to the financing of the United Nations system; the implications of the changing role of the system for the international civil service; and the public image of the United Nations, in particular the challenge of mobilizing and focusing the attention of the media on the Organization's economic and social work.

B. ENSURING AN ADEQUATE FINANCIAL BASE

The United Nations financial crisis continues to deepen because of   *152*
the delays with which Member States have paid their assessed contributions, both for the regular budget and for peace-keeping operations. As at 10 August 1995, unpaid assessed contributions totalled $3.9 billion: $858.2 million for the regular budget (of which $456.1 million relates to the current year (1995) and $402.1 million relates to prior years) and $3 billion

for peace-keeping operations, current and prior shortfalls taken together (see fig. 6).

153   The United Nations is able to continue its peace-keeping operations only because the payment of bills and reimbursements to troop-contributors are being delayed. By the end of the year, unpaid reimbursements to troop-contributors and payments owed for contingent-owned equipment are estimated to reach the $1 billion mark. This situation cannot continue. Troop-contributors have expressed their difficulty with con-

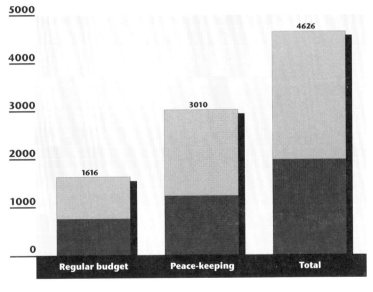

FIGURE 6

**Status of contributions
(peace-keeping and regular budget), 1989-1995 ***

Millions of US dollars

Outstanding
Received

* As at 10 August 1995

tinuing participation in peace-keeping operations if they are not paid on time.

Many Member States have made serious efforts to expe- *154* dite payment of their assessments but, without substantial additional major contributions before the end of the year, the cash balance of the United Nations will be dangerously low. This difficult financial situation, in particular when compounded by the continued unpredictability of the receipt of contributions, has a direct impact on the efficiency of the Organization and makes it more and more difficult to manage it effectively.

Along with these cash difficulties, the Organization has *155* also been facing another serious problem as a result of the growing practice on the part of the General Assembly of authorizing spending on additional or new activities without providing corresponding resources through assessments on Member States. This has further exacerbated the already difficult financial situation, since the only way to provide funding for those activities is to borrow from accounts with cash resources, without any assurance that those accounts will be replenished in order to implement activities for which Member States had initially provided resources.

Unless the receipt of unpaid assessments dramatically im- *156* proves, there will be no choice but to reduce spending further, focusing on those activities for which no assessments have been approved. Activities for which assessments have been approved, but have chronically not been paid by Member States, may have to be curtailed.

Notwithstanding these financial problems, efforts are con- *157* tinuing to make the Organization more efficient and more effective in carrying out the many tasks entrusted to it. In formulating the proposed programme budget for the biennium 1996-1997, particular emphasis has been placed on management improvements, which have resulted in savings without affecting the delivery of mandated activities. On that basis, a budget has been proposed for the next biennium in the amount of $2,510 million (at current rates before re-costing) for approval by the General Assembly this year. This represents a reduction of $109 million, or 4.2 per cent less than was appropriated for 1994-1995 (see fig. 7). The implementation of the 1996-1997 programme budget, once approved by the General Assembly, should not suffer from the same financial uncertainties that the Organization has been experiencing.

158   The objective of the High-level Open-ended Working Group on the Financial Situation of the Organization, which was established by the General Assembly and began meeting in January 1995, is to bring about constructive and positive

FIGURE 7

Revised appropriations for the biennium 1994-1995

Thousands of US dollars

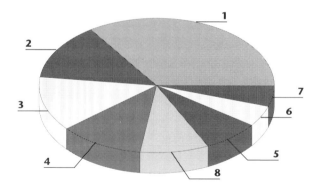

1 Administration and management ($896,821)
2 Staff assessment ($357,798)
3 Regional cooperation for development ($339,333)
4 International cooperation for development ($307,254)
5 Political affairs and peace-keeping operations ($198,338)
6 Human rights and humanitarian affairs ($132,666)
7 Public information ($131,433)
8 Others ($244,629)

changes to provide the Organization with a long-sought-after solid financial base.

C. THE FIFTIETH ANNIVERSARY

During the past year, much of the work of the Preparatory Committee for the Fiftieth Anniversary has focused on the preparations for the Special Commemorative Meeting of the Assembly on the occasion of the fiftieth anniversary of the entry into force of the Charter of the United Nations, to be held at United Nations Headquarters from 22 to 24 October 1995. The Committee has also continued to monitor the progress of the commemorative programme being undertaken by the Fiftieth Anniversary Secretariat. The Committee is expected to conclude its work by adopting, in early September, as part of its report to the General Assembly, a declaration in support of the Organization on its fiftieth anniversary.   *159*

The Fiftieth Anniversary Secretariat, headed by Ms. Gillian Martin Sorensen, has continued to develop and implement an ambitious global commemorative programme of activities and products. The goals identified for the fiftieth anniversary are to promote a more balanced image of the United Nations; to enlarge its constituency of support, especially among youth and non-traditional audiences; to improve worldwide education about the work of the Organization; and to mobilize public support in favour of the United Nations to position it to meet ever-growing demands. In line with these objectives, the Fiftieth Anniversary Secretariat has developed and implemented projects in key programme areas, among which education and communication have been given priority.   *160*

Educational activities include the development of educational kits for primary, intermediate and secondary schools and their distribution in all six official languages. Substantial funds have been made available for free distribution in developing   *161* countries and translation into additional languages as part of a "Global Teach-In" (a day or a week designated for teaching about the United Nations). In cooperation with UNESCO, workshops on the kits and the Global Teach-In have been conducted at several international education conferences. Other cooperative projects with specialized agencies and programmes have focused on youth and teachers. A "Passport to the Future" has been designed to sign on millions of young persons, between the ages of 7 and 14, as "global citizens". The Passport encourages them to demonstrate their concern for a better future by becoming involved in some of the world's most pressing challenges — the environment, human rights and peace — by participating in their local community.

162   Communications activities have included an international public service campaign through video, radio and print, in the six official languages. The campaign is designed to inform the public of the many achievements of the United Nations system, such as those in the areas of democratization and decolonization, women and development, environment, health, refugees, peace-keeping and food security. The videos, which were produced by directors from eight geographic regions, are appearing worldwide on television and airlines and in schools. The print and radio campaign is being distributed to broadcasters and publications in all Member States. A multimedia exhibit has been provided to Headquarters and regional offices and to headquarters of specialized agencies. Publications include a pictorial history of the United Nations, *Visions — Fifty Years of the United Nations*, and a book on the United Nations written by young people for young people, entitled *A World in Our Hands*.

163   Emphasis in all programme activity has been on achieving broad participation. As the Fiftieth Anniversary Secretariat was not in a position to implement and publicize all of the activities

in each Member State, considerable efforts have been made to encourage and provide support to the fiftieth anniversary committees formed by Member States, local United Nations offices and non-governmental organizations in their implementation of these and other activities. In all, 145 countries have established national committees and are carrying out an impressive array of local commemorative events. The Fiftieth Anniversary Secretariat continues to work in close cooperation with them, providing information materials, guiding and supporting the development of activities at both the local and country levels, and recommending specific activities to complement those being implemented at the global level. Over 40 Member States are honouring the United Nations with commemorative coins and virtually every postal administration is issuing commemorative stamps honouring the Organization.

The Secretariat has also worked with many cities — includ- *164* ing the cities that host our Headquarters offices — in development of appropriate commemorations, including conferences and colloquiums, concerts, art exhibits and other cultural and popular events. One among many was the myriad of activities organized at San Francisco to commemorate the fiftieth anniversary of the signing of the Charter.

In addition to the public service announcement campaign, *165* the Fiftieth Anniversary Secretariat has continued to develop a wide range of information products, which are being distributed widely to national committees, United Nations information centres, United Nations field offices, permanent missions, United Nations associations, academic groups and international news media, as well as the general public. These products include the UN50 newsletter, an updated press kit, a 16-page information brochure on the fiftieth anniversary, information about the anniversary available through the computer network and a number of information brochures published jointly with the Department of Public Information, along with audio and video compilations.

166   Overall, the funds required for developing the commemorative programme were secured from private sector support from global sponsors of the fiftieth anniversary as well as from project sponsors. Royalties from the coin programme are providing substantial revenue for educational and communications activities. Additional revenue has been derived from a commemorative watch.

167   United Nations associations and other non-governmental organizations have supported the fiftieth anniversary effort to broaden public understanding of the work and continued relevance of the United Nations through, among other things, education programmes, conferences and activities aimed at young people, such as art projects, essay competitions and model United Nations programmes. In addition, many of these organizations, especially United Nations associations, actively participate as members of the national committees established for the fiftieth anniversary to arrange commemorative programmes within the Member States. Furthermore, in the context of the Special Commemorative Meeting of the General Assembly for the Fiftieth Anniversary, there are plans to organize a one-day non-governmental organization programme in mid-October to examine the role of non-governmental organizations in the work of the United Nations.

D. UNITED NATIONS UNIVERSITY (UNU)

168 The Governing Council of the United Nations University (UNU) held its forty-first session from late November to early December 1994 at Accra. The Council considered proposals to further enhance the effectiveness of the University, led by Rector Heitor Gurgulino de Souza, and to strengthen the University's role and impact in United Nations research initiatives and activities. Several proposals for new academic initiatives were approved by the Council. Among them, the Council decided to establish the UNU International Leadership Academy, which will operate at Amman, with financial support from the Government of Jordan.

The Director-General of UNESCO and the Secretary- *169* General appointed new members of the Council to replace 11 members whose six-year term of office came to an end on 31 May 1995.

The year 1995 marks the twentieth anniversary of the in- *170* itiation of UNU academic activities. It is also the sixth and final year of the UNU research, training and dissemination activities carried out under the second medium-term perspective (1990-1995). The process of preparing the University's third medium-term perspective (1996-2001) for the next six years has accordingly been set in motion. To that end, the University prepared a mission statement as a step towards sharpening the focus of its institutional goals as an international educational institution and autonomous entity of the United Nations in a rapidly evolving global environment.

At its forty-first session, the Council endorsed an institu- *171* tional strategy paper setting out the programmatic development goals to take the University into the twenty-first century. In addition, the Council considered the appraisal report of an internal assessment group of the Council. The report called for the University to take a leading coordinating role in United Nations research initiatives and activities and to act to enhance the overall coherence of the University's academic programme. The assessment underlined the need for a better integration of UNU research, training and fellowship initiatives and for more effective dissemination of UNU publications. Another major recommendation of the report was the further strengthening of the UNU Centre in its key function as a coordinating mechanism of

University academic programmes and research and training centres and programmes. The Council requested that the essential components of the assessment report and the institutional strategy paper and mission statement be integrated as a further step in the process of developing the University's third medium-term perspective.

172   During the period from 1 September 1994 to 10 August 1995, 72 UNU academic meetings were held worldwide. As at 10 August 1995, 58 UNU postgraduate trainees were enrolled in training programmes at cooperating institutions around the world. The areas of training include food and nutrition, geothermal energy, remote sensing, biotechnology and micro-informatics. In 1994, 57 per cent of the training was done at institutions in developing countries and 43 per cent at institutions in industrialized countries. More than 1,340 fellows from over 100 countries have been trained by the University since 1976; an additional 2,300 persons have received training in UNU workshops and seminars. To date, more than 300 books, 5 scientific journals and numerous research papers and studies have been produced from UNU research.

173   Research continued to be carried out within the five programme areas identified by the UNU second medium-term perspective: universal human values and global responsibilities; new directions for the world economy; sustaining global life-support systems; advances in science and technology; and population dynamics and human welfare.

174   The University has made progress in the implementation of its programme on environmentally sustainable development (UNU Agenda 21), which places particular emphasis on human development and capacity-building in developing countries. A series of postgraduate education and capacity-building activities on environmental management has been initiated in Tokyo, together with collaborating institutions in India and Thailand.

The University also launched a major new long-term re- *175*
search effort that brings together private companies, industrial
policy makers and researchers to pursue the achievement of
technological breakthroughs that will facilitate manufacturing
without any form of waste, the so-called Zero Emissions Research Initiative. To mobilize support and to exchange information on the design and implementation of this global multidisciplinary research programme, the University organized the first
World Congress on Zero Emissions at its headquarters in Tokyo
in early April 1995. The World Congress was the first multi-
point Internet video conference undertaken from Japan, linking
scholars and government and business leaders in Asia, Europe
and North America and allowing access to an extended audience in some 100 countries.

To further the development of long-term initiatives related *176*
to the work of the United Nations, the Rector convened a special
advisory team to assist in preparing a "UNU Agenda for Peace,
Security and Global Governance". The advisory team suggested a five-year programme focusing on such topics as ethics,
democracy and governance, human rights, adjudicatory tools
of governance and mechanisms for peace and collective security. These mechanisms include preventive diplomacy, collective security schemes, peace-keeping, post-conflict measures
and disarmament. The programme is currently being implemented.

The University continues to strengthen its interaction with *177*
the United Nations system and is making an intensive and concerted effort to ensure that the results of its work feed into the
deliberations and operational activities of the United Nations.
The University prepared policy papers for presentation at the
International Conference on Population and Development and
the World Summit for Social Development preparatory process. Substantive contributions are being planned or are in

progress with respect to the Fourth World Conference on Women, Habitat II and the ninth session of UNCTAD. The University has also intensified its research efforts in support of the United Nations Secretariat through studies on mine-clearance technology, peace-keeping in Africa and regional security questions in Latin America.

178   The University has produced a number of policy-oriented studies, including "The Fragile Tropics of Latin America: Sustainable Management of Changing Environments"; "International Waters in the Middle East: From Euphrates-Tigris to Nile"; "Managing Water for Peace in the Middle East: Alternative Strategies"; "Hydropolitics Along the Jordan River: Scarce Water and Its Impact on the Arab-Israeli Conflict"; "Sustainable Management of Soil Resources in the Humid Tropics"; "Ocean Governance: Sustainable Development of the Seas"; "Steering Business Toward Sustainability"; "Culture, Development and Democracy: The Role of the Intellectual"; "Global Transformation: Challenges to the State System"; "State, Society and the United Nations System: Changing Perspectives on Multilateralism"; "The United Nations System: The Policies of Member States"; "Arms Reduction: Economic Implications in the Post-Cold-War Era"; "Mega-City Growth and the Future"; "Global Employment: An International Investigation into the Future of Work"; and "The Evolving New Global Environment for the Development Process".

179   From 1 September 1994 to 10 August 1995, UNU received some $19.9 million in endowment fund, operating and specific programme contributions. Nevertheless, the University faces continued resource constraints brought on by lower investment income from its endowment fund and increased competition for limited resources. Mobilization of operational contributions and of untied or unearmarked funding has become increasingly difficult in the last decade.

III. The foundations of peace: development, humanitarian action and human rights

A. IMPLEMENTING "AN AGENDA FOR DEVELOPMENT"

THREE YEARS AGO, at its forty-seventh session, the *180* General Assembly set in motion the process of formulating an Agenda for Development. Since then, considerable effort has been devoted both at the intergovernmental level and by the Secretariat to its elaboration.

In November 1994, in a report to the General Assembly *181* (A/49/665), I presented four principal recommendations on "An Agenda for Development" for the consideration of Member States at the forty-ninth session of the General Assembly.

These were: (*a*) that development should be recognized as *182* the foremost and most far-reaching task of our time; (*b*) that while it must be seen in its many dimensions — in the contexts of peace, the economy, environmental protection, social justice and democracy — development at its core must be about improvement of human well-being, the removal of poverty, hunger, disease and ignorance, ensuring productive employment and the satisfaction of priority needs of all people in a way that can be sustained over future generations; (*c*) that the emerging consensus on the priority and dimensions of development should find expression in a new framework for international cooperation; and (*d*) that within this new framework for development cooperation, the United Nations must play a major role in both policy leadership and operations.

I further outlined the need for a new framework for world *183* development cooperation that requires supporting actions at the national and international levels and a strong and effective multilateral system, at the centre of which would be the United Nations, with its unmatched global network at all levels. The United Nations can promote awareness, build consensus and inform policy in every dimension affecting development and can help rationalize and harmonize the multiplicity of public and private efforts worldwide. An important element in the new framework should be improved cooperation between the United Nations, its specialized agencies and the Bretton Woods institutions.

184   The General Assembly has primary responsibility to bring together all these aspects in an Agenda for Development. The aim should be to provide consistent policy guidance that would contribute to greater coherence and integration of the development work of the United Nations system. This implies strengthening the capacity of the Assembly to provide such harmonized policy guidance by a careful review of the working methods of its Second and Third Committees, so that the debates in those Committees could be sharply focused on key policy issues and their mutual complementarities enhanced. Secondly, a revitalized Economic and Social Council could greatly assist the Assembly by bringing to its attention recommendations leading to the adoption of harmonized and integrated policies. The relationship between those central bodies and the Bretton Woods institutions, on the one hand, and the funds and programmes and specialized agencies, on the other, could be built around shared objectives and a common purpose leading to closer cooperation and joint actions at the country level.

185   Recent pronouncements of the summit meeting of seven major industrialized countries, which was held at Halifax, Canada, in June 1995, as well as of the Ministerial Meeting of the Coordinating Bureau of the Non-Aligned Countries held at Bandung, Indonesia, in April 1995, signify a resolute will-

ingness on the part of the international community at the political level to see a strong United Nations system working in unison for the realization of internationally agreed goals and objectives. Efforts to make United Nations operational activities more efficient and effective begin with the identification of those areas where it has special assets and strengths that can support the process of development. Given shared vision and a common purpose, coordination and integration in the Organization's operational activities can be ensured.

This issue was considered during the coordination segment of the Economic and Social Council in July 1995. At my request, the Administrator of UNDP, who assists the Secretary-General in ensuring policy coherence and the coordination of operational activities for development, initiated a process of consultation among senior United Nations officials on coordination mechanisms that can be instituted on conference follow-up at the inter-agency level, thus mobilizing the United Nations system as a whole through thematic inter-agency task forces at the national, regional and headquarters levels. *186*

During the forty-ninth session of the General Assembly, Member States decided to establish an open-ended working group to elaborate further an action-oriented comprehensive agenda for development, taking into account the reports and recommendations presented by the Secretary-General pursuant to Assembly resolutions 47/181 of 22 December 1992 and 48/166 of 21 December 1993, the outcome of the high-level segment of the 1994 substantive session of the Economic and Social Council, the views expressed by representatives in the high-level debate held during the forty-ninth session of the Assembly, as well as the summary of the World Hearings on Development and proposals presented by Member States and other parties. *187*

188   The Working Group was required to submit a report on the progress of its work to the General Assembly before the conclusion of its fiftieth session. A compendium containing the goals, targets and commitments of major United Nations conferences held and agreements signed since 1990, as well as an assessment of the status of their implementation, was submitted by the Secretariat to the Working Group following its first session. That document was a complement to the background information already identified in Assembly resolution 49/126 of 19 December 1994.

189   At the Working Group's second session, held from 15 to 26 May 1995, Governments presented their views on the structure and content of the Agenda for Development during the formal meetings, which were preceded and followed by inter-sessional consultations. The Working Group reached a consensus on the structure of the Agenda and defined modalities for developing its text during the third and final session, yet to be held. A tentative comprehensive structure was adopted, consisting of three chapters, the first devoted to setting goals and objectives; the second representing the bulk of the Agenda, providing a policy framework and identifying priority actions for development, together with means of implementation; and the third dealing with institutional issues and follow-up.

B.   GLOBAL DEVELOPMENT ACTIVITIES

1.   *Secretariat departments at Headquarters*

190   The Department for Policy Coordination and Sustainable Development, headed by Mr. Nitin Desai, provides support for the central coordinating and policy-making functions vested in the Economic and Social Council and its subsidiary bodies, as well as for the Second and Third Committees of the General Assembly. Ensuring the integration of economic, social and en-

vironmental concerns in policy development and implementation is a crucial objective underlying the structure and mandate of the Department.

The World Summit for Social Development was convened *191* by the General Assembly at Copenhagen from 6 to 12 March 1995 to address the urgent and universal need to eradicate poverty, expand productive employment, reduce unemployment and enhance social integration. The Summit provided an impetus for the world's Governments to give priority to the social aspects of global development and the social impact of international relations, while reaffirming their commitment to individual, family and community well-being as the fundamental concern of their policies.

The Summit was the largest gathering ever of Heads of *192* State and Government: in all, 187 countries participated in the deliberations, which produced the Copenhagen Declaration on Social Development and Programme of Action, and 117 of them were represented by Heads of State or Government. In addition, 2,315 delegates representing 811 non-governmental organizations joined the meeting, demonstrating eloquently the vitality and diversity of people's initiatives and establishing the foundation for a renewed and strengthened partnership between Governments and the actors of civil society. The preparations for the Summit and the actions initiated in pursuance of its mandate have brought into play virtually the entire spectrum of departments, agencies, programmes and offices of the United Nations system and fostered coordination between them and with Member States and non-governmental organizations.

The observance of the International Year for the Eradica- *193* tion of Poverty (1996) will provide an excellent opportunity for the implementation of the commitments made at Copenhagen. Countries are invited to elaborate specific targets during the

Year and to prepare national strategies for the struggle against poverty.

194   The International Year of the Family (1994) has led to a remarkable evolution of the political approach to the family as an object and agent of social policy throughout the world. A greater recognition has been accorded at the global, national and individual levels to the importance of supporting families and bringing about positive changes in the family as an integral part of the efforts to achieve peace, human rights, democracy, sustainable development and social progress, as well as lasting progress on behalf of women, children and other traditionally less advantaged members of society. A large number of local, national and international activities in support of the family were arranged by Governments in more than 150 countries and by various non-governmental, community and intergovernmental organizations in observance of the Year. Those efforts were effectively augmented by supportive action of 34 bodies and agencies of the United Nations, including the regional commissions.

195   The International Conference on Families, held in October 1994 during the forty-ninth session of the General Assembly, marked the first occasion on which the Assembly devoted a discussion exclusively to the family. The Conference itself conveyed the growing conviction that it is in the best interests of individuals and societies to promote democratic families and family-friendly societies. I will submit to the Assembly at its fiftieth session a detailed report on the observance of the International Year of the Family, along with specific proposals on its long-term follow-up.

196   The High-level Advisory Board on Sustainable Development, which was set up following the United Nations Conference on Environment and Development, held in June 1992, to provide independent advice to the Secretary-General on environment and development matters, held its third session from

17 to 21 October 1994. The Board examined four issues: (*a*) sustainable food security for a growing world population; (*b*) the need for mutual reinforcement between international trade and environment policies; (*c*) value-based education for sustainability; and (*d*) ways of forging new alliances for sustainable development. The Vice-Chairperson of the Board apprised the Commission on Sustainable Development, at its third session, of the conclusions reached in its deliberations and on its discussions with me. The Inter-Agency Committee on Sustainable Development of the Administrative Committee on Coordination met in February and July 1995. The Inter-Agency Committee has received strong support from Member States, which have expressed their particular appreciation for the fact that the follow-up to the United Nations Conference on Environment and Development and the work of the Commission on Sustainable Development bring together the entire system in a coordinated and cooperative manner.

Since the adoption of the Barbados Declaration and Pro- *197* gramme of Action for the Sustainable Development of Small Island Developing States in May 1994, efforts have intensified to follow up on the work programme regarding the specific economic, social and environmental concerns of those States. There is increasing interest among the organizations of the system, including the regional commissions, as well as a number of concerned non-governmental organizations, in joint and coordinated activities in this regard. In May 1995, the Department organized a meeting of those organizations and representatives of the Alliance of Small Island States to discuss the status of implementation of the Barbados agreements. The achievement of the goals set out in those agreements, as with Agenda 21 itself, continues to be impeded by financial constraints, as well as by difficulties in the effective transfer of technology for sustainable development.

198   The Office of the Special Coordinator for Africa and Least Developed Countries, as requested by the Secretary-General's Panel of High-level Personalities on African Development, organized a high-level brainstorming workshop on non-governmental organizations and African development on 16 and 17 January 1995. The Office prepared a pamphlet on the conclusions and recommendations of the Panel, as requested by the General Assembly in its resolution 48/214 of 23 December 1993. In addition to disseminating information to countries and organizations, the Office coordinated activities related to the United Nations New Agenda for the Development of Africa in the 1990s, adopted by the General Assembly in its resolution 46/151 of 18 December 1991, including the sixth meeting of the Working Group of the United Nations Inter-Agency Task Force on Africa's Critical Economic Situation, Recovery and Development.

199   My report on the development of Africa, including the implementation of the United Nations New Agenda for the Development of Africa in the 1990s, prepared for the 1995 high-level segment of the Economic and Social Council, identifies key policy issues critical to African development and offers concrete recommendations on what African countries and the international community can do to improve the lives of the people of Africa. It also analyses the progress made and difficulties encountered in the implementation of the New Agenda.

200   The Office of the Special Coordinator provided substantive assistance to donor and African countries in the negotiations on the establishment of a diversification facility in the African Development Bank, which led to General Assembly resolution 49/142 of 23 December 1994, requesting those States participating in the African Development Fund to consider making an initial adequate contribution to finance the preparatory phase of commodity diversification projects and programmes in African countries. The Office organized regular briefings on areas of concern and, together with UNDP and the Governments of Japan and Indonesia, organized the Asia-Africa Forum at Bandung, Indonesia, in December 1994, as a follow-up to the Tokyo International Conference on African Development. The Office also organized, together with the Department for Development Support and Management Services and UNDP, an international workshop on informal sector development in Africa at United Nations Headquarters. The Office participated in a number of intergovernmental and other meetings, including those of OAU.

The Interim Secretariat of the Convention to Combat Desertification opened the United Nations Convention to Combat Desertification in Those Countries Experiencing Serious Drought and/or Desertification, Particularly in Africa, for signature in Paris on 14 and 15 October 1994. As at July 1995, the number of signatories had reached 106 and 2 countries had ratified the Convention. Consistent with General Assembly resolution 49/234 of 23 December 1994, the Intergovernmental Negotiating Committee for the Elaboration of an International Convention to Combat Desertification in those Countries Experiencing Serious Drought and/or Desertification, Particularly in Africa, held its sixth session in New York, from 9 to 19 January 1995, and adopted a work programme for the interim period leading to the first session of the Conference of the Parties, which will be held within 12 months of the entry into force of the Convention. The Intergovernmental Negotiating Committee established two working groups to lay the groundwork for the first session of implementation of the resolution on urgent action for Africa, through the exchange of information and the review of progress made thereon, and through the promotion of action in other regions. It initiated this phase of its work at its seventh session, held at Nairobi from 7 to 18 August 1995.

201

202   "Awareness days" are being held in 20 affected countries in the various subregions of Africa to sensitize key actors at the local level and to enable them to participate fully in the Convention's implementation. Seminars are also being held at the subregional level in southern, eastern and western Africa to facilitate the preparation of relevant action programmes. A number of activities were held in various countries in observance of World Day to Combat Desertification and Drought, 17 June, pursuant to General Assembly resolution 49/115 of 19 December 1994, including seminars, exhibitions and the launching of publications.

203   The first meeting of the Conference of the Parties to the United Nations Framework Convention on Climate Change was convened from 28 March to 7 April 1995 at Berlin. The meeting aimed at setting in motion the processes needed to promote the effective implementation of the Convention — only four years after multilateral negotiations were first launched on the issue of global warming and its impact on the climate. It is to the credit of the international community that the Conference of the Parties, fully aware of the contribution that the implementation of the Convention can make towards sustainable development, has agreed by consensus to forge ahead with concrete efforts aimed at bringing emissions of greenhouse gases in the atmosphere within safe limits.

204   The Department for Economic and Social Information and Policy Analysis, headed by Mr. Jean-Claude Milleron, is the principal unit in the United Nations for the generation and elaboration of economic, demographic, social and environmental data and the analysis of national and regional development policies and trends. It also provides technical support to projects in statistics and population undertaken by developing countries.

A cornerstone of the Department is its wide-ranging *205*
programme of statistical publications, which continued during
the year. In addition to the *Statistical Yearbook*, other annual
reference volumes published included the *Demographic Yearbook, Industrial Commodity Statistics Yearbook, National Accounts Yearbook* and *Energy Statistics Yearbook*. Publications
with a more frequent periodicity included the *Monthly Bulletin
of Statistics, Commodity Trade Statistics* and the *Population
and Vital Statistics Report*. As part of its contribution to the
Fourth World Conference on Women, the Department completed the 1995 edition of *The World's Women: Trends and
Statistics*. This second edition, which was a collaborative effort
among 12 United Nations offices and agencies, not only pre-
sents an array of new data, but also underlines the work that still
must be done to develop gender statistics that are comprehensive and of adequate quality.

The year has seen further progress by the Department in *206*
the development and implementation of new statistical concepts and methodologies in other areas. The 1993 System of
National Accounts was the result of collaboration between the
United Nations, EU, IMF, the World Bank and the Organisation
for Economic Co-operation and Development (OECD). Since
the adoption of the System, the Department has been working
in close cooperation with the regional commissions and other
international organizations on its implementation in selected
developing countries. During the past year, the Department
conducted seminars on the 1993 System of National Accounts
in concept and practice, and on the use of the System of
National Accounts for transition economy countries.

The Department, in cooperation with international organi- *207*
zations and countries, has completed a draft revision of the international concepts and definitions for international trade
statistics. In addition, the Statistical Commission, at its twenty-

eighth session, held in New York from 27 February to 3 March, approved an international compilation of environmental indicators that will be assembled by the Department. Close collaboration with the Commission on Sustainable Development and its secretariat will ensure comparability with its programme on indicators of sustainable development. In the area of integrated environmental and economic accounting, the framework developed by the Department is now being tested through several country projects with the support of United Nations Environment Programme (UNEP) and UNDP. The Statistical Commission also designated the period 1995-2004 as the 2000 World Population and Housing Census Decade. In this area, the Department continued its work on civil registration and vital statistics.

208   The work of the Department in the area of population was given fresh impetus towards the end of 1994 with the success of the International Conference on Population and Development, held at Cairo from 5 to 13 September 1994. The Department, in cooperation with UNFPA undertook substantive preparations for the Conference. Following the Conference, the General Assembly decided, in its resolution 49/128 of 19 December 1994, that the revitalized Commission on Population and Development should be charged with monitoring, reviewing and assessing the implementation of the Programme of Action adopted at Cairo. The Department provides the secretariat for the Commission. At its twenty-eighth session, from 21 February to 2 March, the Commission affirmed the Department as the body with competence to cover the monitoring and appraisal of the broad range of areas covered by the Programme of Action. The Department was also charged by the Secretary-General with the preparation of the report on international migration and development called for by the General Assembly in its resolution 49/127 of 19 December 1994. The report, which was submitted to the Economic and Social Council at its 1995 substantive session, not only addressed the substantive issues involved but also included aspects related to the objectives and modalities for the convening of the United Nations Conference on Migration and Development.

The Department completed its 1994 revision of *World* 209 *Population Prospects*, the official United Nations population figures for all countries of the world. Reflecting the high international standing of these data, the World Bank announced that henceforth it would rely exclusively on the United Nations for population statistics. Studies in the field of population by the Department address such subjects as contraception, women's education and fertility behaviour, abortion, urbanization, population policy, international migration policies, the status of female migrants and the spread of HIV/AIDS. Much of the work undertaken in the course of these studies contributed to the deliberations on the Cairo Programme of Action.

As a further dimension of its responsibility for monitoring 210 the world economic and social situations, the Department produced the *World Economic and Social Survey 1995*. In addition to an analysis of the world economic situation and its short-term prospects and discussions of major global policy issues, the *Survey* examined some longer-term dimensions of economic and social changes in the world. As part of the continuing effort to improve the *Survey*, the 1995 edition devoted greater attention to a discussion of economic and social policies around the world. In a parallel effort to provide both the academic community and the general public with information on issues that would form the backdrop to the World Summit for Social Development, the Department published *The World Social Situation in the 1990s* prior to the Summit.

The Department carried out development projections and 211 perspective studies under Project LINK, an international economic research network of more than 70 country teams. During the past year, the Department convened two meetings of this network — one in Salamanca, Spain, and the other in New York — to assist in the preparation of short-term economic forecasts for the General Assembly and the Economic and Social Council. As part of its longer-term analysis, the Department prepared an update of the "Overall socio-economic perspective of the world economy beyond the year 2000" for the General Assembly at its fiftieth session. The Department has continued its work on the debt crisis, sources of finance for development, coercive economic measures and economic assistance to countries affected by sanctions imposed by the Security Council. It has produced reports on each of these subjects for the Assembly at its fiftieth session.

212   As mandated by the General Assembly in response to the new development thinking that has evolved in recent years, the Department has been expanding its research and analysis on micro-economic issues, focusing on ways in which increased reliance on market forces can contribute to the attainment of development objectives. This work has included studies relating to employment, technology and the use of market-based mechanisms both to meet environmental objectives and to provide public services. The Department has continued to provide operational and technical assistance to developing countries and economies in transition, primarily in the areas of population and statistics and mostly with financing provided by UNDP and UNFPA. Such arrangements applied to more than 100 technical cooperation projects over the past year, with additional assistance on such matters as country strategy notes being provided through resident coordinators on a *pro bono* basis.

213   The Department has sustained its efforts to provide information and analysis through means other than official documents and publications. In order to promote exchanges with others with shared interests, the Department convenes seminars, issues a series of working papers and continues to increase its dissemination of information by electronic means. In 1995 the *United Nations Statistical Yearbook* was again issued on CD-ROM, as well as in its traditional paper form. Version III of *Women's Indicators and Statistics Database (Wistat)* was similarly made available in CD-ROM format, while *Statbase Locator* (an inventory of international computerized databases) was released on diskette. In addition, selected information from the 1994 revisions of *World Population Prospects* and *World Urbanization Prospects* released during the year is available on-line to users of the Internet, through the Department's Population Information Network, which was used extensively during the International Conference on Population and Development. All the official documents of the Conference, as well as the statements made in the plenary, were made available on the Network, which handled more than 28,000 requests while the Conference was taking place.

As part of its effort to improve the availability of economic *214* and social information, the Department, in cooperation with the regional commissions, continues to work on a new system that will encompass the collection, processing, storage, exchange and dissemination of economic and social information. Entitled the United Nations Economic and Social Information System, phase II of the project commenced in 1995 and focuses on implementing the System's core components in selected pilot areas, such as national accounts and the development of prototype techniques.

The Department for Development Support and Manage- *215* ment Services, headed by Mr. Chaozhu Ji, is responsible for providing technical assistance to developing countries and economies in transition in the broad fields of integrated development and public management, thereby assisting Governments in establishing an enabling environment for development.

216   In the planning and management of mineral resources, the Department organized international round-table conferences on foreign investment in exploration and mining in India and Pakistan in 1994. These were to familiarize foreign investors with the new mining policies and regulations in those countries, to encourage investment in development of the mineral sector, to acquaint better the Governments with the mining industry's expectations and with the elements of a successful mining investment promotion drive, and thus to arrive at mutually satisfactory and rewarding policies for mining investments. The conferences culminated in concrete joint venture investments in both countries. The Department has also prepared the Environmental Guidelines for Mining Operations in response to the need stressed in Agenda 21 for the adoption of environmental guidelines for natural resource development.

217   The water resource activities at the individual country level have been extended into subregional and regional initiatives through the use of joint programming with the regional economic commissions. This work has brought the added benefit of preparing the ground for several recently launched Global Environment Facility initiatives in international waters and the Okavango and Lake Chad basins. The detailed implementation experience has also provided the empirical basis for the ongoing global freshwater assessment initiated at the request of the Commission on Sustainable Development.

218   Information exchange dealing with both mineral and water resources is facilitated by the substantive services the Department provides to the Committee on Natural Resources. Dissemination of ideas is also fostered by the *Natural Resources Forum,* the quarterly technical journal produced by the Department.

The Department is collaborating with the African Energy *219* Programme of the African Development Bank in a wide-ranging effort to address the serious problems within the African energy sector. In 1994 the Department undertook a study of energy institutions in 17 African countries to characterize better the strengths and weaknesses of the sector at the country, sub-regional and regional levels. A key recommendation that emerged from the exercise was that an African energy unit should be established, based within the African Development Bank and supported by OAU, the Economic Commission for Africa (ECA) and the Department for Development Support and Management Services. A programme of action is now being elaborated in conjunction with the African Energy Programme of the African Development Bank.

The Department executed a $7 million project in Zim- *220* babwe funded by the Global Environment Facility, which provides a model for other countries with sufficient solar energy. The project addresses the issue of global warming by providing a sustainable model of solar electricity dissemination in Zimbabwe's rural areas where an expanded commercial market is being developed for affordable domestic solar electric lighting systems through the provision of low-interest financing from existing institutions to allow householders to purchase home solar systems.

The United Nations International Conference on Coal *221* Methane Development and Utilization will be held in Beijing in October 1995. A primary objective of the Conference is to assist Governments in developing a legal and regulatory context for the promotion of domestic coal-bed methane resources. The Conference will review the status and potential of ongoing coal-bed methane recovery projects in China. Coal mines in that country characteristically have high seepage rates of methane gas, with consequent danger of atmospheric pollution and a grave risk to the safety of miners and the productivity of the mines. To help address this problem, the United Nations is assisting China through a $10 million programme designed for recovery of coal-bed methane prior to, during and after mining operations. Funded by the Global Environment Facility and executed by the Department for Development Support and Management Services, the programme addresses all types of gas recovery and the feasibility of various options for gas utilization. Another project is developing the geothermal resources of the Tibet region, with $3 million in trust funds contributed by the Government of Italy. This project is leading to institution-building and human resource training both in China, during the execution of the project, and overseas. The project is also oriented towards important investments to be realized in the near future.

222   Under the joint programming exercise, initiated in June 1994, pilot projects implemented by the Department together with the regional commissions include a geothermal project in conjunction with the Economic Commission for Latin America and the Caribbean (ECLAC), a capacity-building project in central Asian countries to deal with transboundary management of water resources and a small-scale mining proposal from ECA designed to train artisanal miners.

223   The Department has taken several steps to strengthen support to Governments in the area of social development policy and poverty alleviation, consistent with priorities enunciated at the World Summit for Social Development. Africa is an area of particular concern. To limit the potential for negative effects of national economic adjustment programmes on vulnerable groups and on delivery of services in social sectors like health and education, the Department has developed a system for monitoring the social effects of such programmes. This has been introduced in projects in Algeria, Cameroon, Côte

d'Ivoire, Gabon, Senegal and Tunisia. In June 1995, the Department collaborated with the Department for Policy Coordination and Sustainable Development and UNDP to organize a workshop at Headquarters on the development of Africa's informal sector. Experts from Governments, the United Nations system and non-governmental organizations and academic institutions discussed experiences and perspectives.

In the fields of public administration and finance, the De- *224* partment is assisting Governments in developing administrative and managerial systems at the central and local levels, in strengthening financial management capabilities, in undertaking public enterprise reform and encouragement of private enterprise and in improving related informational technology. For example, in Viet Nam, the Department is currently providing technical services to the Government's comprehensive public administration programme and in particular to the component on improvement of civil service management.

The Department has completed the establishment of a *225* computerized information system to assist key agencies of government. This public sector planning and management information system facilitates econometric analysis, national budget preparation and modelling, the preparation of debt programmes and investment programme planning and monitoring. The system has already been demonstrated in several countries and is ready for installation upon request.

Laying the groundwork for a session of the General As- *226* sembly on making Governments work better was the focus of a meeting of more than 50 experts worldwide organized by the Department from 31 July to 11 August at Headquarters. The themes for the experts' discussions included policy development, administrative restructuring, civil service reform, the role of public administration in promoting social development, financial management, post-conflict rehabilitation and reconstruction of government machinery, public/private sector interaction and the role of public administration in the management of development programmes. Recommendations from the meeting will be reviewed at a resumed session of the Economic and Social Council later this year.

227   The outbreak of localized conflicts throughout the world has highlighted the interdependence and interaction between peace and improvement of the human condition, as today Governments must often begin to reconstruct their human and administrative infrastructures even before conflict has ceased. The Department's work in assisting Rwanda to restore its technical, human and institutional capacities and rehabilitate its judicial system, in strengthening Yemen's water and sanitation facilities, in preparing a reconstruction and development plan for Bosnia and Herzegovina and in providing support to the rejuvenation of Haiti's public administration — these are all examples of this recognition being acted upon by the United Nations.

228   To help stimulate a better exchange of ideas on post-conflict reconstruction strategies, the Department organized a colloquium in June in Austria, with support from the Government of Austria and in cooperation with the Austrian Centre for Peace and Conflict Resolution. This informal gathering brought together representatives from several Governments, plus a number of United Nations departments and agencies, non-governmental organizations and academic institutions. The conclusions of the meeting and other documentation, including an inventory of possible post-conflict peace-building activities, have been published.

229   In the area of cartography, the Department continues to implement the recommendations presented by the Thirteenth United Nations Regional Cartographic Conference for Asia and the Pacific, which requested the United Nations to support

surveying, mapping and charting activities in the Asia and Pacific region and to facilitate the participation of the least developed countries and the small island developing States of the region in the work of the Conference.

2. United Nations Conference on Trade and Development (UNCTAD)

The work of UNCTAD, under the Officer-in-Charge, Mr. Carlos *230* Fortin, was dominated during the past year by the forty-first session of the Trade and Development Board and its subsidiary bodies, and the United Nations International Symposium on Trade Efficiency, as well as by the preparatory process for the ninth session of the United Nations Conference on Trade and Development. I have proposed for approval by the General Assembly the appointment of Mr. Rubens Ricupero as Secretary-General of UNCTAD. His appointment would be effective as at 15 September 1995.

During this period, the Trade and Development Board un- *231* dertook a preliminary analysis and assessment of the final act of the Uruguay Round of multilateral trade negotiations. The States members of UNCTAD recognized the important role it could play in the post-Uruguay Round period in enhancing the ability of developing countries to take maximum advantage of these new opportunities and in recommending measures to mitigate the consequences on countries that could be adversely affected. The respective roles and functions of UNCTAD and the World Trade Organization have been more clearly delineated.

UNCTAD also started implementation of the decisions *232* taken during the mid-term review of the Cartagena Commitment in May 1994. The commemoration of the thirtieth anniversary of UNCTAD at the first part of the Board's forty-first session in September was the occasion for States members to reaffirm their full support to the organization and to look to its future orientation. Finally, the preparatory process for the ninth session of the Conference, to be held in the spring of 1996, started in a spirit of cooperation and with the conviction that the Conference should address in an innovative and action-oriented way the economic issues facing the international community.

233   The Trade and Development Board, at the first part of its forty-first session, in September 1994, adopted a declaration in which States members reaffirmed their commitment to the primary development objectives of UNCTAD and undertook to reinforce their political support for the organization and for its important role in strengthening the global Partnership for Development by addressing the economic and development problems of all countries, in particular the developing countries.

234   The Board's discussion on interdependence was based on the *Trade and Development Report 1994*. The Board reviewed the east Asian growth and development experience and concluded that there was a wide variety of experience in east Asia: while in some fast-growing economies the policy regime had been more liberal, several Governments had successfully played active and interventionist roles.

235   The Board concluded its policy review of technical cooperation activities of UNCTAD by noting that the agency's technical cooperation was greatly valued by developing countries and countries in transition and had also attracted increasing support in the last few years from donor countries and institutions. Accordingly, the Board emphasized the need to strengthen UNCTAD technical cooperation.

236   At the second part of its forty-first session, in March 1995, the Board endorsed agreed conclusions on trade policies, structural adjustment and economic reform, and on the UNCTAD contribution to the implementation of the United Nations New Agenda for the Development of Africa in the 1990s. The Board

also agreed on preparatory action for a high-level intergovernmental meeting to be held in September to undertake a mid-
term review of the implementation of the Programme of Action
for the Least Developed Countries for the 1990s. It also carried
out a policy review of the work of UNCTAD on sustainable development. On trade policies, structural adjustment and economic reform, a broad convergence emerged on a number of
conclusions. The Board concluded that Governments should
take a positive approach to structural adjustment. A policy
framework favourable to structural adjustment could facilitate
the comprehensive and effective implementation of the Uruguay Round agreements, lower resistance to further liberalization and better prepare economies for future negotiations on
improving market access.

On preparations for the ninth session of the Conference, *237*
the Board reached agreement on the provisional agenda for the
Conference. The theme of the ninth session will be promoting
growth and sustainable development in a globalizing and liber-
alizing world economy. The Government of South Africa announced its decision to make an offer, in principle, to host the
Conference. States members underlined the importance of
holding the session in Africa and expressed their full support
for South Africa as the host country.

The United Nations International Symposium on Trade *238*
Efficiency was held at Columbus, Ohio, from 17 to 21 October
1994. More than 2,000 decision makers from both the public
and private sectors participated in the Symposium and in the
other parallel events: the Global Executive Trade Summit,
the Global Summit for Mayors and the World Trade Efficiency
and Technology Exhibition. The Symposium was chaired by
the Secretary of Commerce of the United States of America.
The unprecedented involvement of the private sector and of
local governments made the Symposium a unique forum for

bringing practical solutions to some of the problems encountered in international trade. The Symposium adopted the Columbus Ministerial Declaration and launched the Global Trade Point Network. Together, these documents constitute a blueprint for efficient international trade in the next century.

239   The Standing Committee on Commodities held its third session from 31 October to 4 November 1994. In its agreed conclusions, the Committee requested UNCTAD to continue its analysis of ways to improve the competitiveness of natural products, giving priority to the theoretical and practical aspects of the internalization of ecological externalities. UNCTAD held a number of commodity-related meetings under its auspices. In January 1994, the fourth session of the United Nations Conference on Tropical Timber adopted the International Tropical Timber Agreement and, as at 31 December 1994, 12 States had signed the new Agreement and one had become formally party to it, although conditions for its entry into force are not yet met. At the end of the second session of the United Nations Conference on Natural Rubber, in October 1994, 53 out of the 67 articles for a successor agreement had been cleared in principle. The Conference resumed its work, under UNCTAD auspices, at a third session, in February 1995, where 31 countries, representing nearly 90 per cent of world trade in natural rubber, adopted the 1995 International Natural Rubber Agreement aimed at stabilizing prices. The new Agreement was opened for signature at United Nations Headquarters on 1 April 1995. Other commodity-related meetings held under UNCTAD auspices dealt with iron ore and tungsten.

240   The Standing Committee on Economic Cooperation among Developing Countries held its second session from 14 to 18 November 1994. The Committee endorsed a set of recommendations aimed at fostering economic cooperation among developing countries. Furthermore, it concluded, *inter alia,* that developing countries should adopt strategies that combine trade liberalization with other measures in the areas of production, investment, transport and communications, marketing and distribution and trade information. Special attention should be given to measures for increasing the effectiveness of trade liberalization regimes in regional integration arrangements and for increasing South-South trade.

At the end of the thirteenth session of the Intergovernmen- *241* tal Group of Experts on Restrictive Business Practices, held from 24 to 28 October 1994, competition experts launched the preparatory process for the Third United Nations Conference to Review All Aspects of the Set of Multilaterally Agreed Equitable Principles and Rules for the Control of Restrictive Business Practices, which is scheduled to take place in November 1995. The main document prepared by the UNCTAD secretariat dealt with the role of competition policy in economic reforms in developing and other countries. The Intergovernmental Group held its fourteenth session from 6 to 10 March 1995. Anti-trust experts made a number of proposals for strengthening multilateral cooperation in the area of competition laws and policies.

The three new ad hoc working groups, established in ac- *242* cordance with a decision of the Board taken at the resumed second part of its fortieth session, in May 1994, commenced their work. The Ad Hoc Working Group on Trade, Environment and Development held its first session from 28 November to 2 December 1994. The Working Group examined international cooperation on eco-labelling and eco-certification programmes, and market opportunities for environmentally friendly products. The session emphasized the importance of improved transparency in eco-labelling and the need for developing countries to be more closely associated with the elaboration of environmental criteria having an impact on trade and development.

243   The Ad Hoc Working Group on the Role of Enterprises in Development held its first session from 3 to 7 April 1995, focusing upon the development of small and medium-sized enterprises. The Working Group examined the role of the State in creating an enabling environment for the promotion of entrepreneurship, as well as the viable development of enterprises, especially small and medium-sized enterprises.

244   The Commission on International Investment and Transnational Corporations held its twenty-first session from 24 to 28 April, its first session in its new role as a subsidiary body of the Trade and Development Board. The Commission examined recent trends in foreign direct investment and exchanged experiences on ways of attracting such investment.

245   In 1994, UNCTAD expenditure on technical cooperation amounted to some $22 million. The largest single source of funds continues to be UNDP, although the trend observed in recent years towards increased contributions by other donors has continued. As part of the programme, UNCTAD provided support to a number of countries in assessing the results of the Uruguay Round, and in preparing themselves for new issues subject to negotiations in the General Agreement on Tariffs and Trade/World Trade Organization. Continued assistance was provided in several aspects of trade policies, including competition policy, the linkage between trade and the environment, and the utilization of the generalized system of preferences. Several new packages under the UNCTAD training programme TRAINFORTRADE were developed and delivered. In the area of commodities, particular attention was devoted to the use of risk-management instruments.

246   With the transfer to UNCTAD of the United Nations activities related to transnational corporations and to science and technology, the corresponding technical cooperation programmes, including advisory services on foreign investment,

have become an integral part of UNCTAD technical cooperation. The UNCTAD software for management and analysis of
debt was enhanced and installed in a number of countries.
UNCTAD has also continued to provide support to countries in
the areas of shipping, port management (notably in Somalia)
and cargo tracking, with the training aspects being undertaken
in most cases through the TRAINMAR programme. The largest
single programme undertaken by UNCTAD is that on customs
modernization and computerization, known as ASYCUDA. In
line with the process leading to and following up after the World
Symposium on Trade Efficiency, support and advice were
given to a number of countries in the establishment of trade
points.

At its tenth executive session, held on 4 May, the Trade and   *247*
Development Board agreed that appropriate exploratory work
should be undertaken on such new and emerging issues on the
international trade agenda within the preparatory process for
the ninth session of UNCTAD. Three categories of issues were
identified. The first consists of issues that give rise to demands
for domestic policy harmonization. Among those issues are investment and competition policies and labour standards. The
second category includes issues that reflect concern about the
lack of coherence among global policy objectives. The third
consists of issues affecting the ability of countries, especially
the least developed countries and others with weak economies,
to pursue national goals effectively.

The Commission on Science and Technology for Develop-   *248*
ment held its second session from 15 to 24 May. (The Commission, a subsidiary body of the Economic and Social Council,
now meets at Geneva as a result of the designation of UNCTAD
as the United Nations focal point for science and technology-
related activities.) Topics considered by the Commission at that
session included the use of science and technology to help meet

basic needs of low-income populations, improving women's access to science and technology, and the use of science and technology towards sustainable land-management practices. The Commission decided to focus its work programme for the next two years on recent developments in information technologies and their implications for economic growth, social cohesion, cultural values and society as a whole.

249   The Standing Committee on Developing Services Sectors: Shipping held its third session from 6 to 9 June to examine progress in policy reforms for enhancing competitive services in the fields of shipping, ports and multimodal transport in developing countries and countries in transition. In particular, support was pledged by major donors for the TRAINMAR programme, through which UNCTAD enhances the management capacities of developing countries in the field of shipping, ports and multimodal transport. The role of UNCTAD in the development of the advanced cargo information system was also praised. As this was the last session of the Committee before the ninth session of UNCTAD, the Committee reviewed work carried out since 1992. It established a set of complementary activities to be taken up by UNCTAD during the period leading up to the ninth session and suggested issues for further deliberation at that session.

250   The Ad Hoc Working Group on Trade, Environment and Development held its second session from 6 to 9 June, to examine the effects of environmental policies on market access and competitiveness. The UNCTAD secretariat was requested to outline positive measures that could be used as alternatives to trade-related measures for environmental protection for consideration at the next meeting of the Working Group, to be held in October.

251   The Standing Committee on Poverty Alleviation held its third session from 12 to 16 June to identify national and interna-

tional measures to alleviate poverty through international trade and official development assistance. As this was the last session of the Committee before the ninth session of UNCTAD, the meeting reviewed the work carried out since 1992 by the Committee and suggested that the ninth session should consider whether the present form of intergovernmental machinery for addressing poverty alleviation in UNCTAD was the appropriate one or whether some alternative arrangement could be envisaged. Poverty and increased marginalization will feature high on the agenda of the ninth session.

In cooperation with UNDP and the United Nations regional economic commissions, UNCTAD organized the Symposium for Land-locked and Transit Developing countries from 14 to 16 June, pursuant to General Assembly resolution 48/169 of 21 December 1993. The objectives of the Symposium were to analyse weaknesses in the operational, administrative, regulatory and institutional framework that is currently in place in the transit sector and to propose the future course of action at the national, bilateral, subregional and international levels. Participating countries agreed to develop a global framework for cooperation on transit transport with the support of the international community. UNCTAD has been requested to convene transit corridor-specific consultative groups that will identify priority areas for action at the national and subregional level and will establish the framework for the implementation of agreed measures. At a meeting of governmental experts from land-locked and transit developing countries, held from 19 to 22 June, the recommendations of the Symposium were widely endorsed. *252*

The Standing Committee on Economic Cooperation among Developing Countries held its third session from 19 to 23 June to discuss ways to enlarge and deepen monetary, financial, investment and enterprise cooperation. The agreed con- *253* clusions contain suggestions for strengthening financial and monetary cooperation among developing countries, as well as at the level of investment and business.

3.   *United Nations Environment Programme (UNEP)*

254   UNEP, headed by Ms. Elizabeth Dowdeswell, is pursuing implementation of the environmental dimension of Agenda 21, adopted by the United Nations Conference on Environment and Development in June 1992.

255   At its seventeenth session, in May 1994, the Governing Council of UNEP recognized the need for a fundamental change in the Programme's focus and priorities, and its relationship with other collaborators, in order to address the changed international environmental agenda emerging from the Conference.

256   In addition to implementing a work programme for 1994-1995 based on a Corporate Programme Framework, UNEP held, between October 1994 and February 1995, extensive consultations with Governments and high-level advisors to develop a refocused programme, based on an integrated approach, for its biennium 1996-1997.

257   The new integrated programme for 1996-1997 as approved by the eighteenth session of the Governing Council of UNEP addresses four principal environmental challenges: (*a*) sustainable management and use of natural resources; (*b*) sustainable production and consumption; (*c*) a better environment for environmental health and well-being; and (*d*) globalization trends and the environment.

258   UNEP collaboration with UNDP has been advanced with the signing of two agreements, one on international information exchange and another on a new partnership for combating desertification. In March, UNEP and the International Union for Conservation of Nature and Natural Resources signed a partnership agreement to strengthen their long-standing world-

wide cooperation in resource conservation and sustainable development. The agreement will facilitate collaboration at the regional level, thereby increasing the capability of UNEP and the International Union to respond to geographically diverse environmental concerns.

A major recent development during the period under review has been the operationalization of the restructured Global Environment Facility, which is implemented jointly by UNDP, UNEP and the World Bank. Within the Global Environment Facility, UNEP will catalyse the development of scientific and technical analysis, and promote and implement environmental management. *259*

The Scientific and Technical Advisory Panel was constituted by the Executive Director in April. UNEP has also worked in conjunction with other major groups in the areas of chemicals, refugees, agricultural development and environmental technology. *260*

UNEP, together with the International Labour Organization (ILO), the Food and Agriculture Organization of the United Nations (FAO), WHO, UNIDO and OECD, established the Inter-Organization Programme for the Sound Management of Chemicals to increase coordination and information exchange on chemicals and chemical wastes. Additionally, UNEP, with the active collaboration of the private chemical industry sector, has issued the Code of Ethics in the International Trade in Chemicals. UNEP was asked to increase its role in managing toxic chemicals and to further the development of international environmental law. Moreover, the Governing Council of the United Nations Environment Programme authorized the Executive Director to begin negotiations, in cooperation with FAO, on the development of a prior informed consent convention relating to the international trade of certain hazardous chemicals. UNEP also participated in a regional seminar at San *261*

Salvador in May on the implementation in Central America and the Caribbean of the Basel Convention on the Control of Transboundary Movements of Hazardous Wastes and Their Disposal, which generated valuable discussion on how to incorporate cleaner production activities in the proposed subregional centres for training and technology transfer under the Basel Convention.

262   In collaboration with the United Nations Centre for Human Settlements (Habitat), UNEP assisted Rwanda to address the issue of environmental damage caused by civil war and the massive movement of refugees.

263   UNEP has joined the World Bank, FAO and UNDP in supporting the Consultative Group on International Agricultural Research in its efforts to confront the new challenges of sustainable agricultural development. UNEP is taking part in the development of a multilateral system on plant genetic resources. As a co-sponsor of the Consultative Group, UNEP has been requested to provide information on the negotiating process leading to the second conference of the parties to the Convention on Biological Diversity.

264   The UNEP Environment Technology Centre became operational in September 1994. Located in Osaka and Shiga prefectures in Japan, the Centre is engaged in assisting developing countries in the transfer of technology to solve urban environmental problems and issues relating to management of freshwater lakes and reservoir basins. After the earthquake in Kobe, the Centre responded by providing staff to assist emergency medical teams.

265   The first UNEP International Seminar on Gender and Environment, held in April 1995, called for shared responsibility between women and men in achieving sustainable development and provided material for the development of a policy statement to the Fourth World Conference on Women in Beijing.

UNEP offered to provide the secretariat for the proposed *266*
global programme of action to protect the marine environment
from land-based activities. The programme was reviewed by a
meeting of government experts held in March. The meeting recognized the need to reduce and eliminate pollution by persistent
organic pollutants. The final document of the draft global programme is to be presented for adoption at an intergovernmental
meeting in October and November.

The work of UNEP with the commercial and investment *267*
banking sector since the United Nations Conference on Environment and Development in 1992 has resulted in a new alliance with major insurance companies. In March 1995, UNEP
announced the forging of a new partnership at its Advisory
Group Meeting on Commercial Banks and the Environment,
with a view to continuing to foster responsible sustainable development policies and practices in the banking sector. UNEP
signed an agreement with the International Olympic Committee to promote environmental protection in international sports
competitions. Together with the Foundation for International
Environmental Law and Development, UNEP convened a first
meeting on liability and compensation in London, gathering
experts from the United Nations, Governments and the academic community.

UNEP provides scientific and administrative support to *268*
the secretariats of environmental conventions. The Lusaka
Agreement on Cooperative Enforcement Operations Directed
at Illegal Trade in Wild Fauna and Flora, which aims to reduce
and ultimately eliminate illegal international trafficking in
African wildlife, was concluded in September 1994 by six eastern and southern African countries. The United Nations International Convention to Combat Desertification in Those Countries Experiencing Serious Drought and/or Desertification,
Particularly in Africa, provides for a substantive role for UNEP

in awareness-raising and the formulation and implementation of programmes to combat desertification. The first meeting of the Conference of the Parties to the Convention on Biological Diversity, held in November and December 1994, chose UNEP to host the permanent secretariat of the Convention. UNEP has initiated a programme to promote the safe use of biotechnology throughout the world as one of its responses to Agenda 21. Under the auspices of the Convention on International Trade in Endangered Species of Wild Flora and Fauna, a Timber Working Group was established in March to study how the Convention should be involved in the protection of timber species.

269   The first Conference of the Parties to the United Nations Framework Convention on Climate Change was held in March and April. UNEP believes that a strong climate research base is needed to ensure the Convention's success and to this end has been playing a central role with the Intergovernmental Panel on Climate Change in collaboration with FAO, the Intergovernmental Oceanographic Commission of UNESCO, the World Meteorological Organization (WMO) and the International Council of Scientific Unions. Over 300 experts from countries that have ratified the Montreal Protocol on Substances that Deplete the Ozone Layer to the Vienna Convention for the Protection of the Ozone Layer made significant progress in proposing possible amendments and adjustments to the international treaty during a one-week session at Nairobi from 8 to 12 May. It was the second time since its inception in 1987 that the Montreal Protocol had been reviewed, demonstrating the determination of the world community to find solutions to many ozone-related issues that should be resolved by the December 1995 meeting at Vienna of the parties to the Protocol. Final recommendations will be made at a meeting at Geneva from 28 August to 1 September 1995, at which proposed amendments and adjustments to the Protocol will be considered, including advanced phase-out of methyl bromide and a revised phase-out schedule for chlorofluorocarbons and halons by the developing countries. Meanwhile, the multilateral fund for the implementation of the Montreal Protocol has disbursed $303 million to finance about 830 projects in 81 developing countries.

An intergovernmental agreement aimed at conserving the *270* migratory waterbirds of Africa and Eurasia was adopted in June at The Hague at a meeting held under the auspices of the Convention on the Conservation of Migratory Species of Wild Animals. This new agreement covers more than 150 species of birds that are ecologically dependent on wetlands for at least part of their annual cycle. The coastal States of the Mediterranean Action Plan — the oldest and strongest of the UNEP regional seas programmes — adopted a cross-sectoral approach to environmental protection and development of the Mediterranean basin at the Ninth Ordinary Meeting of the Contracting Parties to the Convention, held from 9 to 10 June at Barcelona. The scope and geographical coverage of the revised Convention and Action Plan were also expanded to ensure the integration between the marine environment, the coastal areas and the associated coastal watersheds, including water resources, and soil, forest and plant coverage.

The Executive Director of UNEP is chairing the Working *271* Group on Sustainable Freshwater Resources for Africa within the Secretary-General's Special Initiative on Africa. A draft report was submitted to the meeting of the Group held in July at Geneva for the purpose of promoting dialogue and collaborative management of water resources among riparian States sharing international water resources. To that end UNEP has been implementing a series of new projects in integrated management of water resources. In June a meeting of experts was held on a diagnostic study for the Nile basin as the first phase in the development of a comprehensive management plan for the basin.

272   At the first meeting of the Environmental Emergencies Advisory Group, held in January, experts from 24 countries commended the work of the Joint UNEP/Department of Humanitarian Affairs Environment Unit, which was established in 1994 and has since carried out a number of emergency assessments of the oil spills in Arctic Russia.

273   UNEP efforts to link environmental and economic concerns are gaining momentum. At a workshop convened by UNEP and the World Bank in March, international experts urged the leading financial institutions to incorporate social and environmental objectives in their structural adjustment programmes. Another workshop was held in March to review the environmental impact of trade policies. UNEP has agreed to take a leading role in the development of methodologies for sustainability indicators. In a workshop hosted by the Philippines in May and June, government representatives from 33 countries, agencies, development banks and industries developed a framework for the sustainable management of reefs as outlined in the International Coral Reef Initiative: the UNEP regional seas programme was recognized as an appropriate vehicle for that effort. The implementation of Agenda 21 was reviewed in Paris in June by UNEP and 50 major international and national industry associations. This annual consultative meeting of UNEP facilitated information exchange among industries on the activities they have undertaken to promote sustainable production and consumption patterns worldwide.

274   From May to June in Mexico City, 50 experts in urban and environmental management from Latin America analysed major problems hindering the efforts of the region's mega-cities towards sustainability. The result was a document prepared in collaboration with UNEP that will be presented at the Second

United Nations Conference on Human Settlements (Habitat II) to be held at Istanbul in June 1996.

The Governing Council of UNEP held its eighteenth ses- *275* sion at Nairobi, from 15 to 26 May, adopting a record number of 64 decisions, all by consensus. A programme activity budget of $90-105 million was approved for the next biennium. UNEP celebrated World Environment Day on 5 June with the theme, "We the Peoples, United for the Global Environment", in South Africa, with the participation and support of the President of the Republic of South Africa, Mr. Nelson Mandela.

The demands placed on UNEP after the United Nations *276* Conference on Environment and Development in 1992 have not been met with any significant increase in financial resources to the Programme. The further expected reduction of the voluntary contributions to the Environment Fund of UNEP and the unpredictability of payments constitute principal constraints for the future of the Programme and its capability to provide an effective service to the international community.

4. *United Nations Centre for Human Settlements (Habitat)*

At a time when approximately one quarter of the world's popu- *277* lation is either inadequately housed or is homeless, the growing global shelter crisis resulting from uncontrolled urbanization and rural poverty is imparting new urgency to the mandate of the United Nations Centre for Human Settlements (Habitat), under the direction of Mr. Wally N'Dow.

To address these far-reaching challenges, the Centre has *278* embarked on a number of major initiatives. Central to these are preparations now under way for the Second United Nations Conference on Human Settlements (Habitat II), also known as the "City Summit". Through its declaration of principles and commitments and its global plan of action, Habitat II is expected to reaffirm the importance of human settlements in national and international development policies and strategies.

279   The recently concluded second session of the Preparatory Committee of the Conference mobilized those whose collaboration is essential to the forging of new partnerships for managing the urban environment: national Governments, local authorities and their international associations, private-sector enterprises, civic groups and non-governmental and community-based organizations. Through a series of regional meetings, supported and/or organized by the regional economic commissions, countries are now taking stock and identifying common concerns with respect to their regions.

280   Preparations have begun on several Habitat II–related conferences, including the International Conference on Best Practices in Improving the Living Environment, to be convened in Dubai in November. Organizations and agencies of the United Nations system, as well as professional associations and research institutions, are collaborating with the Centre in sponsoring an extensive series of workshops, seminars, colloquiums and round tables related to the Conference's two main themes: adequate shelter for all and sustainable human settlement development in an urbanizing world.

281   The Centre continues to monitor and coordinate the implementation of the Global Strategy for Shelter to the Year 2000, which will also be reviewed by Habitat II in 1996. Technical assistance activities geared to that end were undertaken by the Centre in 91 countries over the reporting period, especially in the areas of urban management, environmental planning and management, disaster mitigation and reconstruction, housing policy and urban poverty reduction. Significant interregional programmes are currently being implemented, in urban management, sustainable cities and the housing and urban indica-

tors programme. Among the major reconstruction projects under way in 1995 were those in Afghanistan and in Rwanda.

Capacity-building activities were expanded in the coun- *282* tries in transition of eastern and central Europe and the countries of the Commonwealth of Independent States (CIS). Progress was achieved in introducing gender issues in human settlement–related training programmes. New initiatives have been launched with UNEP and WHO to promote environmental health in human settlements and work is proceeding on the second *Global Report on Human Settlements*, which will be launched at Habitat II.

Africa is an important focus of the Centre's activities. Over *283* the reporting period, new responsibilities have been entrusted to the Centre by the Inter-Agency Task Force for the United Nations New Agenda for the Development of Africa in the 1990s. The Centre will be the associate lead agency responsible for urban management and human settlement programmes and policies and for the continuum from relief to development.

Securing adequate levels of funding to carry out its ex- *284* panding mandate and role within the development agenda of the United Nations, including support for Habitat II, is one of the most important challenges facing the Centre. The urgent need for United Nations and bilateral donor emergency assistance to redress the effects of civil wars and natural disasters has resulted in continuing reductions in the level of funding available for the Centre's development cooperation activities of a longer-term nature.

C. OPERATIONAL ACTIVITIES FOR DEVELOPMENT

1. *United Nations Development Programme (UNDP)*

285 As the principal arm of the United Nations for the funding and coordination of technical assistance and development, UNDP, under its Administrator, Mr. James Gustave Speth, has contributed to the development debate at both the conceptual and operational levels — internationally and in the countries it serves.

286 To strengthen its own capacity to give policy guidance and support in priority areas, UNDP restructured its Bureau for Policy and Programme Support to include four thematic divisions, on social development and poverty elimination, management development and governance, sustainable energy and environment, and science and technology.

287 Path-breaking legislation on the future of UNDP and on the successor programming arrangements for the next period was approved by the Executive Board of UNDP and UNFPA in June. The decision on the future of UNDP continued the process of redefining its role. The Board recognized poverty elimination as the overriding priority in UNDP programmes and urged concentration on areas where UNDP has demonstrable comparative advantages, in particular in capacity-building.

288 The Board's decision on successor programming arrangements constituted a major turning-point for UNDP, replacing the programming system that had been in effect since the "consensus" decision of 1970. The new system is intended to provide greater flexibility in the assignment of resources, as well as greater incentives for the formulation of focused, high-impact and high-leverage programmes to promote sustainable human development.

289 At the conceptual level, the *Human Development Report*, a report to UNDP, prepared by a team of independent development experts, has contributed to the international development debate. The 1995 *Report* focuses on gender issues and on valuing women's work as a contribution to the Fourth World Conference on Women.

Several Governments have requested assistance in the *290* preparation of their own national human development reports, based on the methodologies used in the *Human Development Report*. National reports have been published in 9 countries in all regions in 1994 and 1995 and are in preparation in close to 40 more, including several in central and eastern Europe and CIS. In other countries, such as Botswana, Egypt and Bolivia, exercises based on the human development methodology for the collection of disaggregated data have been conducted. Overall, the reports and data collection exercises help to identify groups excluded from the benefits of development, whether for reasons of poverty, gender or geographic location, and to propose environmentally sound strategies for their inclusion.

The national long-term perspective studies programme, *291* introduced in 1991, has helped African countries define national priorities to guide their development over a 25-year "futures" horizon. By 1994, the programme was active in 11 countries.

UNDP has assisted many programme countries in the *292* preparation of their positions at global forums. Through the resident coordinator system, UNDP has contributed at the national level to preparations for the Fourth World Conference on Women. Several dozen reports on the status of women were prepared for the Conference, most of them based on gender analysis and the collection of disaggregated data. UNDP facilitated dialogue in each country among the organizations of Government, the United Nations and civil society. UNDP is now integrating the broader concept of gender in the programming process. For example, in 1993, the Government of Turkey, with support from UNDP, launched a programme for the enhancement of women's participation in the nation's development. Training was conducted on such topics as women and employment, women and entrepreneurship, and women and violence. UNDP is also cooperating with UNCHS in the preparations for Habitat II.

293   In 1994, in collaboration with the Inter-American Development Bank and Governments of the region, UNDP co-sponsored development-related preparations for the Summit of the Americas, which mapped out areas for enhanced regional cooperation and development and for movement towards greater participation in development planning and management. In the Asia and Pacific region, UNDP sponsored a regional meeting of development ministers at Kuala Lumpur to facilitate dialogue on strategies for collaboration and for development in the region. It was also heavily involved in the preparations for the International Convention to Combat Desertification and the United Nations Framework Convention on Climate Change, assisting with both the preparation of country positions and the conventions themselves.

294   UNDP experience shows that concepts can only be developed and tested against operational activities. In January 1995, in order to serve development professionals, UNDP pulled together national experience in 13 monographs in the UNDP Series on Sustainable Human Development: Country Strategies for Social Development. The series was launched during the preparatory process for the World Summit for Social Development.

295   Inter-agency Cooperation has been furthered by widening the resident coordinator pool to encompass candidates from the joint consultative group on policy agencies as well as from the Office of the United Nations High Commissioner for Refugees (UNHCR) and the United Nations Secretariat. Since Jan-

uary 1994, a total of six resident coordinators have so far been selected from the United Nations, UNICEF, the World Food Programme (WFP), UNIDO and UNCTAD. It is hoped that this will lead to greater understanding of the priorities of different agencies and an enhanced sense of ownership of the resident coordinator system on the part of the agencies.

In many countries, resident coordinators have established *296* sectoral subcommittees led by the relevant United Nations agency representative to ensure coordination at the sectoral level. Joint training of United Nations agency representatives and resident coordinators at the ILO Turin Centre has been stepped up. A total of 13 workshops had been held by April 1995, with 63 staff from UNDP and 305 staff from other United Nations agencies being trained. To give further support to inter-agency coordination, UNDP has established an Inter-Agency Coordination and External Policy Office within a restructured Bureau for Resources and External Affairs.

Considerable success has been achieved in increasing the *297* clarity of respective roles within the United Nations system. A statement of principles was signed with UNEP outlining re-spective roles and an intention to collaborate between the two organizations. A statement of principles was also signed with FAO on food security, a central aspect of sustainable human de-velopment in many countries. The high-level task force be-tween UNDP and the World Bank was revitalized, resulting in the negotiation of a revised statement of principles for collabo-ration between the two agencies, in particular in the areas of forestry and poverty alleviation. Joint programming in select countries is expected to begin in the coming year. Finally, dis-cussions are taking place between UNDP and UNHCR on the col-laborative efforts to reintegrate populations displaced by war.

The Administrator of UNDP established a task force under *298* the chairmanship of the Associate Administrator for further strengthening the role of the regional economic commissions. Mechanisms are being established — with collaboration between UNDP and the commissions — for coordinating United Nations activities at the regional and subregional levels.

299   UNDP has improved its support to the round-table process in order to achieve more regular meetings and a sharper focus on policy and resource mobilization. The 1994 round table for the Gambia raised $400 million. Four others were organized in Africa in 1994 (Central African Republic, Guinea-Bissau, Mali and Seychelles). The two organized in Asia, for the Lao People's Democratic Republic and Maldives, raised $500 million and $100 million respectively. The 1995 round table for Rwanda raised $587 million.

300   UNDP is playing a more active role in consultative group meetings, focusing on capacity for sustainable human development. At the consultative group for the Philippines, the UNDP-sponsored *Philippine Human Development Report 1994* served as a principal reference for the agenda item on sustainable development.

301   In March, the Copenhagen Declaration on Social Development and Programme of Action adopted by the World Summit for Social Development called on UNDP to organize United Nations system efforts towards capacity-building at the local, national and regional levels. In April, the Administrator sent a detailed proposal for UNDP follow-up strategy to all 133 country offices. In June, the Executive Board of UNDP adopted key decisions on following up the Summit and mandated poverty elimination as its overriding priority within the framework of the goals and priority areas agreed to the previous year in support of sustainable human development. The Administrator has asked the UNDP country offices to consult with national counterparts on how the United Nations system can best assist each country in implementing the recommendations of the Summit,

in particular in developing national strategies and programmes for poverty elimination. Other areas include the macroeconomic framework for a greater emphasis on poverty reduction; social sector policy and planning; systems to assist vulnerable groups; and poverty definitions, indicators and assessments. UNDP has set up a rapid response system to provide information required for Summit follow-up and to support shifts in programme emphasis.

Poverty elimination, as addressed by the Copenhagen Declaration and Programme of Action, requires participation and empowerment of people at all levels. This requires effective outreach mechanisms that make use of local government, institutions of civil society such as village and community groups and institutions of traditional government, national and international non-governmental organizations, United Nations Volunteer specialists and United Nations specialized agencies. Most importantly, it involves empowerment of target communities in the identification and communication of their own needs and in the management of the implementation of projects and programmes geared to eliminating critical constraints to their development. During 1994 and 1995, the United Nations Capital Development Fund provided local development funds in addition to larger-scale infrastructure and credit facilities. These funds involve the community, whether through community groups or local government bodies, in establishing priorities and in implementing micro-scale infrastructure projects. *302*

To target those who are marginalized in economic or social terms but nevertheless have the potential for productive livelihood requires pro-poor macro-policies geared to build on the productivity of the poor. Many UNDP-supported programmes and projects, as in Sri Lanka and Uganda, have demonstrated how to bring participation, employment and empowerment to poor people. In recognition of the importance of rural agricul- *303* ture in the alleviation of poverty, employment creation, the preservation of the environment and bringing women into the mainstream of economic development, guidelines for UNDP, government and other development practitioners, entitled "Sustainable Human Development and Agriculture", have been produced and now serve as a basic reference for programming in UNDP.

304   UNDP took several initiatives in 1994 to promote greater participation by the potential actors and beneficiaries of development. The Conference on Peace and Development, held in Honduras in October 1994, represented the climax of effort by the countries of the region to build consensus on the issues of peace and democratization in Central America. The Conference brought together representatives of Governments, the private sector, cooperatives, trade unions, indigenous communities, universities, regional organizations and the donor community, thus institutionalizing the dialogue with civil society.

305   Employment generation requires deepening collaboration between UNDP and ILO to identify market demand systematically and to create economically viable jobs that foster sustainable livelihoods. For example, in Ethiopia, the Government has formulated a national programme on human resource development and utilization that looks at both the supply and demand for human resources. The employment and livelihoods subprogramme has set a target of creating 24,000 additional jobs per year over five years and focuses on areas such as the informal sector, promotion of small and medium-scale enterprises, agricultural wage employment and rural on- and off-farm employment.

306   Protection and regeneration of the environment has been advanced by UNDP for national capacity-building in the follow-up and implementation of Agenda 21 and the Montreal

Protocol. China has developed, with UNDP support and with the involvement of over 50 government agencies, research institutes and public organizations, an Agenda 21 strategy. UNDP helped to organize a donor conference during which the Government presented 62 high-priority projects covering such areas as sustainable agriculture; cleaner production; clean energy; conservation and sustainable use of natural resources; pollution control; population growth; and an improvement in the status of people's health, education and general welfare.

To meet the growing demand for national capacity to man- *307* age complex environmental concerns, a new Division for Sustainable Energy and Environment was established in August 1994 within the Bureau for Programme and Policy Support. It will further support efforts to incorporate environmental concerns at the earliest possible stages of economic decision-making and promote the full implementation of Agenda 21.

A new initiative for sustainable energy is being formulated *308* to support programme formulation and to provide for greater access to improved energy technology. UNDP along with UNEP, UNIDO and the World Bank are the four implementing agencies assisting some 31 developing countries to eliminate ozone-depleting substances in a programme financed by the multilateral fund under the Montreal Protocol. As at 31 December 1994, total approved budgets amounted to $79.61 million. Eleven country programmes have been approved with UNDP as lead agency and 19 capacity-building (institution-strengthening) projects are under way. Out of a total of 97 projects completed, 20 involve technology transfer investment projects, which have phased out 1,455 tons of ozone-depleting substances.

The governance issues concerning the Global Environ- *309* ment Facility have been resolved and the Facility's Instrument has been approved, delineating the roles of UNEP, UNDP and the World Bank. By December 1994, the UNDP Global Environment Facility pilot phase portfolio consisted of 55 technical assistance projects and 28 pre-investment feasibility studies. In 1995, UNDP launched the post-pilot phase, with 20 projects. As the Programme's main effort to implement Agenda 21, Capacity 21 completed its first full year of operation in 1994, with a solid portfolio of national programmes in all regions. By August 1995, the environmental management guidelines training workshop, a major capacity-building initiative, had been held in 122 countries, involving 3,600 participants.

310   UNDP is supporting public sector reform in many countries. In Viet Nam, UNDP is helping with reform of the legal, financial and monetary systems, with particular emphasis on social adjustment concerns. It has been assigned the main responsibility for support to the Government in the coordination and management of external cooperation resources. Similar activities are under way in Lebanon, Peru and Zambia. In March, a regional meeting of Latin American and eastern European experts was held in Argentina to discuss how prudent use of regulation, competition and social safety nets can be combined to ensure that privatization contributes to sustainable human development.

311   During 1994, the United Nations Capital Development Fund began working with UNDP units dealing with governance in selected developing countries. The aim is to promote decentralization by attracting technical cooperation to the local level and providing the capital assistance necessary for newly established local authorities to gain experience in administering development programmes.

312   Collaborating closely with the Electoral Assistance Division of the Secretariat, UNDP has responded to an increasing number of country requests relating to the introduction or enhancement of the electoral process, including, in Africa, Chad,

Ethiopia, Liberia, Mozambique, Togo and Uganda, and, in Latin America, Brazil and Mexico. United Nations Volunteer specialists served as electoral observers and facilitators in Mozambique and South Africa. Other UNDP-supported initiatives have aimed to ensure access to due process and acquired rights. For instance, an international ombudsman workshop was held in the Russian Federation as part of the democracy, governance and participation programme for the States of eastern Europe and the former Soviet Union.

UNDP is attempting to promote sustainable develop-   *313* ment even in the midst of internal conflict situations. The importance of ensuring that humanitarian relief is linked to sustainable human development is widely accepted as a prerequisite for countries to resume progress and rebuild capacity as soon as possible. A case in point is Somalia, where, despite the difficult security situation, UNDP managed to continue an active rural rehabilitation programme in some parts of the country.

In 1994-1995, UNDP substantively enhanced its assist-   *314* ance in two situations in particular. Firstly, resources for the UNDP programme of assistance to the Palestinian people doubled to $25 million between 1993 and 1994. Secondly, the Government of South Africa and UNDP concluded negotiations and signed the Basic Standard Agreement in October 1994 during the visit of President Nelson Mandela to Headquarters during the general debate of the General Assembly at its forty-ninth session.

In other institutional developments, UNDP has become   *315* the first United Nations organization to be accepted as a member of the Society for Worldwide Inter-Bank Financial Telecommunications, a financial communications system using leased lines owned by banks. This has improved cash management capabilities while achieving savings of $250,000 per

FIGURE 8

Voluntary contributions to the United Nations Development Programme (core and non-core), 1989-1995

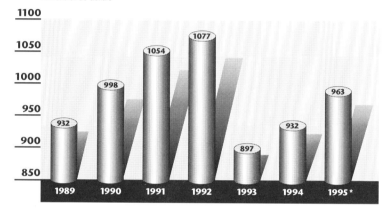

Millions of US dollars

* 1995: expected

year in general operating expenditures and reductions in staff costs.

316   The year 1994 was the mid-point of the current fifth indicative planning figure cycle (1992-1996), and 16 mid-term reviews were completed. It was found that fifth-cycle country programmes were essentially strategic, aimed at a limited number of major national or regional development objectives. As such, they are distinctly more focused than in previous cycles. They aim to reduce the number of individual projects and, as called for in General Assembly resolution 44/211 of 22 December 1989, to move towards the programme approach under national execution, with strong emphasis on national ownership and commitment. For example, in the Lao People's Democratic Republic, individual projects have been reduced from 50 to 15 and in the regional programme for Asia and the Pacific from 350 to 80. National ownership is being reinforced, with an in-

FIGURE 9

**Summary of financial activities:
funds and trust funds administered by the
United Nations Development Programme
1990-1994**

Millions of US dollars

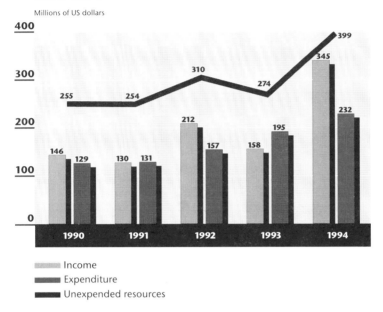

Income
Expenditure
Unexpended resources

crease in the rate of national execution from 34 per cent of approvals in 1991 to 53 per cent in 1994.

In 1994, voluntary contributions by member countries to UNDP core resources amounted to $917.57 million (see fig. 8). Contributions to non-core resources, including UNDP-administered funds, trust funds, cost-sharing arrangements and government cash counterpart contributions, raised the total funds administered by UNDP to over $1.8 billion (see fig. 9). There has been a continued rise in funds received through cost-sharing arrangements, with cost-sharing contributions increasing by 58.7 per cent in 1994 (see fig. 10). Total field programme

317

FIGURE 10

Cost-sharing activities of the United Nations Development Programme, 1992-1995

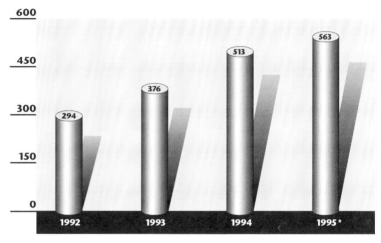

Millions of US dollars

* 1995: expected

expenditures for technical cooperation activities in 1994 amounted to approximately $1,036.50 million.

318   It became clear in 1994 that the UNDP biennial budget would have to be reduced further to keep administrative costs in line with declining core programme resources. This is in spite of the fact that between the biennial budgets for 1992-1993 and 1994-1995 a total of $53.6 million was cut from the administrative budget. Cuts have been made primarily by reducing staff positions both at headquarters (26 per cent) and at the country level (8 per cent).

319   The stagnation of UNDP core resources since 1992 and the current uncertain outlook reflect the global situation with regard to development cooperation. It is a cause for concern that notwithstanding the substantial adjustments undertaken in response to the changed conditions of the post-cold-war era, the resource base for UNDP has been seriously eroded. The 1995 contributions to the central resources of UNDP are expected to amount to approximately $937 million. This is much lower than the originally projected level under Governing Council decision 90/34, which, on the basis of resources of $1 billion, called for an 8 per cent annual increase during the fifth programming cycle (1992-1996). Viewed in the context of that decision, the shortfall for the cycle would amount to approximately $1.4 billion. For this reason, the Executive Board of UNDP decided to reduce national indicative planning figures by 30 per cent from their original levels.

Tragically, 17 UNDP staff members lost their lives in 1994 *320* while serving the cause of development.

2.   *United Nations Children's Fund (UNICEF)*

Ms. Carol Bellamy was appointed the fourth Executive Director *321* of UNICEF, succeeding Mr. James P. Grant, who had led the Organization for 15 years until his death in January 1995. The new Executive Director has indicated that improving the financial management and administrative and programme systems of UNICEF and ensuring more effective and efficient programme delivery will allow UNICEF to move into the next century (see fig. 11).

1995 is the mid-point of the decade-long strategy of the *322* World Summit for Children to meet global objectives for the welfare of children. The international community's goals and objectives for children and the broad outline of a global strategy have been set for the remainder of the decade by the World Summit for Children and by the imperatives of the Convention on the Rights of the Child. The International Conference on Population and Development and the World Summit for Social Development have reiterated the commitment of the international

FIGURE 11

Income of the United Nations Children's Fund, 1990-1994

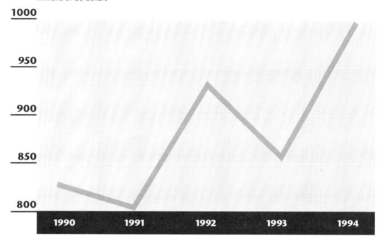

community to these goals. The Fourth World Conference on Women, to be held at Beijing in September 1995, can be expected to take these commitments a stage further, with a heightened emphasis on the need for gender equity and equality and for special attention to the girl-child.

323   The progress report presented to the UNICEF Executive Board on follow-up to the World Summit for Children noted that impressive progress was under way and that the majority of developing countries were on track to achieve a majority of the goals.

324   In 1994, UNICEF supported programmes in 149 countries — 46 in Africa, 37 in Latin America and the Caribbean (including 10 Caribbean island countries), 34 in Asia (including 13 Pacific island countries), 14 in the Middle East and North Africa and 18 in central and eastern Europe, the Commonwealth of Independent States and the Baltic States. The total programme expenditure reached $801 million. The third issue of *The Progress of Nations*, released in June 1995, provided up-to-date data on indicators for monitoring progress towards the goals, ranking countries according to their results.

UNICEF is addressing the main causes of child mortality, *325* with a focus on prevention, including immunization and the prevention and treatment of the major killers — acute respiratory infections, diarrhoeal diseases and malaria in areas of high endemicity. Immunization coverage was sustained globally at the 80 per cent level, but the regional average in Africa remained significantly lower, as it did in 1993. The Bamako Initiative, as a strategy for strengthening local primary health care systems, expanded to 33 countries in Africa, Asia and Latin America. Global and country-level activities continued to achieve goals for the year 2000 of universal iodization of salt and vitamin A distribution to all vulnerable people.

Most countries in East Asia, Latin America and the Middle *326* East achieved the mid-decade goal of universal access to primary education. However, more than one half of developing countries, including high-population countries in South Asia and Africa, still have to make major strides before all their children can be provided adequate opportunities for basic education. Girls' primary education was the dominant component of UNICEF support for education in South Asia, sub-Saharan Africa and the Middle East and North Africa.

UNICEF assisted some 100 countries in achieving their *327* water supply and sanitation goals and worked to refine strategies that emphasize sustainability and maximize health and socio-economic benefits. Progress was made in gaining acceptance of the women's equality and empowerment framework, as well as the life-cycle approach, as tools for promoting gender-balanced programmes for children and development.

328   UNICEF is committed to mainstream development programming, particularly as related to activities in basic social services. While pursuing these long-term development efforts, UNICEF was also called upon to play an active role in responding to many emergencies in which women and children were the hardest-hit victims. Approximately 25 per cent of UNICEF's programme expenditure in 1994 was devoted to providing life-saving essential services for children and women in emergencies.

329   In the former Yugoslavia, UNICEF was charged with a mandate to provide relief assistance in situations of great insecurity for its own staff. In Armenia, Azerbaijan, Georgia and Tajikistan, UNICEF helped to address the special needs of refugee populations and internally displaced people through the reestablishment of the cold chain, the provision of basic vaccines and health supplies, and support for educational systems.

330   UNICEF continues to pay special attention to Africa and other least developed countries. Despite the continuing and threatening emergencies in certain parts of sub-Saharan Africa, there are many positive developments that go almost unnoticed. In the areas of special action for children, 25 of the 46 countries in sub-Saharan Africa have either increased or sustained the immunization levels of 75 per cent or higher reached in 1990; the usage rate of oral rehydration therapy has now reached 50 per cent; salt iodization measures are being implemented in 28 of the 39 countries affected by iodine deficiency disorders; and guinea worm disease is well on the way to being eliminated from most of Africa.

331   Africa remains the continent with the greatest needs. UNICEF devotes some 38 per cent of its financial and human resources to sub-Saharan Africa. It helps build capacities and empower communities and families. In countries emerging from disasters, programmes will aim at strengthening local capacity, solidarity and coping mechanisms, which could become the embryo of new societies. At the national level, UNICEF is strengthening its ability to support Governments in policy development affecting children and in mobilizing resources for children. At the same time, UNICEF is participating actively in a United Nations–wide initiative for Africa, working to strengthen country-level collaboration towards all the elements of sustainable human development, poverty reduction and accelerated economic growth.

Unaccompanied children and internally displaced people *332* were a major challenge for UNICEF in Rwanda, where an unprecedented relief effort was mounted to protect refugees from the rapid spread of disease and famine. In Angola, Burundi and Somalia, UNICEF continued to provide assistance in the areas of health, education and water supply and sanitation. In Mozambique, under a national plan of reconstruction, UNICEF reoriented its emergency activities towards rebuilding basic services for health, water supply and sanitation and education. In Liberia and Sierra Leone, despite facing an increasingly difficult situation, UNICEF continued to provide essential emergency services. Trauma counselling and physical rehabilitation for handicapped children were priorities, as were programmes for violently abused women and girls and vocational training for child soldiers.

The Convention on the Rights of the Child has been em- *333* braced by more States than any other human rights treaty in history. By August 1995, 177 parties had ratified the Convention, with only 17 countries needed to attain the goal of universal ratification by the end of 1995.

At its forty-ninth session, the General Assembly discussed *334* for the first time the issue of children's rights and adopted resolutions on the protection of children affected by armed conflicts; the need to adopt efficient international measures for the prevention and eradication of the sale of children, child prostitution and child pornography; implementation of the Convention on the Rights of the Child; and the plight of street children (resolutions 49/209 to 49/212, all of 23 December 1994). UNICEF was asked to play an active role in support of those resolutions. Furthermore, UNICEF, in collaboration with the Centre for Human Rights, has been assisting the Committee on the Rights of the Child in monitoring implementation of the Convention. UNICEF is supporting the comprehensive study of the impact of armed conflict on children in response to General Assembly resolution 48/157 of 20 December 1993.

335   The World Summit for Social Development has provided new impetus to the work of UNICEF on behalf of children within the United Nations system, setting that work within a wider international effort towards poverty eradication and social development. After two years of systematic mobilization and persistent technical refinement in which UNICEF played an active role along with UNDP and UNFPA, the "20/20" initiative was adopted at the World Summit for Social Development as a legitimate and useful instrument for guiding, assessing and monitoring overall official development assistance and national budgetary allocations to basic social programmes.

3.   *United Nations Population Fund (UNFPA)*

336 During 1994, UNFPA, directed by Dr. Nafis Sadik, supported population programmes in 137 countries and territories. The Fund operates field offices, each headed by a country director, in 60 of those countries. The year 1994 will be remembered as the year the international community changed the way it looks at population issues. That change in perception actually evolved over two decades and culminated in the adoption of the Programme of Action of the International Conference on Population and Development, held at Cairo in September of that year.

The Programme of Action was the product of more than   *337*
three years of intense deliberation and negotiation between
Governments, non-governmental organizations, community
leaders, technical experts and interested individuals. The Programme of Action goes beyond mere numbers and demographic targets and places human beings and their well-being
at the centre of all population and sustainable development activities. It also sets out quantitative and qualitative goals and objectives to be reached by all countries by the year 2015: to provide universal access to reproductive health and family
planning services; to reduce infant, child and maternal mortality; and to provide access to primary education for all girls and
boys.

The Conference, and the Programme of Action it pro-   *338*
duced, spawned a series of internal and external assessments of
UNFPA. For example, each UNFPA geographical division conducted internal reviews of existing policies and programmes
and convened regional meetings to consider the implications of
the Conference for their respective regions.

UNFPA held a series of joint workshops with partner agen-   *339*
cies in the United Nations development system to examine how
best to translate the recommendations of the Programme of Action into actions at the country and local levels. These workshops focused on the key areas of the Fund's programme —
reproductive health and family planning (with WHO); information, education and communication (with UNESCO and
WHO); and population data, policy and research (with ILO) —
and involved advisers from the UNFPA technical support
services/country support team system, including technical support services specialists from the respective United Nations
agencies and organizations. These regional and technical consultations helped UNFPA assess the policy and programme
implications of the Conference for the future work of UNFPA.

340   The programme priorities and future directions of UNFPA in the light of the Conference were considered by the UNDP/UNFPA Executive Board at its annual session in June 1995. The Executive Board, in its decision 95/15, supported the broad outline of the future programme of assistance of UNFPA, which must be implemented in full accordance with the Programme of Action of the Conference, and endorsed the Fund's core programme areas of reproductive health, including family planning and sexual health, population and development strategies, and advocacy. The Board also recommended, in its decision 95/20, that the Economic and Social Council and the General Assembly endorse the agreement between UNDP and UNFPA to designate UNFPA resident country directors as UNFPA representatives.

341   On 19 December 1994, the General Assembly adopted resolution 49/128, entitled "Report of the International Conference on Population and Development", in which it emphasized the importance of continued and enhanced cooperation and coordination by all relevant organs, organizations and programmes of the United Nations system and the specialized agencies, and requested them to take appropriate measures to ensure the full and effective implementation of the Programme of Action. In resolution 49/128, the Assembly decided that the Population Commission should be renamed the Commission on Population and Development and that it should meet on an annual basis beginning in 1996.

342   On behalf of the Secretary-General and at the request of the Administrator of UNDP, the Executive Director of UNFPA convened in December 1994 the first meeting of the Inter-Agency Task Force on the Implementation of the Programme of Action of the International Conference on Population and Development. The meeting, attended by 12 United Nations organizations, worked to establish a common framework for follow-

up to the Conference and other conferences in the social sector. The Task Force decided to use working groups to develop operational guidelines for use by resident coordinators to promote inter-agency collaboration at the country level in the following areas: (*a*) a common data system at the national level in the field of health, notably in the areas of infant, child and maternal mortality; (*b*) basic education, with special attention to gender disparities; (*c*) policy-related issues, including the drafting of a common advocacy statement on social issues; (*d*) women's empowerment; and (*e*) reproductive health.

To achieve the goals of the Conference, it is necessary to *343* mobilize resources from Governments and non-governmental organizations. At the request of the Secretary-General, the Executive Director of UNFPA convened a consultation on resource mobilization on 20 January 1995. The participants suggested using existing mechanisms at the country level, such as the resident coordinator system, the World Bank consultative groups, and UNDP round tables, for the purpose of mobilizing country-specific resources. It was agreed that global consultation on this topic should be convened periodically, preferably at the time of the annual sessions of the Commission on Population and Development.

In conjunction with the International Conference on Popu- *344* lation and Development and the World Summit for Social Development, UNFPA organized two international parliamentarian meetings, dealing specifically with population issues relevant to the themes of the conferences. Moreover, UNFPA established an NGO Advisory Committee to advise on how to make better use of and interact more effectively with non-governmental organizations and the private sector.

In 1994, UNFPA organized programme review and strat- *345* egy development exercises in nine countries, providing useful inputs to the formulation of the country strategy notes. By the end of 1994, UNFPA had undertaken a total of 76 such exercises.

346   The Executive Board of UNFPA, in its decision 94/25, encouraged UNFPA, given the situation in Rwanda, to support, on an exceptional basis, in appropriate ways and in collaboration with other relief agencies, emergency assistance to the people of Rwanda from the population programme resources of the third UNFPA country programme for Rwanda. Subsequently, UNFPA approved a project in Rwanda for emergency/ rehabilitation assistance to the national maternal and child health and family planning programme, with UNICEF and UNFPA as executing agencies, and two emergency assistance projects to meet the reproductive health needs of Rwandan refugees in Burundi and the United Republic of Tanzania. The projects in Burundi and the United Republic of Tanzania, which were formulated in collaboration with UNHCR, UNICEF, the African Medical and Research Foundation and local non-governmental organizations, are progressing reasonably well. The Executive Board, in its decision 95/14, approved the continued implementation of decision 94/25, allowing for flexibility in sectoral expenditure of resources from the third UNFPA country programme for Rwanda and for overall expenditures of up to $7.8 million.

347   At the global level, UNFPA continued to support the Special Programme of Research, Development and Research Training in Human Reproduction of WHO. UNFPA also participated in the United Nations Joint and Co-sponsored Programme on HIV/AIDS. The Fund's Global Initiative on Contraceptive Requirements and Logistics Management Needs in Developing Countries in the 1990s, co-funded by a number of multilateral and bilateral donors and non-governmental organizations, organized in-depth studies on contraceptive requirements in Brazil, Bangladesh and Egypt, generating interest by several other countries with regard to contraceptive require-

ments. The Global Initiative also produced technical reports and organized consultative meetings and workshops.

The income of the Fund in 1994 was $265.3 million, com- *348* pared to a 1993 income of $219.6 million, an increase of 20.8 per cent (see fig. 12). Total expenditures for projects, from regular resources, increased from $134.3 million in 1993 to $204.1 million in 1994, an increase of $67.1 million, or 50 per cent. Expenditures for reproductive health and family planning programmes increased by 46 per cent, from $68.7 million in 1993 to $100.1 million in 1994, and accounted for nearly half of all of the Fund's project expenditures. Expenditures for information, education and communication activities increased by 80 per cent, from $21.3 million in 1993 to $38.3 million in 1994, and accounted for 19 per cent of total project expendi-

FIGURE 12

Voluntary contributions to the United Nations Population Fund (core and non-core), 1990-1994

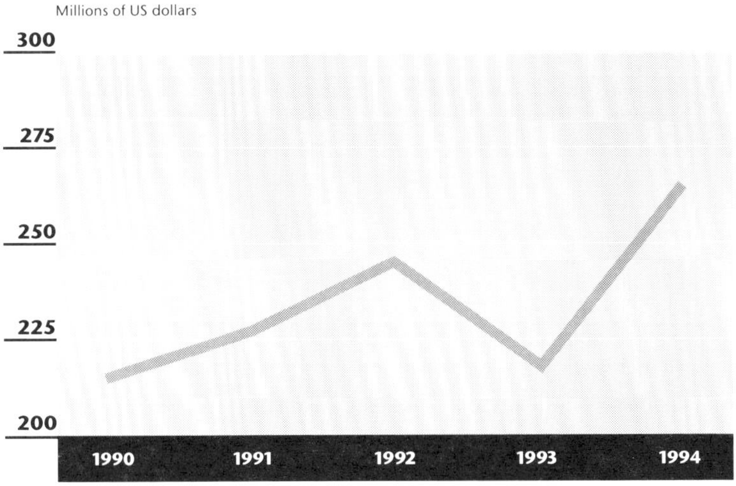

Millions of US dollars

tures. The remaining expenditures were divided among basic data collection (6.6 per cent); population dynamics (5.7 per cent); formulation, implementation and evaluation of population policies (8.1 per cent); multisectoral activities (5.5 per cent); and special programmes (5.4 per cent).

349   In 1994, the Asia and the Pacific region received 31.5 per cent of UNFPA programme allocations, the sub-Saharan Africa region received 31.1 per cent, the Latin America and Caribbean region 13.5 per cent and the Arab States and Europe 11.5 per cent. Support for interregional and global programmes amounted to 12.4 per cent of allocations. The Fund continued to concentrate over 71 per cent of its resources in countries most in need of assistance in the population field and notably in the poorest developing countries. In 1994, there were 58 priority countries for UNFPA assistance: 32 in sub-Saharan Africa, 17 in Asia and the Pacific, 5 in Latin America and the Caribbean and 4 in the Arab States.

4.   *World Food Programme (WFP)*

350   Directed by Ms. Catherine Bertini, WFP, the food aid arm of the United Nations system, remains on the front line of the United Nations battle against hunger and poverty. WFP concentrates its efforts on the neediest people in the neediest countries of the world.

351   In 1994, food assistance provided by WFP reached 57 million poor and hungry people. Eighty-two per cent of total WFP resources went to low income food deficit countries; the share to least developed countries was 52 per cent. Such resources support both relief and development.

352   On the development side, WFP food aid has been an effective means of transferring income to the poor and encouraging collective action in poor communities. Currently, some 225 development projects with an aggregate commitment of $2.6 billion are being supported in over 80 developing countries (see fig. 13).

On the emergency side, WFP responds to food shortages *353* by relying on its network of country offices and on its expertise in transport, logistics and procurement. During 1994, WFP provided relief assistance at a value of over $1 billion to the victims of man-made and natural disasters in over 40 countries.

In 1994, WFP managed $1.5 billion of resources — in *354* food commodities and cash — in support of the hungry and poor throughout the developing world. Over 32 million victims of man-made and natural disasters benefited from WFP assistance in 1994. Some 16 million people participated in food-for-work projects in support of agricultural and rural development.

FIGURE 13

World Food Programme expenditure, 1990-1994

Millions of US dollars

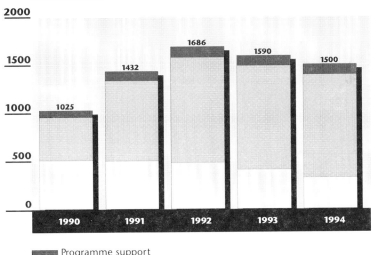

Programme support
Relief
Development

Over 8 million people received supplementary feeding through WFP-assisted education, training, health and nutrition projects.

355   About 80 per cent of WFP relief assistance in 1994 was provided to victims of disasters coming out of civil strife or cross-border wars — some 8.5 million refugees and 16.5 million internally displaced people, representing 50 per cent of the world's population of those two groups. More than 7 million people were victims of drought and other natural disasters. Some 64 per cent of total WFP relief operations were in support of needy people in Africa. The single biggest operation was in Burundi and Rwanda, costing $242 million, or 22 per cent of total relief expenditures. This operation, associated with tragic loss of life on a massive scale, continues to be an urgent focus of attention for the United Nations today, not only in Burundi and Rwanda but also in Kenya, Tanzania, Uganda and Zaire. The Liberia regional programme, costing $96 million, provided assistance to refugees and displaced persons in Liberia and in four neighbouring countries involved in the crisis.

356   Elsewhere in the world, major emergencies faced by WFP included the former Yugoslavia, where people continued to face food shortages and real poverty as a result of unresolved conflicts. WFP operations in that region amounted to $149 million. Afghanistan represents another country that is still in a state of chronic food insecurity in the absence of peace. The WFP regional operations in support of Afghan refugees and displaced people cost $95 million in 1994.

357   The number, scale and duration of emergencies and disasters, particularly those caused by armed conflict, have escalated alarmingly in recent years. In 1994, two out of three tons of WFP-provided food aid were distributed as relief assistance, and only one ton was used in support of development projects. Five years ago it was the reverse. With fewer resources for development, "silent" emergencies, in which people live in abject

poverty and chronic food insecurity, can quickly turn into acute emergencies. Relief assistance alone does not change the vulnerability of poor people to the next emergency. WFP is therefore making a deliberate effort to identify ways to increase the linkages between its relief and development assistance by integrating disaster mitigation elements into development projects, developing capacity-building elements into relief operations, and strengthening disaster preparedness through vulnerability mapping, better early warning and institutional development.

The Programme's approach to reducing problems associ- *358* ated with humanitarian emergencies is to collaborate in efforts aimed at prevention rather than cure. Wherever possible, food aid is used to support development goals. Africa and Asia continue to receive the largest shares of WFP development assistance — 40 per cent and 39 per cent, respectively. However, WFP development resources continue to decline in both absolute and relative terms with respect to emergency operations. Of the target of $1.5 billion for WFP regular development resources for the biennium 1993-1994 (approved by the Economic and Social Council and the FAO Council, and endorsed by the General Assembly and the FAO Conference) only two thirds was realized. As a result, the implementation of projects was often delayed. Moreover, WFP has been unable to support all approved projects at the level originally planned, as donors have increasingly tied and designated their development funds.

Food purchases have increased significantly during the *359* last five years. In 1994, WFP purchased a record 1.4 million tons of food, almost half of all the commodities distributed by the Programme. Sixty per cent of the food commodities were bought in developing countries, maintaining the Programme's position as the largest contributor to South-South trade in the United Nations system.

360   WFP cooperates with other multilateral, bilateral and non-governmental organizations at all stages of its activities. In 1994, significant progress was made in ensuring greater collaboration in relief operations. Joint assessments of refugee food needs (with UNHCR) and emergency needs (with FAO) continued to be an essential part of the work of WFP. WFP-assisted development projects in 17 countries benefited from collaboration with the International Fund for Agricultural Development (IFAD). WFP signed a first memorandum of understanding on joint working arrangements for emergency relief operations with a major international non-governmental organization and will seek to conclude similar agreements with other non-governmental organizations in the future.

361   The approach of WFP has been notably strengthened by the adoption of principles and guidelines for a country-based programme, which includes resourcing levels, and a criteria for project approval. Resource arrangements are being addressed to improve predictability, accountability and transparency, as well as actual resource levels. The General Regulations of the Programme are being amended in the light of General Assembly resolutions 47/199 of 22 December 1992 and 48/162 of 20 December 1993.

5.   *United Nations International Drug Control Programme*

362   During the reporting period, the United Nations International Drug Control Programme, headed by Mr. Giorgio Giacomelli, continued to carry out its activities on the basis of a three-tiered strategy articulated at the country, regional, and global levels.

363   At the country level, the Programme elaborated guidelines to assist Governments in the preparation of national drug control master plans, that is, national agendas that address both illicit demand and illicit supply reduction. Support by the Pro-

gramme led to the development of master plans in 14 countries and territories in the Caribbean. Master plan assistance was also provided to Algeria, Guatemala, Namibia, Pakistan, the United Arab Emirates and Viet Nam. The Programme assisted the Government of Colombia in developing drug control components within that country's 10-year National Alternative Development Plan, to become effective on 1 January 1996.

In 1994, the Programme funded a comprehensive ground *364* survey of the extent of opium poppy cultivation in Afghanistan. The results — to be confirmed in a 1995 survey — reveal a dry opium production volume substantially in excess of previous estimates of 2,000 metric tons; based on the revised estimates, Afghanistan would be the world's largest illicit producer of opium.

At the regional level, the Programme held in South Africa *365* in November 1994 a regional workshop aimed at strengthening judiciary cooperation against drug trafficking in southern Africa. Governments in the region adopted a communiqué against corruption and a plan of action comprising measures to strengthen drug trafficking interdiction in the subregion.

In May 1995, at Beijing, the first ministerial meeting *366* took place between the Lao People's Democratic Republic, Myanmar, China and Thailand, all of which are parties to the memorandum of understanding on control of illicit drugs in South-East Asia. The meeting approved the accession of Cambodia and Viet Nam to the memorandum of understanding and endorsed an Action Plan on subregional cooperation in drug control matters. In China, law enforcement capabilities in Yunnan Province were strengthened with equipment from the Programme and training needs were identified. Law enforcement officers in the border areas of China and Myanmar launched the establishment of an information exchange system. After the signing of a regional memorandum of understanding in 1994, Argentina, Bolivia, Chile, Peru and the Programme developed an action agenda for implementation in 1995-1997 emphasizing law enforcement and harmonization of demand reduction techniques.

367   By 30 June 1995, the Baltic States, 9 Central European countries and 12 countries of CIS had received legal assistance from the Programme. The central Asian republics have emerged as a high priority for the Programme, and accordingly a multisectoral subregional programme, requiring support from the international community, has been developed.

368   In 1994-1995, the Programme continued its series of demand reduction expert forums, with technical consultations held in Brazil, the Bahamas, Cameroon, India and Morocco. In the context of the United Nations Decade against Drug Abuse, a World Forum on the Role of Non-Governmental Organizations in Drug Demand Reduction was held at Bangkok in December 1994 with participants from 115 countries. The Forum resulted in a declaration that reinforces the partnership between the United Nations and non-governmental organizations in demand reduction.

369   In April 1995, the Programme helped organize in Brazil the Second International Private Sector Conference on Drugs in the Workplace and the Community, with one result being the identification of essential elements of corporate policy needed for drug abuse prevention. In February 1995, the Programme and the International Olympic Committee signed a cooperation agreement to promote sports in the prevention of drug abuse.

370   At the global level, the Programme conducted research and synthesized the results into technical information and research papers. In order to address complex issues in drug control, the Programme prepared studies on the present status of knowledge on the illicit drug industry and the economic and social impact of drug abuse and control, as well as an interim report on the economic and social consequences of drug abuse, presented to the Commission on Narcotic Drugs at its thirty-eighth session, in March 1995.

The Programme's laboratory continued to expand its *371* Quality Assurance Programme, aimed at assisting laboratories to develop effective laboratory practices in the analysis of drug-related matters. Eighty laboratories worldwide are participating in the International Proficiency Testing Scheme, which assesses the performance of laboratories and enhances output accuracy.

One of the major issues addressed by the Commission on *372* Narcotic Drugs in 1994 and 1995 was the implementation of General Assembly resolution 48/12 of 28 October 1993 on measures to strengthen international cooperation against the illicit production, sale, demand, traffic and distribution of narcotic drugs and psychotropic substances and related activities. The Executive Director of the Programme convened two meetings in 1994 of an intergovernmental advisory group and produced a report which was examined by the Commission at its thirty-eighth session. That report included specific recommendations on ways to strengthen international action in drug control. The Commission, in its resolution 13 (XXXVIII), invited States to consider the recommendations; it also requested the Executive Director to further refine them in the light of States' comments for submission to the General Assembly at its fifty-first session.

In response to General Assembly resolution 48/12, the In- *373* ternational Narcotics Control Board, an independent treaty organ, outlined its assessment and major findings with respect to the drug control treaties in its report for 1994. The Board also issued a special supplement on the effectiveness of the treaties, highlighting areas in need of strengthening.

374　　　In September 1994 and February 1995, at the request of the Commission on Narcotic Drugs, the Programme convened a working group on maritime cooperation to further international cooperation in combating illicit drug traffic by sea. The recommendations and principles adopted by the working group and endorsed by the Commission represent a milestone in efforts to contain the problem of illicit drug shipments that traverse international waters.

375　　　Also in February 1995, the Administrative Committee on Coordination held a high-level meeting at Vienna that addressed system-wide cooperation in drug control. The meeting resulted in recognition of the need for United Nations programmes, funds and agencies to incorporate drug control components into their programmes and broad support for the leadership role of the Programme in drug control coordination.

376　　　The total budget of the Programme for 1994-1995 amounted to $205 million, of which approximately 93 per cent was funded from voluntary contributions. The main share of these resources, $162 million, was used for over 300 operational activities in 50 countries, aimed at countering illicit drug production, trafficking and consumption. In view of the continuous rise in drug-related problems throughout the world and the trend of dwindling resources available for drug control, I urge Member States to provide the political and financial support needed to pursue international priorities in drug control.

6.　*Technical cooperation programmes of the United Nations Secretariat*

377　The focal point at United Nations Headquarters for technical cooperation for development efforts of developing countries and countries in transition is the Department for Development Support and Management Services. Total project expenditures for the Department in 1994 approximated $101 million for close to 1,044 projects in over a dozen sectors. Of that amount, UNDP funded about $51 million. The Department disbursed 44 per cent of its expenditures in Africa. In order to carry out its projects, over the past year the Department fielded over 900 international experts and consultants to work in collaboration with national personnel. The Department calls on a worldwide roster of over 4,330 consultants, 2,350 consulting companies and 6,330 suppliers of equipment. The Department also helps Governments to identify, select and purchase the most appropriate services and equipment for their development projects and supports capacity-building for work in those areas. Training is a vital component of such activities; in 1994, training placements were made for some 2,500 persons from over 130 countries.

With the approval of the General Assembly, the Secretariat 378 has proceeded with the decentralization to the regional commissions of staff and resources in the fields of natural resources and energy. These activities are managed by the Management Board of the United Nations Technical Cooperation Programme in Natural Resources and Energy, chaired by the Under-Secretary-General of the Department for Development Support and Management Services, with the participation of the regional commissions. This coordinating body has enhanced the responsiveness and effectiveness of assistance provided by the Organization in these areas.

Considerable progress has been made in forging closer 379 links between the Department and UNDP. This strengthened cooperation has resulted in an increased role by the Department in "upstream" advice in development planning and management and in technical backstopping activities at the programme and project levels.

7. United Nations Office for Project Services

380 The United Nations Office for Project Services, formerly a part of UNDP, was established, with the approval of the General Assembly, on 1 January 1995. Consistent with my overall plan for the restructuring of the Secretariat, I proposed to separate the Office for Project Services from UNDP with the objective of strengthening the operational activities of the United Nations system for development. Within this framework, the Office for Project Services is now the principal entity in the United Nations system furnishing project management, implementation and support services.

381 The Office for Project Services is headed by the Executive Director, Mr. Reinhart Helmke, who reports to me through the Management Coordination Committee, as well as to the Executive Board of UNDP and UNFPA.

382 The Management Coordination Committee, comprising the Administrator of UNDP as chairman, the Under-Secretary-General for Administration and Management, the Under-Secretary-General for Development Support and Management Services and the Executive Director of the Office, has met twice during the reporting period to deliberate on a number of important policy and coordination issues relating to Office operations.

383 The Committee reviewed the business plan of the Office, its new financial regulations, its relationship with UNDP and the Department for Development Support and Management Services, operational follow-up activities relating to the World Summit for Social Development, held in 1994, and a set of strategic policy guidelines defining the scope of activities of the Office, including client partnerships and principal areas of concentration. Four main areas of concentration were identified for activities of the Office: executing development projects, coordinating rehabilitation and reconstruction efforts, managing environmental programmes and administering development loans. The proposed new financial regulations for the Office were approved by the Executive Board at the beginning of 1995, affording a new framework from which businesslike management practices can be instituted.

The portfolio of projects of the Office has grown consistently over the past 20 years, reaching more than $1 billion in 1994. Delivery in 1994 stood at $403.1 million, up 5.3 per cent from 1993. The number of projects in the portfolio also increased to nearly 1,900, as compared with roughly 1,700 during the previous year. In 1994, activities where the country portfolio was in excess of $10 million were under way in more than 20 countries. *384*

In addition to implementing projects on behalf of United Nations agencies and programmes, the Office also administers management service agreements (MSAs) on behalf of multilateral development banks, bilateral donors and recipient Governments. Against a portfolio budget of $639 million, services provided under MSA arrangements totalled $142 million in 1994. Expenditures incurred by the Office during that year under the Global Environment Facility and the Montreal Protocol to the Vienna Convention for the Protection of the Ozone Layer amounted to more than $30 million. *385*

In view of the experience it has acquired in managing post-conflict rehabilitation since the late 1980s, the demand for the services of the Office in designing and implementing comprehensive and integrated recovery programmes is increasing. The applicability of the lessons learned in the Horn of Africa, in Central America and in Asia are now being tested, for the first time, in eastern Europe (Ukraine) and in central Asia (Tajikistan). *386*

In keeping with its field orientation and in order to render its services more efficient, the Office has decentralized a num- *387* ber of functions. In addition to the Management Support Unit established in Central America in 1993, the Office has set up a post in Kuala Lumpur, from which it manages programmes in South-East Asia.

D. REGIONAL DEVELOPMENT ACTIVITIES

388   The regional commissions were established by the General Assembly to serve as the main regional centres for economic and social development. They operate at a level between global United Nations entities and country operations. As such, the regional commissions promote regional initiatives and strategies, contribute to in-depth studies of various issues and support intergovernmental initiatives to elaborate norms, standards and legal instruments. In addition, regional commissions are a forum for dialogue for subregional groupings and help prepare regional positions to world conferences and summit meetings held by the United Nations (see fig. 14).

1.   *Economic Commission for Africa (ECA)*

389   Assisting Member States in Africa to reinforce promising trends and overcome the obstacles to accelerated growth and socio-economic development has defined the analytical, advocacy and advisory work of ECA under its Executive Secretary, Mr. K. Y. Amoako. This provided the backdrop to the thirtieth session of the Commission, held from 24 April to 3 May 1995, the theme of which was "promoting accelerated growth and sustainable development in Africa through the building of critical capacities". At that session the Commission reviewed progress in the elaboration of the Framework Agenda for Building and Utilizing Critical Capacities in Africa and directed that the Framework Agenda be completed before the next session, in 1996.

390   The session also adopted a declaration on external debt of African countries which called for improvement in the Naples

FIGURE 14

**Regional commissions:
revised appropriations for the biennium 1994-1995**

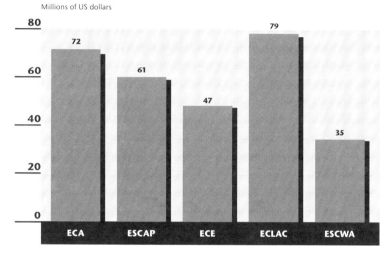

Millions of US dollars

Terms, including an 80 per cent reduction in the total non-concessional debt of African countries, and urged the cancellation of concessional debt rescheduled in the Paris Club. It adopted a special memorandum on the mid-term global review of the implementation of the Programme of Action for Least Developed Countries for the 1990s scheduled for September 1995. The session noted with satisfaction the commitment of African countries to carry out necessary reforms to attract private investment, and invited all African countries and their development partners to participate in the regional forum on private investment which will be held in early 1996 at Accra.

At the same session the Commission strongly endorsed the need to promote food security and self-sufficiency in Africa. In this regard, the Commission called on Member States to create a macroeconomic environment conducive to the development *391* of the food and agricultural sector and requested relevant United Nations agencies to strengthen programmes designed to promote food security and self-sufficiency in Africa.

392   With the coming into force in May 1994 of the Abuja Treaty establishing the African Economic Community, the Commission intensified its efforts in support of the implementation of the Treaty. Together with the Organization of African Unity and the African Development Bank — its partners in a Joint Secretariat — the Commission participated in setting up a committee to formulate proposals for resource mobilization in support of the African Economic Community and formulating a framework for a working relationship between the sub-regional economic communities and the Joint Secretariat. Furthermore, the Commission undertook studies on the rationalization and harmonization of regional economic groups in West and Central Africa in the context of the establishment of the West African Economic and Monetary Union and the Central African Economic and Monetary Union.

393   The Second United Nations Transport and Communications Decade for Africa aims at facilitating development of transport and communications in Africa. A mid-term evaluation report of the Decade programme was examined by the Tenth Meeting of African Ministers of Transport and Communications held in May 1995. The main recommendations from the evaluation were that the programmes should be streamlined, resource mobilization efforts for Decade projects should be intensified and the beneficiaries of the Decade programme should assume ownership. The Commission implemented four important projects in the transport and communication sectors: human resource and institution development in transport and communications; a transport database; the reactivation of the Trans-African Highway Bureau; and the Yamoussoukro Declaration on a new air transport policy for Africa.

With a view to assisting Member States in formulating 394
policies and strategies for sustainable development of natural
resources, the Commission published a document entitled
"Policies and strategies for the development and utilization of
natural resources and energy in Africa". The Commission also
organized, in collaboration with the World Meteorological
Organization, an international conference entitled "Water
Resources: Policy and Assessment", held at Addis Ababa from
20 to 25 March 1995. The Conference articulated a strategy to
rehabilitate, build or adopt the institutional financial manpower
and technological capacity of countries to assess water resources needs for socio-economic development.

In response to the decisions of Member States expressed at 395
the Regional Ministerial Conference on Development and
Utilization of Mineral Resources in Africa, the Commission
undertook two studies on prospects for increased production
and intra-African trade in copper and copper-based products
and prospects for increased production and intra-African trade
in aluminium commodities and metal products. The studies
have been well received by Governments, private companies
and entrepreneurs, as well as regional and subregional organizations.

The Commission continued its efforts to promote the de- 396
velopment of scientific and technological capacities. It thus
conducted studies on incentives for development and the application of science and technology, indicators for science and
technology in Africa and foreign direct investment as a vehicle
for science and technology development. Furthermore, the
Commission, in collaboration with OAU, organized a round
table on the science and technology protocol of the African
Economic Community from 21 to 27 September 1994.

In the context of the implementation of the Second Indus- 397
trial Development Decade for Africa, the Commission assisted

Member States in the formulation of appropriate industrial policies and effective implementation of industrial programmes. The twelfth meeting of the Conference of African Ministers of Industry at Gaborone in June 1995 examined, among other things, the progress made by African countries in the implementation of their national and subregional programmes for the Decade and the role of the private sector in the implementation of the goals of the Decade.

398   The Commission has launched a new series entitled the *Human Development in Africa Report*. The 1995 edition of the report was devoted to the themes of "Goals of the child", "Health for all" and "Basic education for all". The Commission has intensified its activities in assistance to Member States in integrating population development factors into socio-economic development programmes and policies; preparation of studies and/or workshops on family planning and reproductive health, fertility and mortality; and the implementation of the Dakar/Ngor Declaration on Population, Family and Sustainable Development and the Programme of Action of the International Conference on Population and Development.

399   The sixteenth meeting of the African Regional Coordinating Committee for the Integration of Women in Development was held from 20 to 22 April 1995 at Addis Ababa. It endorsed the African Platform for Action for Women adopted at the Fifth African Regional Conference on Women held at Dakar in November 1994. The African Platform for Action is the region's common position for the Fourth World Conference on Women. At the same time, the Commission continued its efforts related to the establishment of an African women's bank by convening an Ad Hoc Group Meeting in August 1994 to examine the feasibility of the creation of the bank. Entrepreneurs from some African countries have indicated their willingness to promote the bank. At its 1995 session, the Conference of Ministers requested further studies to clarify certain issues concerning the establishment of the bank. The Commission's operational role in the advancement of women was matched by the deepening of its analytical work on women's issues in Africa. For example, the Commission's *Economic and Social Survey of Africa 1995* features a special study on gender disparities in formal education in Africa.

The Commission, in collaboration with the General *400* Agreement on Tariffs and Trade (GATT), UNCTAD and OAU, organized in Tunisia in October 1994 the International Conference to Assess the Impact of the Uruguay Round on African Economies. The aim of this Conference was to evaluate the technical requirements of African countries in adapting to the post–Uruguay Round international trade environment.

During the period from December 1994 to June 1995, the *401* Commission fielded over 65 short-term technical advisory missions. The main institutional vehicle for providing these advisory services is the ECA Multidisciplinary Regional Advisory Group. ECA rendered assistance to some Member States in the area of environmental management. It fielded advisory missions to Eritrea on protection of the marine environment and to Seychelles on water and environment. The Commission collaborated with UNEP in the preparation of studies on the contribution of the coastal/marine sector to the gross national product in the Gambia and the United Republic of Tanzania.

The Commission has provided assistance to Member *402* States in areas of public sector management, including development of indicators for public enterprise performance; strengthening of national statistical institutions; establishing information management systems; and agricultural management and policy planning. In Eritrea, for example, ECA has provided technical assistance for public enterprise reform and management, and assisted in establishing a national development information system and network linking various departments of the Government. In Angola, ECA is evaluating the development priority areas to form the basis of a policy framework for its technical assistance to the country's socio-economic development.

403   Reflecting the diversity of requests for its support, the Multidisciplinary Regional Advisory Group also provided technical assistance to universities or institutes in some Member States. These included the Institute for Diplomacy and International Studies at the University of Nairobi, the International Relations Institute of Cameroon and the University of Ghana, Legon. Technical assistance to these institutions included short-term training and assistance in the establishment of new centres within these institutions. Advisory services were also rendered to intergovernmental, regional and subregional organizations and institutions. These included the subregional economic groupings, the ECA-sponsored institutions, the Intergovernmental Authority on Drought and Development and the Semi-Arid Food Grain Research and Development Centre. During the period under review, the Commission had a total of 115 projects, of which 44 were terminated and 71 remained under implementation. A total amount of $5,606,603 was made available to the Commission under extrabudgetary resources for the implementation of the projects.

2.   *Economic Commission for Europe (ECE)*

404   The aim of ECE is to further harmonize policies, norms and practices among the countries of the region and to strengthen their integration and cooperation.

405   Under the direction of Mr. Yves Berthelot, the Commission achieves this aim through policy analysis and dialogue on macroeconomic and sectoral issues; the elaboration of conventions, norms and standards; and a newly developed programme of assistance to the transition process.

ECE has continued to accord priority to the protection of 406 the environment and the promotion of sustainable development, in particular in a transboundary context. Since 1979, ECE member countries have worked energetically to take up the environmental challenges of the region. In particular, the Commission has elaborated nine international, legally binding instruments on air pollution, environmental impact assessment, industrial accidents and transboundary waters.

Preparations are under way for two new protocols on per- 407 sistent organic pollutants and on heavy metals to the 1979 Convention on Long-range Transboundary Air Pollution. These legal instruments constitute a unique legal framework for meeting environmental challenges. In order to make the conventions and protocols fully operational region wide, the Commission, in its decision G(50), called upon all its member States which had not already done so, to consider the earliest possible ratification of, or accession to, these instruments.

The Committee on Environmental Policy, with the assist- 408 ance of its Working Group of Senior Governmental Officials on Environment for Europe, the central coordinating body for the Environment for Europe process, advanced in the preparations for the Sofia Ministerial Conference on Environment for Europe, to be held in October 1995. Among the main issues to be considered by the Conference are the follow-up to the 1993 Environmental Action Plan for Central and Eastern Europe, the assessment of the state of the environment for Europe and financing environmental improvements.

The Committee on Environmental Policy, in cooperation 409 with OECD, has made progress in extending the OECD country environmental performance reviews to central and eastern Europe. The first two joint pilot reviews of Poland and Bulgaria have already taken place. The third review in cooperation with OECD will take place in Belarus next year. As part of its own environmental performance review programme the Commission has undertaken a review of the situation in Estonia, to be concluded by the end of 1995 and published in early 1996.

410   During the past year, the Committee on Human Settlements continued its preparatory work for the United Nations Conference on Human Settlements (Habitat II). The Regional Preparatory Meeting for the Conference was held and a task force was established to assist the Committee in carrying out the preparatory work. An analytical report was prepared containing an overview of human settlements development in the ECE region and was submitted to the Preparatory Committee for Habitat II.

411   During the past year, the ECE Inland Transport Committee has continued to serve as a forum for cooperation in the field of transport. The Committee finalized and adopted two new legal instruments, bringing their total number to 50, and adopted amendments to a number of existing ones. Significant progress was made in the preparation of the European Agreement on Main Inland Waterways of International Importance.

412   Moreover, the Inland Transport Committee progressed in the establishment of international norms and standards for the construction of road vehicles, covering active and passive safety, environmental protection and energy consumption. The Committee has also paid special attention to activities in relation to road safety under the recently revised Vienna Convention on Road Signs and Signals and other related legal instruments. The second Road Safety Week was organized under the auspices of ECE from 27 March to 2 April 1995 and aimed at waging simultaneous campaigns addressed to young road users in each ECE member State. Substantive progress was also made in the elaboration of international norms and standards for the transport of dangerous goods by road and inland waterways and in their harmonization with those concerning the

transport of such goods by rail, sea and air. The Committee acted on the basis of the recommendations developed by the Committee of Experts on the Transport of Dangerous Goods, a subsidiary committee of the Economic and Social Council.

The Inland Transport Committee finalized the customs *413* container pool convention and prepared a draft convention on international customs transit procedures for the carriage of goods by rail. It was decided to undertake the revision of the Customs Convention on the International Transport of Goods under Cover of TIR Carnets (TIR Convention) in view of the current problems in its implementation. A report on the facilitation of border crossing in international rail transport was prepared. A programme of action in the area of inland transport, aimed at assisting the countries of central and eastern Europe in their transitions to market economies, is being implemented.

Work has progressed as a follow-up to the decision taken *414* by the Commission at its forty-ninth session, in April 1994, to convene a Regional Conference on Transport and the Environment in 1996. The Preparatory Committee for the Conference has thus far held five meetings and achieved agreement on a text of draft guidelines for a common strategy on transport and the environment.

The integrated presentation of international statistical *415* work in the ECE region has been expanded beyond the statistical work of ECE, the European Communities and OECD to include statistical activities in the region undertaken by the Statistical Division and the Population Division of the United Nations Secretariat, the specialized agencies, the Council of Europe, CIS and other international organizations.

ECE supports a trade facilitation programme through its *416* Working Party on Facilitation of International Trade Procedures. Considerable progress was made in the development of the United Nations Electronic Data Interchange for Administration, Commerce and Transport (EDIFACT) messages. Members of the Working Party and the secretariat participated in the United Nations International Symposium on Trade Efficiency held at Columbus, Ohio, in October 1994. A Compendium of Trade Facilitation Recommendations was developed. A memorandum of understanding between ECE, the International Electrotechnical Commission (IEC) and the International Organization for Standardization (ISO) was developed and approved in order to better define the division of responsibilities between these organizations.

417   *The Guide on the Adaptation of Real Property Law of Countries in Transition,* prepared under the auspices of the Working Party on International Contract Practices in Industry, was also well received. In the field of trade and investment promotion the secretariat continued to publish quarterly the *East-West Investment News* and to update its database on foreign direct investment projects and supporting legislation in countries in transition.

418   The economic analysis conducted by ECE and published in the *Economic Bulletin for Europe* and the *Economic Survey of Europe in 1994-1995* provides in-depth analysis of current economic developments in Europe, the States of the former Soviet Union, and North America. Special emphasis is given in both publications to developments in the transition economies of eastern Europe and the former Soviet Union and to their progress in creating market economies. This year's *Economic Bulletin* pays special attention to the foreign trade and payments of the transition economies and to the level of external support they have been receiving. The latest Survey, in addition to a detailed review of macroeconomic developments, contains an assessment of the reform process over the last five years and a review of international migration in eastern Europe and the Commonwealth of Independent States.

Under the second phase of the Energy Efficiency 2000   *419*
project, ECE has continued to assist countries in transition to
develop their capacity to enhance energy efficiency and to
implement energy efficiency standards and labelling.

In collaboration with national Governments, local institu-   *420*
tions and UNDP, ECE has also formulated projects for enhancing energy efficiency in the context of programmes of conver-
sion of military bases and manufacturing facilities to peaceful
purposes in central and eastern Europe.

The Gas Centre was established in 1994, supported by   *421*
financial contributions from major European and North American Governments and gas companies. A major regional initiative, the Gas Centre brings together almost all of the key natural
gas market players in the Commission. It has already been successful in opening dialogue among the private and public gas
companies and the Governments in the region.

The Working Party on Engineering Industries and Auto-   *422*
mation prepared and published two studies entitled "World engineering industries and automation — performance and prospects, 1993-1995" and "World industrial robots: statistics
1983-1993 and forecasts to 1997". The engineering industries
continued to influence the restructuring of industry and, in
particular, the process of investment and privatization. In this
respect, special emphasis was given to the creation of small and
medium-sized enterprises in economies in transition. At its fiftieth session, the Commission recognized the publication *Rehabilitation Engineering* as an ECE contribution to the World
Summit for Social Development.

The Working Party on the Chemical Industry discussed   *423*
the policy-oriented issues currently facing the chemical industry and stressed the importance of the work related to sustainable development and, in particular, the Chemical Industry — Sustainable Economic and Ecological Development

(CHEMISEED) programme. Fifteen member countries identified 40 sites polluted by chemicals for the pilot project demonstrating environmental clean-up procedures.

424   The Working Party on Steel strengthened its regional programme on metallurgy and ecology through: the organization of a Seminar on the Steel Industry and Recycling; the addition to the work programme of a Seminar on Processing, Utilization and Disposal of Waste in the Steel Industry; a bibliography of environmental publications in the steel sector; and activities aimed at the harmonization of regulations on environmental protection. *The Global Study on the Steel Industry in Europe* was prepared in cooperation with the European Commission, the European Bank for Reconstruction and Development (EBRD), the World Bank and the International Iron and Steel Institute. The study also served as the basis for the examination of the restructuring of steel industries in the economies in transition.

425   The Working Party on Standardization Policies reviewed developments in the fields of coordination, harmonization, conformity assessment and metrology at the international, regional and national levels and paid particular attention to assistance to the countries in transition with a view to adapting existing structures to market conditions and to assisting newly independent States to build adequate institutions. At its forty-ninth session, the Commission adopted the recommendation on the meteorological assurance of testing proposed by the Working Party as separate decision H(49).

426   In the light of the decision taken by the FAO Council in June 1994 concerning the restructuring of FAO, and in particular the increased decentralization to the regional and subregional offices, the joint ECE/FAO Agriculture and Timber Division was dismantled in 1995. In accordance with the decision of the Commission at its fiftieth session, in April 1995, interim

arrangements have been made to ensure the continuation of the ECE/FAO joint activities on agriculture and the environment and on the economic analysis of the agri-food sector. The Commission will consider a proposal of the Executive Secretary to merge the ECE Committee on Agriculture with the FAO European Commission on Agriculture.

The ECE regional advisory services programme has *427* elaborated a national plan of assistance to the Republic of Georgia. The first phase is scheduled to be implemented before the end of July 1995. The experience of this plan will be evaluated and applied to other cases of high priority.

3.   *Economic Commission for Latin America and the Caribbean (ECLAC)*

The period covered by this report was marked by a certain *428* turbulence in economic performance in Latin America and the Caribbean. This context, in turn, was reflected in the activities of ECLAC, headed by Mr. Gert Rosenthal, which tries to respond to both long-term and emerging development issues in the region.

In the past year, the ECLAC secretariat, which includes *429* the Latin American and Caribbean Institute for Economic and Social Planning (ILPES) and the Latin American Demographic Centre (CELADE), focused on a number of development issues concerned with medium-term growth (macroeconomic management, innovation, enhancing savings and channelling them to productive investment) and intraregional economic cooperation. In addition, the secretariat was involved in numerous regional preparatory activities for global events, particularly the World Summit for Social Development and the Fourth World Conference on Women.

At the time of writing the present report, ECLAC was *430* undertaking a major mid-decade evaluation of the strategies of adjustment, stabilization and structural reforms pursued by the region. The exercise is expected to be particularly timely in the face of recent events affecting some Latin American economies. The document is planned to be reviewed by the member Governments during the forthcoming session of the Commission to be held at San José, Costa Rica, in April 1996.

431   ECLAC continued to be a meeting place for officials. In addition to some 35 seminars held during the past 13 months, the secretariat prepared and held the sixth session of the Regional Conference on the Integration of Women into the Economic and Social Development of Latin America and the Caribbean, held at Mar del Plata, Argentina, from 25 to 29 September 1994. The secretariat played a similar role in the twenty-first meeting of Presiding Officers of the Regional Conference on the Integration of Women into the Economic and Social Development of Latin America and the Caribbean, held at Santiago, Chile, on 3 and 4 July 1995. Support was provided to the third Regional Meeting of Ministers and High-level Authorities of the Housing and Urban Development Sector in Latin America and the Caribbean, held at Quito, Ecuador, from 16 to 18 November 1994.

432   ECLAC has been actively involved in the follow-up activities to Agenda 21, most notably in those dealing with environmentally sustainable management of natural resources and various sectors of activity, and the development of statistics and environmental accounts. The extensive list of publications and research works include a study on water resources management in Latin America and the Caribbean from the perspective of programme 21, and a study entitled "Hazardous products and wastes: impact of transboundary movements towards the Latin American and Caribbean region and possibilities for preventing and controlling it". The Commission made relevant contributions to the preparatory work of the World Summit for

Social Development through the formulation of poverty reduction strategies within the context of its major statement on changing production patterns with social equity. Among the publications most recently issued are: *Proposals for a modern social policy to foster social development* and *Educational inequalities: problems and policies.* Work is ongoing on a project that explores the relationships between this statement and the promotion of economic, social and cultural rights in the region.

ECLAC has also continued to perform its established role *433* of monitoring the economic and social performance of the region. To the Commission's list of traditional annual publications that fulfil this function — the *Preliminary Overview of the Economy of Latin America and the Caribbean*, the *Economic Survey of Latin America and the Caribbean* and the *Statistical Yearbook for Latin America and the Caribbean* — the *Social Panorama of Latin America* has now been added in keeping with the increased level of recognition that the matter is gaining in the region. Work continued on the setting up of the Short-term Indicators Database, the incorporation of new international statistical classifications and the development of a data bank on the external debt of Latin American countries. In addition, assistance was provided to Latin American countries in implementing the new System of National Accounts.

The Executive Secretary participated in the Meeting of *434* Heads of State of the Río Group (September 1994), the Hemispheric Summit of Heads of State (December 1994) and the Ibero-American Summit of Heads of State and Government (July 1995).

4.   *Economic and Social Commission for Asia and the Pacific (ESCAP)*

Against the backdrop of the sustained dynamism of the Asia- *435* Pacific region, ESCAP, headed by Mr. Adrianus Mooy, has continued to focus attention on enhancing economic growth and social development among the countries of the region.

436   In that connection, at its fifty-first session, concluded on 1 May 1995 at Bangkok, the Commission decided to hold a ministerial conference on regional economic cooperation and directed the secretariat to initiate necessary preparations.

437   The Commission also placed emphasis on promotion of subregional economic cooperation in various fields, including trade and investment. A second consultative meeting among executive heads of subregional organizations and ESCAP was hosted by the secretariat of the Association of South-East Asian Nations (ASEAN) at Jakarta in January 1995.

438   The Commission emphasized the pivotal role of industrial and technological development in sustaining the growth momentum in the region. The Commission's work in this area was guided by several mandates and directives as enshrined in the Seoul Plan of Action for Promoting and Strengthening Regional Cooperation for Technology-led Industrialization in Asia and the Pacific, the Action Programme for Regional Economic Cooperation in Investment-related Technology Transfer, the Beijing Declaration on Regional Economic Cooperation and the Delhi Declaration on Strengthening Regional Economic Cooperation in Asia and the Pacific towards the Twenty-first Century.

439   Another important development has been the fifteenth session of the Standing Committee of the Bangkok Agreement, held at Bangkok in February 1995, which decided to launch the third round of negotiations, with a mandate to address both tariff and non-tariff barriers and to explore the possibility of including the services sector in due course.

440   The Commission endorsed the Jakarta Declaration and Plan of Action for the Advancement of Women in Asia and the Pacific adopted at the Second Asian and Pacific Ministerial

Conference on Women in Development, held at Jakarta in June 1994. The Jakarta Declaration and Plan of Action served as the regional input to the draft global platform of action for adoption by the forthcoming Fourth World Conference on Women. Following the Ministerial Conference, regional meetings of coordinating bodies of non-governmental organizations and national machineries for the advancement of women were convened to accelerate implementation of the Plan of Action.

An Asian and Pacific Ministerial Conference in Prepara- *441* tion for the World Summit for Social Development was organized at Manila in October 1994, at which the Manila Declaration and Agenda for Action for Social Development in the ESCAP region were adopted. As part of the preparatory activities, a symposium of non-governmental organizations was convened by ESCAP prior to the Ministerial Conference.

The Commission's initiatives with regard to its declaration *442* of the Asian and Pacific Decade of Disabled Persons, 1993-2002, continued to generate significant activities at national and regional levels aimed at improving the status and participation of disabled persons. To date, 30 members and associate members have signed the Proclamation on the Full Participation and Equality of People with Disabilities in the Asian and Pacific Region.

The Commission continued to support national efforts and *443* activities to promote participatory human settlements development. Preparatory work has begun for convening an Asia-Pacific Urban Forum in 1995 which will serve as a key preparatory activity to the second United Nations Conference on Human Settlements (Habitat II) in 1996. The Commission is also working closely with the Regional Network of Local Authorities for the Management of Human Settlements (CITYNET) and the Asian Coalition for Housing Rights to assist member countries in addressing urban poverty issues, particularly as they relate to low-income housing and settlements improvement.

444   In implementing the Bali Declaration on Population and Sustainable Development and the Programme of Action of the International Conference on Population and Development, various inter-country research projects and training courses were conducted; technical assistance was also provided relating to such areas as family planning, population ageing, migration and urbanization, the role and status of women and demographic analysis. Activities of the Asia-Pacific Population Information Network (POPIN) focused on upgrading technical skills in database development and improving population information management and sharing.

445   Under the theme of environment and sustainable development, the Commission focused attention on the preparations for the Ministerial-level Conference on Environment and Development in Asia and the Pacific, which will be organized by ESCAP at Bangkok in November 1995, and the prevention of desertification including preparation of the Regional Implementation Annex for Asia to the United Nations Convention to Combat Desertification in Those Countries Experiencing Serious Drought and/or Desertification, particularly in Africa.

446   Under the theme of transport and communications, the Commission pursued its activities related to the implementation of the Asian Land Transport Infrastructure Development Programme, comprising the Asian Highway and Trans-Asian Railway projects. Current activities under this project include a study on developing land transport linkages of Kazakstan, Turkmenistan and Uzbekistan with seaports of the Islamic Republic of Iran and Pakistan in the south and China in the east; a study on the development of a highway network in Asian republics; a Trans-Asian Railway route requirements study; and

implementation of ESCAP resolution 48/11 on road and rail transport modes in relation to facilitation measures.

Following the theme topic of the fiftieth session of the *447* Commission "Infrastructure development as key to economic growth and regional economic cooperation", and Commission resolution 50/2 on the "Action plan on infrastructure development in Asia and the Pacific", the Commission at its fifty-first session adopted the New Delhi Action Plan on Infrastructure Development in Asia and the Pacific. The Commission decided to convene a ministerial conference on infrastructure in 1996 to launch the New Delhi action plan and to review phase II (1992-1996) of the Transport and Communications Decade for Asia and the Pacific.

Special efforts were made to improve policies for tourism *448* development, taking into consideration the socio-economic and environmental impact of tourism. Studies on the cultural and environmental impact of tourism provided policy recommendations for the cultural and environmental management of tourism development. ESCAP convened the first meeting of the Working Group on the Greater Mekong Subregion Tourism Sector in April 1995.

The statistics subprogramme of the Commission focused *449* on promoting the improvement of capabilities of national statistical offices in the region for timely and accurate collection and dissemination of statistics needed for development planning and decision-making. Technical meetings were organized to support country work in the implementation of the 1993 System of National Accounts (SNA), in statistics on gender issues and in environment statistics and environmental and resource accounting. Assistance was also provided through advisory services, including those in population statistics, data-processing and national accounts.

450   The Commission's reaffirmation of its predominant role in promoting regional cooperation in Asia and the Pacific was manifested in the decision by the Russian Federation to seek a revision in its status in order to become a regional member. The application of the Russian Federation was unanimously endorsed by the Commission, which recommended a resolution on the matter for submission to the substantive session of 1995 of the Economic and Social Council.

451   To meet the need for an integrated and effective approach to development at the regional level, an inter-agency meeting on strengthening coordination at the regional level was convened by ESCAP in May 1994. This meeting established the Regional Inter-agency Committee for Asia and the Pacific under the chairmanship of the Executive Secretary of ESCAP. The first meeting of the Committee was concluded at Bangkok in June 1995.

5.   *Economic and Social Commission for Western Asia (ESCWA)*

452   The impact of international and regional issues does not only concern the political environment, but also affects the whole economic and social fabric in ESCWA countries. Thus, ESCWA, headed by Mr. Hazem El-Beblawi, undertook multidisciplinary coverage of work programme components, combining them in a few compact areas. Thus, the Commission's work programme was formulated around five themes featuring interrelated activities.

453   Under the first thematic subprogramme, Management of natural resources and environment, issues concerning the assessment and proper management of land, water and energy resources were addressed, as well as environmental degradation resulting from inadequate management of these resources.

In the field of environment, ESCWA participated in sev- *454*
eral meetings and workshops such as the Technical Secretariat
of the Council of Arab Ministers Responsible for Environment.
A report was completed on progress made in the ESCWA plan
to implement Agenda 21 in the region which was presented to
the Commission at its eighteenth session, in May 1995, as well
as to the Commission on Sustainable Development and the
Economic and Social Council. Furthermore, ESCWA, in its
capacity as a member of the Executive Committee of the Joint
Committee on Environment and Development in the Arab
Region, participated in its fifth meeting at Cairo in July 1995.
The meeting discussed the implementation of the decisions of
the second meeting of the Joint Committee and preparations for
a meeting on biodiversity in the Arab region. The meeting also
included discussions on two technical reports on the establishment of an integrated environmental information network
in the Arab region.

A report was prepared by ESCWA on activities related to *455*
the protection of the ozone layer, while issues pertaining to resource conservation were addressed through studies on wildlife
conservation for sustainable development in the Arab countries
and the assessment of the fisheries sector in the United Arab
Emirates. In the field of water resources, ESCWA organized a
meeting at Amman from 12 to 14 September 1994 of the Inter-
agency Task Force on modalities of cooperation and coordination among United Nations specialized agencies and Arab
regional agencies involved in various water-related activities.
The meeting recommended that ESCWA serve as the secretariat for the Inter-agency Task Force. A long-term project on the
assessment of water resources using remote-sensing techniques is under way.

The second thematic subprogramme, Improvement of *456*
the quality of life, includes activities to provide support for

ESCWA member States in preparing, at the national and regional levels, for world conferences and meetings. Reports were submitted to the Commission at its eighteenth session on all preparatory and follow-up activities for meetings and conferences such as the International Conference on Population and Development, the International Year of the Family, the World Summit for Social Development, the United Nations Conference on Human Settlements (Habitat II) and the Fourth World Conference on Women.

457   The Commission participated in the preparatory committee for the World Summit for Social Development and in the Summit itself. It also participated in the Ninth United Nations Congress on the Prevention of Crime and the Treatment of Offenders, held at Cairo from 29 April to 8 May 1995. Other major activities included the preparation of the Arab Declaration for Social Development, which was presented to the Council of Arab Ministers for Social Affairs, the launching of a social development database, the preparation of a project document on human development in the Arab States and a workshop on sustainable human development experiences, held at Cairo from 14 to 19 May 1995. ESCWA also undertook a study on the impact of the recent crisis on the social situation in the ESCWA region, which analysed the socio-economic impact of crises in the region, with particular emphasis on population migration, the quality of life and vulnerable and disadvantaged groups. ESCWA organized, in this context, a seminar entitled "The Role of the Family in Integrating Disabled Women into Society", at Amman from 16 to 18 October 1994.

458   In the area of women and development, ESCWA organized the Arab Regional Preparatory Meeting for the Fourth World Conference on Women, which was held at Amman from 6 to 10 November 1994 and was attended by 420 participants representing all Arab countries. The meeting reviewed the implementation of the Nairobi Forward-looking Strategies for the Advancement of Women and the ESCWA Strategy for Arab Women to the Year 2005. The meeting also finalized the Regional Plan of Action for the Advancement of Arab Women. ESCWA also organized a meeting on the Arab family in a changing society at Abu Dhabi in December 1994, in the context of preparations for the Fourth World Conference on Women. Other activities within this framework included national workshops in nine ESCWA countries to review the national plans of action in the light of national reports on the situation of women. Information on women's issues was addressed through a publication on Arab women in ESCWA member States. This publication includes statistics, indicators and trends. A database on statistics on women was also launched.

In the field of rural development, two long-term rural community development projects are being implemented in Egypt and the Syrian Arab Republic. ESCWA continued to issue its annual publication *Agriculture and Development in Western Asia* (No. 16, December 1994); and it prepared a *National Farm Data Handbook for the Syrian Arab Republic.* Other publications issued by the secretariat include: *Land and Water Policies in the Near East Region; Marketing of Agricultural Products in Lebanon; Evaluation of Agricultural Policies in the Syrian Arab Republic: Policy Analysis Matrix Approach; Prospective Development of the Agricultural Institutions in the Occupied Palestinian Territories*; and *Rehabilitation of Veterinary Services.* *459*

Information on human settlements issues was disseminated through the publication of a newsletter jointly published by ESCWA, the United Nations Centre for Human Settlements and the League of Arab States. ESCWA participated in preparatory meetings for Habitat II and convened at Amman, in March 1995, a regional preparatory meeting for the Conference. *460*

461   In the area of industrial development, ESCWA completed a publication entitled *Proceedings of the Expert Group Meeting on the Creation of Indigenous Entrepreneurship and Opportunities for Small and Medium-scale Industrial Investments*. In preparation for the Fourth World Conference on Women, the Commission issued a publication entitled *Participation of Women in Manufacturing: Patterns, Determinants and Analysis*. Several training-of-trainers workshops on how to start a business in war-torn areas were held in Bethlehem, Gaza, Nablus and Beirut. Moreover, a pilot workshop on upgrading entrepreneurial skills of managers of small and medium enterprises under changing conditions, was held at Amman in September 1994. A study was completed entitled "Impact of the single European market on the industrial sector in the ESCWA region"; and two project documents were completed for the establishment of business incubators in the occupied Palestinian territories.

462   The third thematic subprogramme, Economic development and cooperation, involved activities dealing with such central issues as promoting economic and technical cooperation and integration among ESCWA countries, promoting coordinated regional strategies, training officials in developing national capabilities in managerial skills, and reviewing and analysing economic performance, policies and strategies.

463   The *Survey of Economic and Social Developments in the ESCWA Region, 1993* was issued in November 1994. The *Survey* for 1994 was completed in July 1995. Within the same context, a study was completed on "Review of developments and issues in the external trade and payments situation of countries of Western Asia", which included a chapter on the implications of the Uruguay Round on development in the region. A study was also completed entitled "Review of developments and trends in the monetary and financial sectors in the economies of the ESCWA region".

The proceedings of four workshops/conferences were *464* published, namely: the Western Asia workshop on strategies for accelerating the development of civil registration and vital statistics system; the Second Arab Conference on Perspectives of Modern Biotechnology; the workshop on the implication of the new advanced materials technologies for the economies of the ESCWA countries; and the workshop on the integration of science and technology in the development planning and management process in the ESCWA region.

In the area of transport and communications, a report was *465* submitted to the Commission at its eighteenth session on the "Follow-up action of the implementation of the Transport and Communications Decade, second phase: 1992-1996". Furthermore, studies were completed on "Development of free zones in Western Asia"; "Development of the telecommunications sector in the ESCWA region"; and "Present status, development trends and future prospects of telecommunications in the ESCWA region"; and the ESCWA *Transport Bulletin for 1994* (No. 5) was issued. Additionally, the ESCWA secretariat conducted an expert group meeting on the Development of a Multi-modal Transport Chain in Western Asia, held at Amman from 24 to 27 April 1995.

In the field of statistics, ESCWA continued the develop- *466* ment and maintenance of databases on energy and industry. A workshop on the implementation of the 1993 System of National Accounts was held at Amman from 12 to 19 December 1994 and another workshop on industrial statistics took place at Damascus from 26 November to 6 December 1994. Training was also provided on the use of statistical computer packages, geographical information systems and the application of the International Comparisons Programme.

The fourth thematic subprogramme, Regional develop- *467* ment and global changes, encompassed activities dealing with exogenous factors and global changes affecting the region. The major activity under this subprogramme is an ongoing multi-disciplinary study on the impact of the single European market on different sectors in the ESCWA region.

468   Issues concerning Palestine, the Middle East peace process and the least developed member States were the focal points for the fifth thematic subprogramme, Special programmes and issues. In its studies, the Agriculture Section covered the rehabilitation of the fisheries sector in the Gaza Strip and of veterinary services in the occupied territories. In addition, a proposed action programme for the restructuring of Palestinian agricultural public institutions was also prepared. The Industry Section undertook workshops on the development of small enterprises in the occupied Palestinian territories.

E. THE HUMANITARIAN IMPERATIVE

469   This past year has seen a frightening persistence and intensity of conflicts that affect an unprecedented number of innocent civilians. The reality of contemporary warfare is that more than 90 per cent of casualties are non-combatants who are often deliberately targeted because of their ethnic or religious affiliation. As a consequence, victims continued to flee their homes and communities in staggering numbers in 1995, reaching a global total of some 25 million refugees. A still larger number of persons have been displaced or are directly affected by warfare within their own countries.

470   Increasingly, humanitarian organizations are compelled to operate in war-torn societies where conflicting parties are often openly contemptuous of fundamental humanitarian norms. In such circumstances, a major challenge is the need to safeguard the well-being of civilians while providing assistance in a manner consistent with humanitarian principles.

In addition, the international community is faced with the *471*
paradox of needing ever larger resources to address the immediate survival needs of victims, while simultaneously recognizing that such action may deflect attention and support from initiatives essential to undoing the root causes of vulnerability
and strife. Faced with these conflicting trends, humanitarian
organizations have been reassessing the processes that shape
the nature and impact of their interventions.

Recent experience illustrates the importance of a well- *472*
organized and adequately resourced mechanism for coordination, both within the multi-actor humanitarian arena and with
other elements of the international system involved in crisis
management and pre-emptive action. This is particularly evident
in rapid and simultaneous mass population movements, where
it is often difficult to move quickly enough to mobilize and deploy resources in a manner that will prevent avoidable deaths.
However, notwithstanding the importance of support from the
international community, it is the people of the country directly
affected who are primarily responsible for their own recovery
and that of their communities.

The volatile context within which humanitarian assistance *473*
is provided is a major determinant in the overall capacity of the
United Nations system to pre-empt and respond to crises in a
manner that minimizes avoidable suffering.

The scale and depth of suffering in conflict situations con- *474*
fronting the international community today is too often a consequence of a disregard for fundamental humanitarian principles.
In many instances, the suffering endured by civilians is not an
incidental element of political and military strategies but constitutes its major objective. The conflicts in Bosnia and Herzegovina and Rwanda are alarming examples of what occurs
when civilians are subjected to the full brutality of contemporary warfare and gross violations of human rights. Determina-

tion must be shown to enforce the rule of law and to hold accountable those who are responsible for heinous crimes.

475   The limited means of humanitarian organizations to provide protection is particularly glaring in conflict settings and in situations characterized by extreme violations of human rights. The Rwandan experience illustrates the way in which the capacity of the United Nations to provide protection and assistance is undermined when inputs and distribution mechanisms are used for purposes that are inimical to humanitarian objectives. Finding the means to reach those in need without entrenching the power of abusive elements is one of the most difficult challenges facing the humanitarian community in recent times.

476   The indifference of warring parties for even the most basic humanitarian principles has continued to make conditions under which relief workers must operate extremely dangerous. As the number of conflicts increases so too does the number of practitioners who have been killed or wounded, sometimes deliberately, while carrying out their humanitarian tasks. Frequent disruption and diversion of emergency relief supplies have occurred. Access has on many occasions had to be negotiated. Dependence on the agreement of armed groups often makes the provision of humanitarian assistance tenuous and subject to unacceptable conditions. If this trend continues, it could undermine the capacity of the agencies to carry out humanitarian work. Safeguarding both the concept and the reality of "humanitarian space" remains one of the most significant challenges facing the humanitarian community.

477   Another major obstacle facing humanitarian organizations is the absence of sufficient political will and support for action to address the underlying causes of crises. The provision of humanitarian assistance in a vacuum is tantamount to managing only the symptoms of a crisis. Experience shows that, in most

instances, the effectiveness of humanitarian endeavour in conflict settings is predicated to a considerable extent on successful action by the international community to resolve the problems that provoked the crisis.

In some situations, such as in Angola and Mozambique, a 478 determined effort has been made to stop the fighting and to consolidate the peace. In other settings, such as Haiti, assertive action has been taken to end oppression and the potential for violent conflict. This is in dramatic contrast to other settings, such as the Sudan, where conflict has smouldered for 28 of the last 39 years. In Burundi and Liberia, a volatile mix of circumstances points to the need for action to strengthen the push for peace.

The humanitarian agenda is often shaped by political atti- 479 tudes to particular crises, strategic interests in specific areas and the attention span of the media. Such factors, which are for the most part beyond the control of humanitarian organizations, contribute strongly to the low level of attention and support provided to victims of "silent" emergencies. Ideally, and in a more humane world, assistance would be provided according to need and the core principle of impartiality would have greater relevance when responding to emergencies.

Other factors that have an impact on the effectiveness of 480 relief and protection organizations include the relationship between the level of resources and attention devoted to the prevention of, preparedness for and recovery from disasters and the amount of resources required to meet the daily needs of people in camp situations (see fig. 15). Rwanda is but one example of current trends. Some $1 billion was spent in the first six months of the crisis. Most of this was used for the immediate survival needs of the millions who were uprooted and displaced in 1994. Although resources were requested at an early stage for confidence-building measures to facilitate and encourage the

FIGURE 15

United Nations consolidated inter-agency humanitarian assistance appeals, 1992-1995

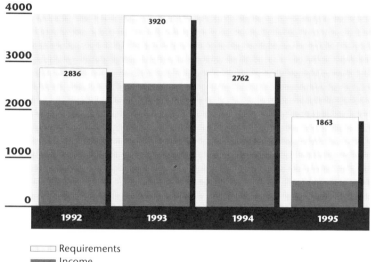

Millions of US dollars

Requirements
Income

return of those who had fled and for action focused on the problem of genocide, only a minuscule amount has been made available for activities essential to ameliorating and resolving the underlying cause of the cyclical strife that now characterizes Rwanda and other parts of the Great Lakes region.

481   However, some vital progress has been made both in responding rapidly and effectively to the needs of victims and in generating a more cohesive approach within the United Nations system. The Inter-Agency Standing Committee has played an incisive role, having on many occasions enabled consensus and decisions on pressing country-specific issues to be arrived at quickly and with immediate impact. Its uniqueness and success stem in part from the presence of, and close working relations with, certain major umbrella non-governmental organizations.

In 1994, the Committee agreed on a number of measures for strengthening field coordination of humanitarian assistance in complex emergencies, in particular in the pre-emergency and initial response phases. A set of guidelines relating to the humanitarian mandate as well as the appointment of and terms of reference for humanitarian coordinators were approved and the Emergency Relief Coordinator was also designated as the focal point for internally displaced persons. Most importantly, procedures for the most expeditious agreement on the division of labour between agencies have also been approved by the Committee.

Within the Secretariat, the Department of Humanitarian *482* Affairs, the Department of Political Affairs and the Department of Peace-keeping Operations have established a mechanism for the joint analysis of early warning of a looming crisis, within a broader framework for the coordination of operational planning and implementation among the three departments. Among the United Nations agencies also, agreement as to the responsibility and criteria for "sounding the alarm" in impending crises has enabled appropriate preventive and preparedness actions (such as contingency planning measures, primarily at the in-country level) to be initiated.

Timing is also critical in the fielding of humanitarian assist- *483* ance operations. The Department of Humanitarian Affairs has established a Rapid Response Unit to field experienced personnel to work with the United Nations resident or humanitarian coordinator and to build up systematic support for field-level coordination activities. At Kigali in April 1994, the United Nations advance humanitarian team, staffed by United Nations agency representatives and Department of Humanitarian Affairs personnel, re-established a United Nations humanitarian presence during a very difficult period and was able to lay the groundwork for the expansion of humanitarian activities as the situation permitted. In Haiti, a combined Department of Humanitarian Affairs/UNDP team was deployed to support the United Nations Coordinator for Humanitarian Assistance in the immediate aftermath of the United Nations action of September 1994. During the crisis in Chechnya, Department of Humanitarian Affairs staff were dispatched to neighbouring republics, where they worked closely with UNHCR and United Nations agency representatives in addressing the needs of internally displaced persons.

484   The Central Emergency Revolving Fund has consistently proved its value in facilitating both a rapid and joint response by United Nations agencies to fast-breaking emergencies. Delays in its reimbursement have, however, offset its usefulness on a number of occasions. The past year also saw the first use of the interest on the Fund to support immediate coordination arrangements in the field, with the establishment of the United Nations Rwanda Emergency Office at Kigali.

485   With a growing number of major emergencies of all varieties requiring international assistance, the Department of Humanitarian Affairs, led by Under-Secretary-General Peter Hansen, has continued to strengthen its coordination support capacity and to act as a focal point for the development of new initiatives taken jointly by the international emergency response community towards the improved effectiveness of international relief operations. Activities since my last report include the expansion of the number of countries participating with members in the United Nations Disaster Assessment and Coordination Team, including six disaster-prone developing countries from the Latin American region, and the development of guidelines and standards for the assessment of international relief requirements in multisectoral emergencies and for the mobilization of resources, the rapid initiation and support of field coordination, the exchange of know-how and techniques, and the development of standard operational procedures in the deployment of international response teams.

In this endeavour, the Department of Humanitarian Affairs *486* has worked closely with and supported the activities of international networks of emergency teams such as the International Search and Rescue Advisory Group and the Standing Coordinating Group on the Use of Military and Civil Defence Assets in Disaster Relief. With regard to the provision of specialized human, technical and logistical resources to support the coordination of international relief operations, the Department has initiated memoranda of understanding with Governments and organizations to allow it expeditious access to their emergency relief capacities. This forward-looking, systematic approach used by the Department has proved its worth in a number of sudden-onset emergencies during the year.

Natural disaster reduction remains a core activity of *487* humanitarian assistance, which tackles the root causes of disasters, and an essential ingredient of rehabilitation and reconstruction planning. The Under-Secretary-General has, therefore, brought together the Department of Humanitarian Affairs' Disaster Mitigation Branch and the secretariat for the International Decade for Natural Disaster Reduction under the umbrella of a Disaster Reduction Division. Thus the Department is able to serve all aspects of natural disaster reduction at all levels within the framework of a coherent United Nations strategy (see table 1).

Between May 1994 and July 1995, the Department of *488* Humanitarian Affairs launched 27 appeals for international assistance on behalf of countries affected by natural, technological or environmental disasters. It coordinated international assistance following more than 85 disasters in 50 countries. Some 243 situation reports were issued on the consequences of those disasters, to which the international community reported contribu-

TABLE I
Natural disasters: casualties,
damage and contributions

	1992	1993	1994
Number of disasters	45	8	75
Number of dead	6 971	13 542	7 572
Number of missing	258	1 631	1 989
Amount of damage[a] · · · · · · · · · · · · · · ·	2.06	15.80	9.00
Contributions reported to DHA[b] · · · · · · ·	257.4	77.5	114.0
Contributions channelled through DHA[b] · ·	3.73	4.23	7.50

[a] Billions of United States dollars.
[b] Millions of United States dollars.

tions amounting to more than $115 million, $6.3 million of which were channelled through the Department. During the same period, the Department arranged 38 relief flights from its emergency stockpile at Pisa, Italy, in response to the immediate requirements of those affected by disaster.

489   However, while much vital progress has been made in augmenting the capacity of humanitarian agencies to respond quickly and coherently to the immediate needs of victims of all kinds of emergencies, the task of assisting countries to emerge from crises continues to pose significant challenges. This is particularly evident in situations of systemic breakdown when the task of rebuilding civil society is dependent on the commitment of the international community to address the underlying cause of crises. The ability of aid agencies to support a recovery process is, of course, largely determined by the extent to which affected communities engage in activities geared to making the transition from dependency on relief to sustainable development.

490   As is now widely acknowledged, the relationship between relief and development, particularly in conflict settings, is complex and needs constantly to be assessed to ensure that interventions are mutually reinforcing. In many instances, gains made

by the humanitarian community in stabilizing a situation are not accompanied by the inputs necessary to nurture a recovery process. Indeed, protracted crises often experience funding shortfalls, thereby negating tenuous advances in the reduction of vulnerabilities of either a social, economic or political nature. The tragic experiences of people in Liberia, Rwanda and the Sudan illustrate the need for sustained and concerted action focused on breaking the dynamic of violence.

On a more positive note the experiences of Haiti and *491* Mozambique during this past year demonstrate the advantages of assertive action that actively nurtures the quest for peace. Likewise, the opportunity to consolidate the long-awaited peace in Angola must be fully exploited and necessary support provided for vital rehabilitation and reconstruction activities. As in other post-cease-fire situations, it is important that the international community maintain the momentum for peace; too often, critical activities, including de-mining and the homeward return of refugees, the displaced and former combatants, are jeopardized because of insufficient support for programmes that are essential for the revitalization of community life. Aware of the challenges confronting war-torn societies, humanitarian and development staff of the United Nations system are currently reviewing mechanisms to ensure that their respective funding and operational activities are complementary and enhance peace-building initiatives.

1. Cooperation with regional arrangements or agencies

In the field of natural disaster reduction, the primary function *492* of the Department of Humanitarian Affairs is to promote new initiatives. This includes project activities in 28 of the more disaster-prone developing countries, including 11 new ones during the year under review.

493   The main objectives have been to establish and apply the most effective methods for hazard and risk assessment, to promote wider interchange of knowledge and systematic application of appropriate technology, to carry out more active pooling, analysis and dissemination of early warnings, and to stimulate the development of scenario-specific disaster mitigation and preparedness plans with emphasis on maximizing the use of local resources and community involvement, while providing access to external expertise where essential. A special focus has been placed on Africa, where three subregional seminars have stimulated new national initiatives in disaster reduction. In Latin America and the Caribbean, new projects have been formulated for five countries and comprehensive programmes continue in four others. For Asia, projects are continuing or are in the process of formulation for six countries, including a new four-year programme encompassing the South Pacific island States, which has been widely sponsored and warmly welcomed by the participating countries and regional agencies. Attention is also being given to the eastern European, Middle East and CIS countries, with projects launched or in process of formulation in five States. The above activities have been carried out in close cooperation with UNDP and UNEP to promote the inclusion of development and environment issues wherever applicable. Eleven other international agencies and more than 30 non-governmental organizations have been associated.

494   In the framework of the Department for Humanitarian Affairs' project on the use of military and civil defence assets in disaster relief, arrangements have continued for strengthening cooperation between the Department of Humanitarian Affairs and NATO, the Western European Union (WEU) and the Inter-American Defense Board. Within the provisions of the Oslo Guidelines, mechanisms for such cooperation are being tested and improved through joint training, contingency planning and field exercises. Regional cooperation was tested in particular during an exercise hosted by the Russian Federation focusing on international assistance following a simulated major nuclear power plant accident. Standing operating procedures for the use of military and civil defence assets in disaster relief are being refined to enhance the humanitarian aspects of the NATO Partnership for Peace programme. The EU Humanitarian Office, a member of the Standing Coordinating Group, has funded the activities of the project related to relief air operations and to regional cooperation in Africa and Asia.

UNDP and the Department of Humanitarian Affairs have *495* established a Joint Environment Unit that strengthens the international capacity to respond to environmental aspects of disasters, while making the most effective use of limited resources. The Unit represents a practical synergy between the two organizations that ensures a targeted and comprehensive approach to the growing problem of environmental emergencies while at the same time avoiding duplication of effort. As such, the Joint Environment Unit is fully integrated into the Department of Humanitarian Affairs. UNEP provides staff and funding for the project, while the Department provides access to resources, expertise in disaster management and procedures for effective mobilization and coordination of relief.

The Department of Humanitarian Affairs also continues to *496* work closely with the Caribbean Disaster Emergency Response Agency, with which the Department has an agreement for early warning and exchange of information when disaster strikes.

2. *Proactive humanitarian action*

Part of the Department of Humanitarian Affairs' core coordina- *497* tion function involves participation in the planning and execution of "proactive" humanitarian action, though this term carries different meaning when applied to the onset of complex crises, on the one hand, or natural disasters, on the other. Examples of humanitarian activities that might prevent or reduce the scale of suffering include the provision of assistance that could pre-empt mass population movements or support that facilitates the reintegration of demobilized soldiers. Prevention of natural disasters might involve the strengthening of structures against earthquakes or the resettlement of populations away from flood zones or earthquake fault lines.

498   A functioning early warning system is critically important for the timely planning and implementation of pre-emptive action. The Humanitarian Early Warning System has been created to provide up-to-date warnings of country crisis situations through analysis of its database, drawing upon the various early warning mechanisms of other United Nations agencies as well as non–United Nations information sources. The system is made up of a database that includes both statistical and other country-specific information, graphically presented trend evaluation and an analysis process that examines statistical and event information. The System completed its prototype in January 1995 and has expanded its country coverage as well as its depth of information on each country. It became fully operational in July.

499   In the field of natural disasters, activities generated by the International Decade for Natural Disaster Reduction are focused specifically on preventive measures. The momentum created by the World Conference on Natural Disaster Reduction, held at Yokohama in May 1994, has been successfully sustained by means of a participatory and continuous dialogue of traditional and new partners within the International Framework of Action. Consequently, the Yokohama Strategy for a Safer World: Guidelines for Natural Disaster Prevention, Preparedness and Mitigation, in particular its Plan of Action, has

been transformed into a comprehensive and structured sequence of sectoral and cross-sectoral activities at all levels. During the second half of the International Decade for Natural Disaster Reduction, and commensurate with the proposals of the World Conference, emphasis is being shifted to concrete activities at the country and local levels. In order to maintain this broad-based inter-agency approach, the Inter-Agency Steering Committee has been extended until the end of the Decade.

Also in line with the Yokohama Strategy, the interdependency of natural disaster reduction, environmental protection and sustainable development is being reflected through improved cooperation between the International Framework and the major development activities inside and outside the United Nations system. Thus the Department of Humanitarian Affairs is acting, through the International Decade for Natural Disaster Relief secretariat, as task manager for natural disasters for the Commission on Sustainable Development. The process that has been outlined for the remaining years of the Decade will provide the opportunity to present its closing event with sound proposals for the full integration of disaster reduction into national planning and international development cooperation. It reflects the challenging objectives that have been laid out by the "Agenda for Development" (A/48/935). *500*

3. *Relief operations*

The four major operations during the past year have taken place *501* in Chechnya, Ukraine (Chernobyl), Kenya and the Sudan.

Chechnya

Following a request from the Russian Federation for international assistance for persons displaced from Chechnya to the neighbouring federal republics of Ingushetia, North Ossetia and Daghestan, last January I authorized a United Nations inter- *502* agency mission to the region. This resulted in the issue of a "flash appeal" in February to mobilize immediate resources for the emergency needs of 220,000 people. Subsequently, the United Nations consolidated appeal for persons displaced as a result of the emergency situation in Chechnya, Russian Federation, covering the period from 1 January to 30 June 1995, was launched at Geneva in March. Because of the continuing crisis, the appeal was updated in June and its coverage was extended by six months to the end of 1995.

503   The extended United Nations humanitarian programme now covers the emergency needs of the 118,000 internally displaced persons identified as being the most vulnerable and seeks donor support for financial coverage of the 30 per cent shortfall of the total $25 million needed to allow relevant agencies to complete emergency assistance projects, as originally envisaged. Activities being implemented include assistance in areas such as shelter, water and sanitation, food, health and care for children in especially difficult circumstances. A high level of inter-agency cooperation has been achieved through a triangular structure among agencies operating in the field, the Humanitarian Coordinator in Moscow and the headquarters of the United Nations agencies, the International Organization for Migration (IOM) and the Department of Humanitarian Affairs. However, the situation affecting refugees and internally displaced persons in the three republics is still precarious. While the majority of those affected have sought shelter with host families, this additional burden has placed severe pressure on already meagre resources. Overcrowding has stretched the social services available to persons in the region. Food and medicines are in short supply and the onset of winter weather will result in additional hardships for the victims of the conflict unless urgent preventive action is taken. In particular, additional funding support is urgently required in order for agencies

to stockpile contingency food supplies for the winter months.

At the end of June, peace negotiations between the Russian   *504*
authorities and the Chechen delegation commenced at Grozny under the auspices of OSCE. A cease-fire came into effect on 2 July.

Chernobyl

While the tenth anniversary of the accident at the Chernobyl   *505*
nuclear power plant is approaching, the extent of its impact on the populations of Belarus, the Russian Federation and Ukraine is only now being fully realized. Over 300 children now suffer from thyroid cancer, a disease practically non-existent in children before the accident, and hundreds of thousands live in constant fear of still unknown effects the accident may have on their long-term health. The fertility rate, especially in Belarus, has declined dramatically, while the morbidity and mortality rates have increased. This trend is unlikely to reach its peak until well into the next decade.

In September 1994, the United Nations Coordinator on   *506*
International Cooperation on Chernobyl convened an expanded meeting of the quadripartite committee for coordination on Chernobyl. The meeting assessed the results of ongoing United Nations activities relating to Chernobyl and discussed the need for initiatives to commemorate the tenth anniversary of the accident in April 1986 and, in that connection, to draw attention to the continued need for funding of programmes to overcome the effects of the Chernobyl accident.

Members of the Inter-Agency Task Force on Chernobyl   *507*
continue their efforts to bring Chernobyl projects to fruition, but the lack of funds has brought several programmes to a halt. Particularly affected is the International Programme on Health Effects of the Chernobyl Accident under the auspices of WHO.

Although generous financial support by a handful of countries allowed the full and rapid implementation of the priority activities, there are now no resources to maintain the programme and initiate much-needed follow-up activities that have a direct impact on the health of the affected population.

508   In November 1994, nine community centres (three each in Belarus, the Russian Federation and Ukraine) were officially opened, marking the completion of phase I of the UNESCO programme to overcome the psychological effects of the accident. However, the implementation of phase II of the project, as well as other related projects, will depend on the possibility of raising additional funds. The FAO/International Atomic Energy Agency (IAEA) joint division completed successful projects on the use of radio-caesium binders to reduce contamination of milk and on the cultivation of rape-seed on contaminated soils. As a result of the projects, large areas that were hitherto regarded as unsafe can now be used for agricultural production. In 1995, IAEA also began, in cooperation with the French Institut de Protection et de Sureté nucléaire, a project on environmental impact assessment.

509   Plans are now under way for events to commemorate the tenth anniversary of the Chernobyl accident. WHO will arrange a conference at Geneva in November on the health aspects of the accident, the United Nations will participate in a conference to be arranged at Minsk by the Government of Belarus and EU, while IAEA will arrange a summing-up conference at Vienna from 8 to 12 April 1996. A further meeting of the quadripartite committee will be held in the autumn of 1995 and will have as its main objective to identify those projects which remain of vital importance to the affected population and to agree on ways to ensure their funding.

Kenya

The United Nations consolidated inter-agency appeal for Kenya *510* launched in February 1994 covered the period from January to December of that year, targeting a population of 1,620,000. Donor response totalled $54,860,331, an amount equal to almost 57 per cent of the total requested in the appeal. The food situation remains mixed, as agricultural conditions in some regions have improved while others remain uncertain. Aggregate production in 1994/95 is provisionally estimated at close to 3.5 million tons, almost 1 million tons above the previous year's reduced level. Good rains and high world prices for coffee are helping to maintain recovery in agriculture. Over 200,000 Somali refugees remain in Kenya, adding some strain to the food situation and increasing tension at border areas. Political tensions continue, as do both ethnic tensions in the Rift Valley and violence in Mombasa between Islamic groups.

The Sudan

The Secretary-General's report of 12 September 1994 on emer- *511* gency assistance to the Sudan (A/49/376) stated that, despite progress made in the Sudan relief operation and Operation Lifeline Sudan, considerable needs still remained to be addressed, and the international community was urged to respond generously to the emergency needs and recovery of the country. In January 1995, the Department of Humanitarian Affairs issued the 1995 United Nations consolidated inter-agency appeal for the Sudan, in which United Nations agencies requested $101.1 million to meet the urgent humanitarian needs of 4.25 million people.

The donor response to the yearly United Nations consoli- *512* dated appeals between 1992 and 1994 has generally been quite positive: in 1992 it was 73 per cent of the amount requested. In 1993, however, it was 64 per cent, but although there were considerable delays in the donor response to the 1994 appeal, at the close of the year approximately 85 per cent had been received. Such fluctuations have serious ramifications for programme effectiveness.

513   Regrettably, the early part of 1995 showed only limited contributions to the appeal, so that by mid-July a considerable shortfall in donor response (less than 27 per cent of total requirements) was seriously compromising the United Nations ability to provide the urgently needed humanitarian assistance. This is all the more alarming as the shortfall occurred after increased cooperation during the previous two years with both the Government of the Sudan and the southern factions, as well as the improved cereal harvest in 1994, had permitted the United Nations to scale down its funding requirements by 45 per cent of the prior year's revised figure.

514   Since the launching of the 1995 appeal, Operation Lifeline Sudan activities have been hampered by renewed fighting, in particular in the provinces of Equatoria, Upper Nile, Junglei and northern Bahr El-Ghazal, where tens of thousands of persons have been dispossessed and dispersed. Renewed hostilities, combined with a lack of donor funding, have greatly reduced the effect of improved food production and forced people to abandon their homes and fields. In total, the United Nations estimates that there are just under 1.2 million internally displaced persons in the Sudan. The conflict has also forced the evacuation of relief workers from numerous localities, while in already three instances this year, relief workers have been kidnapped and held for periods ranging from a few days to almost two months. In another case an armed attack on a United Nations barge convoy disrupted a highly successful and cooperative logistics operation. With respect to other components of the Operation Lifeline Sudan logistics plan, operations remain dependent on air transport as the Operation has not received

agreement on the use of road corridors. Moreover, both financial constraints and a recent increase in the denial of air access have cut into the Operation's effectiveness. Further affecting the United Nations and non-governmental organizations' capacity to respond were the various incidents of misuse, misappropriation and looting of food and other relief supplies, which continue despite agreements to the contrary, although improved monitoring and coordination mechanisms have reduced the overall number of incidents since last year.

Positive developments registered before the mid-year *515* mark related notably to the two-month cease-fire between the Government and rebel factions mediated by the former United States President Jimmy Carter in consultation with the Inter-governmental Authority on Drought and Development, under whose aegis peace efforts have been organized since late 1993. Despite sporadic fighting, United Nations agencies were able to take advantage of opportunities for accelerating primary health care programmes during this initial period as well as during a subsequent two-month extension. Further efforts to renew the cease-fire in late July did not meet with success.

Since 1989, when Operation Lifeline Sudan began as a *516* short-term programme to deliver food and other life-saving provisions, it has developed considerably. While still providing food aid and basic health care to reduce mortality and morbidity among the affected population, the Operation now implements a much broader programme that extends to household food security, water and sanitation, basic shelter, food for work in support of agricultural production and health sector rehabilitation, primary education, support to psychologically traumatized children, capacity-building and promotion of humanitarian principles.

With increased access to a war-affected population of *517* approximately 4.25 million throughout the country, Operation

Lifeline Sudan reaches more people than ever before. Originally serving some 8 sites in southern Sudan, its operations have since come to include as many as 104 locations. This has been due in large part to greater flexibility shown by all the concerned parties.

518   It will be recalled from last year's report that the Intergovernmental Authority on Drought and Development had by March 1994 assumed a separate, though complementary, role in the regional peace process by facilitating negotiations on humanitarian access and related issues organized by the United Nations with the Government and the principal southern factions. Subsequent to agreements reached in March and May 1994, fixing modalities for humanitarian access across lines of conflict was identified as the priority for further negotiations. As no progress has been achieved during the intervening period, preliminary discussions intended to permit a resumption of tripartite talks were undertaken with the parties at Khartoum and Nairobi in late July and early August by the United Nations Special Envoy for Humanitarian Affairs for the Sudan, at which the question of operational modalities for international non-governmental organizations working out of Khartoum was discussed and all parties encouraged to work closely with the United Nations Special Envoy and senior Operation Lifeline Sudan personnel at Khartoum and Nairobi to secure an improved basis for progress.

519   With some exceptions, notably the suspension of an international non-governmental organization from the Operation owing to a breach of operational procedures, as well as the need to agree on guidelines for non-governmental organizations working out of Khartoum, cooperation among national, United Nations and non-governmental organizations working in the Sudan remains excellent. As in the past, the Operation provides the framework for the humanitarian efforts of 30 international

non-governmental organizations working in the region. While the Nairobi office has established letters of understanding with non-governmental organizations, which reflect the ground rules for Operation Lifeline Sudan operations, UNICEF Khartoum has sought to support government counterparts and local non-governmental organizations in relief and rehabilitation initiatives. Special efforts have been made to promote an improved framework for international non-governmental organizations to operate from Khartoum, including in the displaced person camps and the transitional zones. However, the continued strict controls on access and movement of the international non-governmental organizations in Khartoum have hampered attempts to bring to bear the comparative advantages they can offer.

While the number of approximately 1.2 million benefici- *520* aries identified as requiring emergency food aid in 1995 is a significant reduction compared with the needs of 1994, insecurity continues to plague the food delivery systems. In addition, whereas carry-over food stocks from 1994 were sufficient to cover most of the emergency food aid needs for 1995, international assistance to support monitoring, operational support costs and special transport costs had received less than 30 per cent of required donor support by July, causing the World Food Programme (WFP) to scale back monitoring activities by 50 per cent. Despite these constraints, by the end of July over half of the estimated 109,398 tons of food needs for 1995 had been transported by WFP and partner non-governmental organizations to areas in need.

For Operation Lifeline Sudan non-food assistance out of *521* Khartoum and all operations in the southern sector out of Nairobi, UNICEF has a lead responsibility. Overall 4.25 million people have been targeted for 1995, of whom 2.7 million are accessed from Khartoum and 1.7 million from Nairobi.

522   In May 1995, the Department of Humanitarian Affairs organized a consultation of key donors and aid organizations at Geneva to review funding status and programme implementation, the status of recommendations made by donors in 1994 and the timetable for a comprehensive review of Operation Lifeline Sudan.

523   A detailed critical review of the Operation is planned for later this year. As its main objectives, the review will analyse the Operation, its appropriateness in achieving maximum access to populations in need and in ensuring respect for fundamental humanitarian principles; assess the effectiveness of its coordination structures, in particular the relationship among the United Nations, donors, non-governmental organizations and Sudanese counterparts; and assess efficiency, identifying constraints and achievements.

524   In the first half of 1994 alone, some 96,000 tons of emergency food aid were delivered to affected areas of the Sudan by WFP and international relief agencies, in a major initiative that benefited substantial numbers of the affected population and not least the 500,000 persons who were then on the verge of starvation. In the latter part of the year WFP continued those efforts and expanded, in particular, its surface delivery capacity in southern Sudan.

4.   *Relief operations in the Near East (UNRWA)*

525 The activities of the United Nations Relief and Works Agency for Palestine Refugees in the Near East (UNRWA), headed by Commissioner-General Ilter Türkmen, focused during the reporting year on providing constructive support to the Middle East peace process.

526   The Agency took immediate steps to develop an effective working relationship with the Palestinian Authority and to meet the Authority's requests for assistance to the fullest extent possible. On 24 June 1994, an exchange of letters took place between the Commissioner-General of UNRWA and the Chairman of the Palestine Liberation Organization (PLO) for the purpose of facilitating the continued provision of UNRWA services to Palestine refugees in areas under the control of the Palestinian Authority. On an ad hoc basis UNRWA provided land and buildings, temporary shelter and emergency humanitarian aid to assist the Authority in establishing its operations in the Jericho area. UNRWA actively pursued coordination of its services with those provided by the Authority, developing effective relations with it in the education, health and relief and social service sectors. The Agency also played an active role in multilateral forums established to support the peace process, such as the multilateral working group on refugees, as part of the United Nations delegation.

Within the context of developments in the peace process, *527* UNRWA began the process of relocating its headquarters from Vienna to Gaza by the end of 1995. The relocation should serve to demonstrate the commitment of the United Nations to the peace process, underline its confidence in the Palestinian Authority and contribute to the economic development of the Gaza Strip.

UNRWA developed a detailed budget and action plan for *528* the move, including the design of a new headquarters building in Gaza. The Agency was taking the necessary steps to obtain the $13.5 million in funding needed for the move and to meet the schedule for the move. As at August 1995, the Agency had received $4.07 million in pledges and contributions for the move.

At my request, UNRWA undertook to administer the pay- *529* ment of the salaries of 9,000 members of the Palestinian Police Force from funds contributed by donors. The technical mechanism underlying the effort was established in a memorandum of understanding signed by UNRWA and the Palestinian Police Force in September 1994. From that date until March 1995 a total of $29.8 million was disbursed in the operation, in which UNRWA worked closely with the office of the United Nations Special Coordinator in the Occupied Territories. In its resolution 49/21 O of 13 April 1995, the General Assembly requested UNRWA to continue to facilitate the payment of Palestinian Police Force salaries until the end of 1995. An additional $4.9 million was paid for the July 1995 police salaries.

530   In September 1994, UNRWA launched the second phase of its Peace Implementation Programme with the objective of providing continuing infrastructure development and job creation to Palestine refugees throughout the Middle East. Funded projects included construction of schools, health clinics, women's programme centres and sewerage and drainage works, as well as renovation of shelters. Besides improving living conditions for refugees, related projects created an estimated 5,500 jobs over an average four-month period in Gaza alone. The programme met with a positive response on the part of donors, receiving a total of $109 million in funding as at May 1995. The Agency's project for a 232-bed general hospital in Gaza, begun in October 1993, continued during the reporting year. The hospital is due to be completed in early 1996 and recruitment of senior staff is under way.

531   While taking on new roles and responsibilities in response to changing conditions, UNRWA continued to fulfil its basic mission of providing essential health, education and relief and social services to 3.1 million Palestine refugees located in Jordan, Lebanon, the Syrian Arab Republic and the West Bank and Gaza. Some 410,000 elementary and preparatory school pupils were enrolled in the Agency's 643 schools during the academic year 1994/95. The Agency handled nearly 6.5 million patient visits during 1994 through its network of 123 health centres and health points. More than 181,000 of the neediest Palestine refugees received special assistance from the Agency during the year, including food rations, shelter rehabilitation and subsidized medical care. Additional facilities and services provided on an ongoing basis through the Agency's core programmes included vocational training, graduate scholarships, family planning services, special infant care, community rehabilitation centres, women's programme centres and income-generation schemes.

UNRWA's regular and emergency cash budget for the bi-ennium 1994-1995 was $570 million. The Agency ended 1994 with an actual funding shortfall of $7 million. Because of the deficit the Agency was forced to carry over the austerity measures imposed in 1993 in response to an earlier deficit, which included a salary freeze, a reduction in administrative costs and cuts in the budgets for additional teacher posts, hospitalization and medical supplies. An informal meeting of UNRWA's major donors and host Governments held at Amman in March 1995 resulted in pledges that helped to reduce the projected deficit for 1995. At the Amman meeting the donors reiterated their commitment to the continued provision of UNRWA services and approved a five-year planning horizon proposed by the Agency. *532*

F. PROTECTION AND RESETTLEMENT OF REFUGEES

The core functions of the Office of the United Nations High Commissioner for Refugees (UNHCR), headed by Mrs. Sadako Ogata, are those assigned by its 1950 statute: providing international protection to refugees and seeking permanent solutions to their problems. As part of its duty to ensure that voluntary repatriation schemes are sustainable, UNHCR has also become involved in assisting and protecting returnees in their home countries. In recent years, the General Assembly and the Secretary-General have called with increasing frequency on UNHCR to protect or assist particular groups of internally displaced people who have not crossed an international border but *533* are in a refugee-like situation inside their countries of origin, as well as other populations affected by conflict.

534   The genocide in Rwanda and the flight last year of over 2 million Rwandan nationals into neighbouring countries in the Great Lakes region of Africa was one of the darkest episodes in recent history and one that posed an unprecedented challenge for UNHCR and other humanitarian agencies. Other regions, including the former Yugoslavia, south-west Asia, the Horn of Africa and parts of western Africa, have also continued to suffer from massive population displacements, while a major new crisis erupted in the northern Caucasus in December 1994.

535   Although the refugee population worldwide had decreased to 14.5 million by the beginning of this year because of repatriation solutions in various parts of the world, the total number of people of concern to UNHCR had risen to some 27.4 million. This included 5.4 million internally displaced persons, 3.5 million others of humanitarian concern, predominantly populations affected by conflict, and some 4 million returnees requiring assistance to re-establish sustainable reintegration in their countries of origin. In 1994, UNHCR provided material assistance to a total of 17.6 million people, as compared to 13.8 million in 1993. This included 8.9 million in Africa, 5 million in Asia, 3.5 million in Europe and 115,000 in Latin America.

536   The present period of volatility and readjustment in world affairs has been characterized by increasing levels of human displacement. In the face of this reality, UNHCR has continued to hone its emergency response capacity and to pursue preventive and solution-oriented approaches. It has aimed to assure a high level of emergency preparedness, to provide assistance and protection in such a way as to avert, where possible, the occurrence of new refugee flows and to promote concerted efforts to achieve durable solutions, notably voluntary repatriation. In so doing, it has collaborated increasingly closely with political, peace-keeping and development initiatives and organs of the United Nations, with other intergovernmental and regional bodies and with a wide range of non-governmental organizations.

1.   *Emergency response*

As a result of its efforts since 1991, UNHCR's standby capacity has achieved a high level of preparedness in terms of both personnel and stockpiles of emergency relief supplies that it can deploy rapidly in an emergency. During 1994 and the first half of 1995 alone, its emergency response teams were deployed to 17 operations around the world. *537*

While continuing to take the lead in the international response to refugee emergencies, UNHCR has endeavoured to ensure the effectiveness of its interventions and the durability of results by building partnerships with other United Nations agencies and by coordinating its activities in complex emergency situations with the Department of Humanitarian Affairs. In its emergency operations in the former Yugoslavia, the Great Lakes region and other parts of Africa, and the central Asian republics, UNHCR has continued to strengthen its collaboration with United Nations agencies and programmes, in particular WFP, UNICEF, WHO and the United Nations Population Fund (UNFPA), in activities such as food aid, immunization and health care, water supply and sanitation, mother and child medical care, family planning and education. *538*

Faced in the Great Lakes region with the most severe refugee emergency in recent history, the Office was again obliged to innovate. With its own staff resources heavily committed in the region and elsewhere, it appealed to donor Governments to assume an operational role by providing self-contained services in a number of critical assistance sectors through the deployment of resources drawn largely from their military and civil defence establishments. The use of these so-called *539* "service packages" in the Rwanda emergency has demonstrated how, under certain conditions, unique military skills or assets can support UNHCR emergency relief activities. The positive impact of service packages in responding to the critical conditions that characterized the massive exodus of Rwandans has led UNHCR into a process of consultation with Governments and the Department of Humanitarian Affairs on how, when necessary and appropriate, this mechanism can best be used.

2. *The search for solutions*

540   Over 2 million refugees returned to their countries of origin in 1994, most notably to Mozambique, Afghanistan and Myanmar. Return movements have continued in 1995, with prospects also opening up for the large-scale return of some 300,000 refugees to Angola. Solutions have continued to be consolidated in several other regions, especially in Central America, where the process launched by the International Conference on Central American Refugees was brought formally to a close in June 1994 and a framework agreed for the post-Conference period, and in south-east Asia with the agreement of the Steering Committee of the International Conference on Indo-Chinese Refugees to aim for the completion of activities under the comprehensive plan of action by the end of 1995.

541   Solutions to complex, refugee-producing emergencies require concerted efforts whereby humanitarian activities are complemented by both political initiatives to resolve conflict and development efforts to ensure a sustainable livelihood for the most severely affected areas and people.

542   In many areas of the world, UNHCR works increasingly closely with peace-keeping or peacemaking initiatives undertaken by the United Nations. It has continued to work with the United Nations peace-keeping operation in the former Yugoslavia where, as lead agency for the provision of humanitarian

assistance, it has brought urgently needed assistance to over 2 million victims of war. Elsewhere, be it in Angola, Liberia, the Great Lakes region, the Horn of Africa, Guatemala, the Caucasus or central Asia, it has worked either within the framework of or in tandem with United Nations efforts at conflict resolution.

In its search for solutions to the problems of refugees and other displaced persons of concern to it, UNHCR has also placed considerable emphasis on developing closer collaboration with regional bodies. A regional conference was hosted jointly by UNHCR and OAU at Bujumbura in February this year to ensure a concerted approach to the crisis in the Great Lakes region. Working relationships have also been enhanced with other regional bodies, as, for example, in Georgia, where UNHCR and OSCE cooperate closely on efforts to resolve the Abkhazia and South Ossetia conflicts. Similar collaboration has been taking place in Nagorny Karabakh and Chechnya. *543*

UNHCR continues to attach great importance not only to conflict-resolution initiatives, but also to achieving a better interface between relief, rehabilitation and development. In the experience of the Office, the implementation of the concept of a continuum from relief to development should, on the one hand, enable humanitarian assistance to promote viable reintegration of displaced people into a process of social and economic recovery and, on the other, bring development endeavours closer to people-centred concerns and aspirations. Without this, solutions to humanitarian crises may regress into new, divisive communal problems. *544*

UNHCR has thus continued to reinforce its community-based approach to reintegration assistance through the implementation of quick impact projects and has pursued discussions with other departments and agencies, notably the Department of Humanitarian Affairs and UNDP, on how institutional gaps *545* can be bridged to ensure a meaningful continuum from relief to development. It has also sought to strengthen its relationship with the financial institutions, notably the World Bank. UNHCR efforts to support reconciliation and rehabilitation in post-conflict societies have been evident in the case of Mozambique, where its strategy for the reintegration of the 1.6 million refugees who have returned since the signing of the Peace Agreement aims, with the endorsement of the Government and major donors, at establishing linkages to longer-term development programmes.

3. *Preventing refugee crises*

546 Recognizing that, without effective preventive action, problems of human displacement will continue to spread, the Office has strengthened its institution-building and training activities in various parts of the world. In addition, UNHCR and IOM have continued their collaboration in mass information campaigns targeted, in particular, at potential migrants from the Russian Federation and other countries of CIS.

547   The scale of actual and potential problems of displacement in the former Soviet Union has led to an important initiative, which seeks to address current problems of displacement and prevent their proliferation. Further to General Assembly resolution 49/173 of 23 December 1994, UNHCR is engaged in preparations for a conference that will establish a programme of action to address the problems of refugees, returnees and displaced persons in the CIS countries and relevant neighbouring States. It is expected that the programme of action will include measures to prevent unnecessary movements and address the consequences of past, present and future displacements.

548   Most frequently, however, the efforts of the Office have come into play in situations where large-scale human displacement has already occurred. In such situations, UNHCR has continued to promote and participate in strategies that may help contain fragile situations. It has attempted to address or attenuate, wherever possible, the causes of refugee flows or, failing that, to reduce the necessity for affected populations or individuals to seek asylum across international borders. As part of these efforts, UNHCR has, at my request, continued or expanded its involvement in assisting and seeking solutions for groups of the internally displaced. In addition to its programme of humanitarian assistance for over 1.5 million internally displaced persons in the former Yugoslavia, UNHCR has, for example, been engaged in activities on behalf of substantial numbers of internally displaced in Angola, Ghana, Sierra Leone, Rwanda, Afghanistan, the Caucasus and the Russian Federation. These activities are frequently carried out in cooperation with other concerned United Nations bodies in the context of comprehensive approaches to displacement and conflict resolution.

4.   *Protecting the victims*

The scale of recent humanitarian crises has drawn renewed at-   *549*
tention to the protection needs of victims of persecution and conflict. Among the challenges that have come to the fore are the provision of international protection to those seeking asylum from internal conflict, the often compelling protection needs of the internally displaced, the need to ensure the security and rights of the inhabitants of refugee camps and the need to restore effective national protection for those who have returned to fragile situations in their home countries. The importance of UNHCR's protection role has thus remained primordial in all phases of its activities, be it in responding to emergencies or in pursuing and consolidating solutions.

In the contemporary situation, large numbers of people in   *550*
need of international protection have been forced to flee their countries because of situations of conflict. In view of political

initiatives undertaken by the international community to resolve such situations, certain asylum countries have resorted with increasing frequency to providing temporary protection rather than making formal determinations of refugee status under the 1951 Convention relating to the Status of Refugees. UNHCR, together with States, has been exploring this concept, notably in relation to those who have fled the former Yugoslavia, in an effort to ensure that international protection continues to be granted to all who need it.

551   One premise upon which temporary protection is based is the expectation of resolving, within a reasonable period, the underlying cause of the outflow. UNHCR has insisted that temporary protection must not be unduly protracted before more permanent status is granted to the victims in situations where the grounds for flight have not been resolved. In addition, UNHCR has emphasized that the beneficiaries of temporary protection are, in many cases, refugees within the meaning of the 1951 Convention.

552   As the Rwanda crisis has recently demonstrated, mass flight from situations of inter-communal conflict can lead to the politicization of refugee camps and to attendant abuses of human rights. UNHCR has endeavoured to ensure that the security and human rights of refugees, including their right freely to decide to return home, are protected in such situations. In response to security problems in Rwandan refugee camps in Zaire and following close consultations with the Secretary-General, measures were taken by UNHCR to improve law and order and prevent intimidation and violence against refugees and candidates for voluntary repatriation through the deployment of Zairian forces, monitored by an international security liaison group.

553   The protection responsibilities of UNHCR also include protecting the human rights of returnees and other displaced persons of concern to the Office. UNHCR has thus continued to play a role in monitoring the situation of returnees and ensuring that national protection is restored. Recent experience in Central America has been particularly encouraging in this respect. The international colloquium held in Costa Rica in December 1994 to commemorate the tenth anniversary of the Cartagena Declaration adopted the San José Declaration on Refugees and Displaced Persons, which addresses the key issue of harmonizing legal criteria and procedures to consolidate the durable solutions of voluntary repatriation and local integration.

In pursuing its preventive and solution-oriented activities, *554* UNHCR has welcomed United Nations efforts to establish a more effective operational capacity in the field of human rights, be it through intensified human rights field operations or through the establishment of international tribunals to prosecute the perpetrators of grave violations of human rights and humanitarian law. UNHCR has sought to strengthen collaboration with human rights treaty bodies and other human rights mechanisms, and has sought to establish active collaboration with the United Nations High Commissioner for Human Rights, especially at the level of field operations. Ongoing contacts with human rights working groups, rapporteurs, experts and monitors are also an integral part of the approach of UNHCR to link human rights concerns with the protection of refugees.

G. PROTECTION AND PROMOTION OF HUMAN RIGHTS

The United Nations High Commissioner for Human Rights, *555* Mr. José Ayala Lasso, is the United Nations official with principal responsibility for the Organization's human rights activities and, with the Centre for Human Rights, forms a unity of action. The staff of the Centre provides support for the activities of the

High Commissioner and the various programmes, procedures and organs of the human rights programme.

1. *New directions for the human rights programme*

556 Over the last 12 months, the Organization's human rights work has taken action in response to the need, as seen by Governments and United Nations organs, to reach out and apply abstract human rights principles in concrete situations. A growing number of countries have requested advisory services and technical cooperation in building up national human rights infrastructures. In the last year well over 100 human rights technical cooperation projects have been implemented in some 50 countries. In order to assist in carrying out human rights technical cooperation programmes and at the request of Governments concerned, the United Nations has established human rights field presences in Burundi, Cambodia, Malawi and Rwanda. This represents a new departure in delivering human rights assistance. The human rights officers involved seek, through training, law reform, education and information, to contribute to building the structures of a society respectful of human rights and to prevent violations. Their very presence has proved to be a confidence-building measure for fragile societies.

557 The committees established by human rights treaties are also focusing their recommendations on ways the United Nations can help States live up to their human rights obligations. Further, the committees themselves are undertaking field missions to understand better the conditions in which human rights must be protected, to try to defuse situations of tension and to help develop concrete solutions to problems. They are also increasingly active in the field of early warning and preventive action.

558 Monitoring human rights violations on the ground in order to provide accurate information to the international community and to contribute to bringing serious situations to an end is

another area in which our activities have grown. In 1993, the first monitors were sent to the field and today more than 120 human rights monitors are to be found in the territory of the former Yugoslavia and in Rwanda. Further, and following a resolution of the Commission on Human Rights, agreement has been reached to send two monitors to Zaire. The role of monitors is not only to report on violations, but also to be active agents of prevention.

2.   *Activities of the United Nations High Commissioner for Human Rights*

The activities of the High Commissioner for Human Rights *559* have opened new domains for United Nations action to promote human rights and have given direction and provided initiative throughout the human rights programme. Strengthening international cooperation for human rights has been a main theme. In visits to over 30 States on all continents, the High Commissioner has sought to reinforce commitment to international and national protection of human rights through discussion with government officials, members of parliament and the judiciary. The High Commissioner has sought to strengthen the role of civil society in protecting human rights through contacts with nongovernmental organizations, the academic community, the press and the public. These missions include appeals for ratification of treaties, for cooperation with all United Nations human rights mechanisms, inclusion of United Nations standards in national law and the establishment of national institutions to protect human rights. Human rights problems are dealt with frankly and appropriate actions suggested, including the revision of laws, release of detainees and adoption of other measures.

The High Commissioner's efforts to strengthen international *560* cooperation extend also to cooperation with United Nations agencies and programmes, international and regional organizations and with international and national non-governmental organizations. The High Commissioner has met with regional human rights organizations in Europe and the Americas, and he has drawn the attention of high-level international development and financial meetings to the need to support human rights activities.

561   An important aspect of the High Commissioner's activities is to help ensure that the human rights perspective is included in international conferences and that the high level of existing United Nations human rights standards is maintained. The High Commissioner took initiatives in this regard in relation to the World Summit for Social Development and the Fourth World Conference on Women. With regard to the latter, the High Commissioner has given particular attention to encouraging the inclusion of all aspects of the equal status and human rights of women and the girl-child in its deliberations.

562   The High Commissioner has also continued his activities aimed at responding to serious situations of violations and at preventing violations from developing or becoming widespread. The High Commissioner has continued to strengthen the activities of his offices in Burundi and Rwanda, has dispatched a high-level personal representative to visit the Russian Federation, including Chechnya, and has appointed a personal representative to the Office of the Special Representative of the Secretary-General in the Former Yugoslavia to deal with human rights issues.

563   Preventing violations often goes hand in hand with providing advisory services and technical cooperation in human rights. In this connection the High Commissioner has established a special programme to promote and support national human rights institutions. Other areas of activity are combating all forms of discrimination, including racism, racial discrimination, xenophobia and related forms of intolerance; promoting

the equal status and rights of women; the rights of the child; and the rights of minorities and indigenous people. Of special importance is the responsibility given to the High Commissioner by the General Assembly to coordinate the implementation of the plan of action of the United Nations Decade for Human Rights Education. The High Commissioner places importance on promoting the right to development and cultural, economic and social rights. A strategy for the implementation of the right to development and protection of cultural, economic and social rights is being developed to identify, in cooperation with relevant agencies, treaty-based bodies and experts, ways of improving the implementation of those rights.

3. *International human rights treaty system*

Some progress has been made in ratifications within the international human rights treaty system. As at 10 August 1995, 177 States had accepted to ensure and respect the wide range of basic human rights laid down in the Convention on the Rights of the Child. This means that the rights of more than 90 per cent of the children in the world today are protected by the Convention. This is in itself a notable achievement; every effort should be made to gain universal ratification by the end of 1995. Ratification of other treaties has not progressed so rapidly: as at 10 August, 132 States were party to the International Covenant on Economic, Social and Cultural Rights; 131 to the International Covenant on Civil and Political Rights; 143 to the International Convention on the Elimination of All Forms of Racial Discrimination; and 141 to the Convention on the Elimination of All Forms of Discrimination against Women. Only 90 States had ratified the Convention against Torture and Other Cruel, Inhuman or Degrading Treatment or Punishment and only 4 had ratified the International Convention on the Protection of the Rights of All Migrant Workers and Members of Their Families.

564

565   In September 1994, I wrote to all Member States urging ratification of outstanding human rights treaties. In February 1995, I wrote to Heads of State or Government appealing for ratification of the Convention on the Rights of the Child. I am pleased with the numerous positive responses and I have asked the High Commissioner for Human Rights to follow up on my letters and to offer assistance where required. Nevertheless, new efforts must be made to achieve universal ratification of these important instruments.

566   At the heart of the international human rights treaty system are the six expert committees charged with monitoring respect for human rights as laid down in the respective treaties: the Human Rights Committee; the Committee on Economic, Social and Cultural Rights; the Committee on the Rights of the Child; the Committee on the Elimination of Racial Discrimination; the Committee on the Elimination of Discrimination against Women; and the Committee against Torture. Together, they review the human rights situation in some 60 countries a year. The committees and their members represent a precious source of information and expertise.

567   The committees have been improving their methods of work, providing more focused recommendations and carrying out field missions with increasing frequency. Three objectives are shaping their work: increased interaction and participation of the specialized agencies and non-governmental organizations; the establishment of closer connections between the findings of the treaty body concerned and the programme of advisory services and technical cooperation; and the establishment by treaty bodies of procedures aimed at preventing human rights violations and preventing existing problems from escalating into conflicts.

568   In connection with situations that require special or urgent action, the committees have requested special reports on an

urgent basis (former Yugoslavia, Croatia, Bosnia and Herze-govina, Haiti, Iraq, Peru, etc.), undertaken good offices mis-sions (Belgrade, Kosovo) or carried out technical assistance missions (Croatia, Panama). Special appeals have also been issued with regard to Indonesia, concerning East Timor and Pakistan.

In June I met, for the first time, with the chairpersons of all 569 six treaty-based bodies. The discussion focused on the role of those bodies in early warning and preventive action, on the greatly increased capacity of those bodies to monitor accurately the human rights situation in a wide range of countries and the assistance those bodies needed from the Secretariat to carry out those expanded responsibilities successfully. I expressed my full support for their important activities and my personal com-mitment to securing universal ratification of human rights trea-ties. I look forward to closer cooperation with the treaty bodies in the future.

4.   *Activities of the Commission on Human Rights and its subsidiary bodies*

The Commission on Human Rights is a unique world forum for 570 the public discussion of important human rights issues between Governments, international organizations and non-governmental organizations. Over the years the Commission has created numerous human rights fact-finding mechanisms charged with reporting on various human rights situations or types of serious violations, dealing with individual appeals and making suggestions for action to improve respect for human rights. The human rights situation in 12 countries is under re-view by these procedures. In addition, 14 thematic mandates have been established dealing with particularly serious viola-tions, wherever they may occur, running from arbitrary execu-tions, torture, disappearances, exploitation and sale of children, to violence against women and racism, racial discrimination and xenophobia. This year saw the appointment of a special rapporteur on Burundi and one on the adverse effects on human rights of the illicit movement and dumping of toxic waste and dangerous products. Each year thousands of urgent individual cases are transmitted to Governments and some 40 field missions are carried out. In May a special meeting on these procedures took place to improve their operation, to seek ways of integrating women's human rights into their work and to decide on their contribution to the Fourth World Conference on Women.

571   The Commission on Human Rights, through various working groups, also pursued the adoption of a declaration on the rights and responsibilities of individuals, groups and organs of society to promote and protect universally recognized human rights and fundamental freedoms; a draft optional protocol to the Convention against Torture and Other Cruel, Inhuman or Degrading Treatment or Punishment concerning visits to prisons or places of detention; and a draft optional protocol to the Convention on the Rights of the Child on involvement of children in armed conflicts. Work is also under way on guidelines for a possible optional protocol to the Convention on the Rights of the Child on the sale of children, child prostitution and child pornography, as well as the basic measures needed for the prevention and eradication of those practices.

572   The Commission has given close attention to the equal status and human rights of women. The Commission's Special Rapporteur on violence against women, its causes and consequences, submitted her preliminary report to the Commission at its last session. The document deals with the different forms of violence that occur in the family and the community and are perpetrated or condoned by the State, and sets out the framework for the future work of the Special Rapporteur. The Special Rapporteur has also been actively involved in the integration of

women's rights into the mainstream of United Nations activities in the field of human rights, as called for in the Vienna Declaration and Programme of Action. The High Commissioner and the Centre for Human Rights have been helping to focus the attention of the various human rights organs and bodies on the human rights input to the Fourth World Conference on Women and on the preparation of parallel human rights activities.

The United Nations has continued to work for the protection of the rights of indigenous people. The Working Group on Indigenous Populations is the main forum for interaction between human rights experts, Governments and representatives of indigenous people; some 400 representatives of indigenous people take part each year. The General Assembly has proclaimed the period 1995-2004 as the International Decade of the World's Indigenous People and the Commission on Human Rights is studying the draft declaration on the rights of indigenous people. Work continues towards the establishment of a permanent forum for indigenous people, as called for by the Vienna Declaration. *573*

Minorities are another especially vulnerable group often needing international action to help protect their rights. A new body, the Working Group on Minorities, has been set up with a wide mandate aimed at promoting respect for the 1992 Declaration on the Rights of Persons Belonging to National or Ethnic, Religious and Linguistic Minorities and examining possible solutions to problems involving minorities. Further, the General Assembly has asked the High Commissioner to promote the implementation of the principles contained in that Declaration. *574*

The programme of action for the Third Decade to Combat Racism and Racial Discrimination is a key element in promoting equality. The General Assembly has recommended that various measures and actions be taken on the national, regional and international levels. High priority is to be given to provid- *575* ing assistance and relief to victims of racism and all forms of racial discrimination. The possibility of convening a world conference on the elimination of racism, racial and ethnic discrimination, xenophobia and other related contemporary forms of intolerance is being studied.

5.　*Advisory services and technical cooperation*

576　The World Conference on Human Rights, held at Vienna in June 1993, gave heightened emphasis to the need for the international community to respond to the requests of States for technical cooperation to strengthen the institutions of human rights and human rights practices. The concrete response to this is to be found in the programme of technical cooperation in the field of human rights implemented by the Centre for Human Rights. The programme supports a wide range of projects aimed at, among other things, developing national plans of action for human rights, providing assistance in drafting constitutional provisions relating to human rights, reforming legislation, human rights aspects of elections, prison reform, developing and strengthening national institutions, strengthening the judiciary, training judges, prosecutors and lawyers in human rights, and training police and the armed forces. Technical cooperation projects also support regional human rights institutions such as the African Commission on Human and Peoples' Rights, the African Centre for Democracy and Human Rights Studies and the Arab Institute for Human Rights. Many of these activities are financed through the United Nations voluntary fund for technical cooperation in the field of human rights under the guidance of its board of trustees, composed of eminent international experts.

577　The preventive capacities of this programme have grown in importance. Contributions have been made during the past year to support the peace process in Palestine through the training of the Palestinian Police Force, to strengthening the human rights structures in the Caucasus (Armenia, Azerbaijan, Georgia), to the peace-keeping operation in Mozambique through human rights training for the ONUMOZ civilian police component and in the former Yugoslavia through training for UNPROFOR officials and the national police of the former Yugoslav Republic of Macedonia. Assistance continues in Cambodia and in Rwanda and Burundi.

6. *Early warning mechanism*

The Centre for Human Rights has increasingly brought its human rights expertise to bear on various activities dealing with early warning or with information relating to emergency situations. The Centre has participated in the Administrative Committee on Coordination Working Group on Early Warning of New Flows of Refugees and Displaced Persons and its subgroup on indicators. The Centre has also contributed to the development of the set of indicators for the Humanitarian Early Warning System led by the Department of Humanitarian Affairs and to the framework for coordination project for planning and implementation of complex operations in the field. The Centre is also an active participant in the relief net project coordinated by the Department and contributed to the May 1995 meeting on early warning activities related to the CIS region. *578*

During the last year the United Nations faced a major challenge in responding to the increasingly varied demands for action made upon it by Governments and United Nations bodies. Initial difficulties encountered in fielding complex human rights missions have now been overcome and the High Commissioner is seeking the cooperation of countries in building a solid basis for future action in the following areas: (*a*) logistical assistance capacity on a standby basis to provide material, communications and other support needed to contribute to emergency or preventive field missions; (*b*) the establishment *579* and maintenance of an international roster of specialized staff to be available at short notice for human rights field missions (investigation teams, human rights field officers, legal experts etc.); and (*c*) increased contributions to the voluntary fund for technical cooperation in order to cover the financial needs of advisory service field missions and assistance.

580   Other action must be envisaged to enable the human rights programme to respond to the new demands of the Vienna Declaration, the High Commissioner's mandate and other decisions of policy-making bodies. The structure of the programme and of the supporting secretariat is being carefully reviewed in order to rationalize the work programme and to provide the substantive and technical support needed by the programme.

IV. Expanding preventive diplomacy and conflict resolution

A. IMPLEMENTING "AN AGENDA FOR PEACE"

IN RESPONSE to my report entitled "An Agenda for Peace", *581* the General Assembly adopted resolutions 47/120 A and B on 18 December 1992 and 20 September 1993, respectively. In the first resolution the Assembly gave me a clear mandate to pursue preventive diplomacy and to strengthen the Secretariat's capacity in an early-warning mechanism, in particular collection and analysis of information, for situations likely to endanger international peace and security. The Security Council has also held a number of meetings to examine specific proposals made in "An Agenda for Peace", and the President of the Council has issued some 10 statements or letters as part of the review process.

On 3 January 1995, I issued a position paper entitled "Sup- *582* plement to 'An Agenda for Peace' " (A/50/60-S/1995/1), in which I set forth additional recommendations, highlighting the areas where unforeseen, or only partly foreseen, difficulties had arisen and where there is a need for Member States to take the "hard decisions" noted in my 1992 report (A/47/277-S/24111). I also drew conclusions with regard to the crucial distinction between peace-keeping and enforcement action, as well as to the circumstances in which military force is a useful tool of diplomacy and those in which it is counterproductive.

In response to the Supplement, and after intensive discus- *583* sions on 18 and 19 January 1995, the Security Council issued a presidential statement (S/PRST/1995/9) in support of that position paper. The Council welcomed and shared the priority I had given to action to prevent conflict. Furthermore, it encouraged all Member States to make the fullest possible use of instruments of preventive action, including the good offices of the Secretary-General, the dispatch of special envoys and the deployment, with the consent as appropriate of the host country or countries, of small field missions for preventive diplomacy and peacemaking. Among other things, the Security Council hoped that the General Assembly, as well as other organizations and entities, would accord the Supplement a high degree of priority. It is encouraging to see that the lessons of contemporary peacekeeping have begun to appear not only in United Nations documents but in the training manuals of a number of Member States as well.

584   In the General Assembly, the Informal Open-ended Working Group on An Agenda for Peace continued its work during 1995 on issues contained in "An Agenda for Peace" and the Supplement.

585   Encouraged by such interest and in the belief that it is evidently better to prevent conflicts through early warning, quiet diplomacy and, in some cases, preventive deployment, than to undertake major politico-military efforts to resolve conflicts after they have broken out, I intend to redouble my efforts to perform the task entrusted to me under the Charter. If the United Nations is to play a timely and constructive role in averting or mitigating the destructive effects of complex crises, it is essential that the various elements of the Organization have an early, common view of the nature of the problem and the options for preventive action. In the Supplement, I noted that the multifunctional nature of both peace-keeping and peace-building had made it necessary to improve coordination within the Secretariat, so that the relevant departments function as an integrated whole under my authority and control.

586   It is in this context that, following an initiative of the Department of Humanitarian Affairs, the three substantive departments of the Secretariat, the Department of Humanitarian Affairs, the Department of Political Affairs and the Department of Peace-keeping Operations, have developed a flow-chart of actions — information sharing, consultations and joint action — for the coordination of their respective activities in the planning and implementing of complex operations in the field. This mechanism, known as the "Framework for coordination", covers the departments' activities during routine monitoring and early-warning analysis, assessment of options for preventive action where possible, fact-finding, planning and implementation of field operations, and conduct of evaluations or lessons-learned exercises.

An important element of the Framework for Coordination *587* is the provision for staff-level consultations by the three departments, as well as the United Nations Development Programme, the Commission on Human Rights, the Department of Public Information and other parts of the Organization, to undertake joint analyses of early-warning information from a variety of sources, and to formulate joint recommendations for possible preventive measures. The individual departments — particularly the Department of Political Affairs — will retain the authority to implement preventive action, under my direction.

To ensure continuous consultation between the Secretary- *588* General and the Security Council and to assist the latter in being informed about the latest developments, particularly in the area of peace-keeping operations, I have appointed one of my Special Advisers, Mr. Chinmaya Gharekhan, as my personal representative to the Council. Troop-contributing Governments are also understandably anxious to be kept fully informed. Therefore, I have endeavoured to meet their concerns by providing the Governments with regular briefings and by engaging them in dialogue about the conduct of the operation in question. Members of the Security Council have been included in such meetings, which the Council recently decided to formalize. It is important, however, that this reform should not lead to any blurring of the three distinct areas of authority, which include overall political direction that belongs to the Security Council; executive direction and command for which the Secretary-General is responsible; and command in the field, which I entrust to the chief of mission.

589 All the efforts of the Security Council, the General Assembly and the Secretariat to control and resolve conflicts need the cooperation and support of other players on the international stage. Chapter VIII of the Charter defines the role that regional organizations can play in the maintenance of peace and security. Forms of cooperation between the United Nations and regional organizations include consultations, diplomatic support, operational support, co-deployment and joint operations. While the capacity of regional organizations for peacemaking and peace-keeping varies considerably, none has yet developed the capacity and experience the United Nations has in those fields. The United Nations is ready to help them when requested to do so and when resources are sufficient. To advance these efforts, I intend to hold another high-level meeting with regional arrangements and organizations as a follow-up to the meeting I convened on 1 August 1994.

B. PREVENTIVE DIPLOMACY AND PEACEMAKING

590 It has become clear that preventive diplomacy is only one of a class of actions that can be taken to prevent disputes from turning into armed conflict. Others in this class are preventive deployment of military and/or police personnel; preventive humanitarian action, for example, to manage and resolve a refugee situation in a sensitive frontier area; and preventive peace-building, which itself comprises an extensive menu of possible

actions in the political, economic and social fields, applicable especially to possible internal conflicts.

All these preventive actions share the following charac- *591* teristics: they all depend on early warning that the risk of conflict exists; they require information about the causes and likely nature of the potential conflict so that the appropriate preventive action can be identified; and they require the consent of the party or parties within whose jurisdiction the preventive action is to take place.

The element of timing is crucial. The potential conflict *592* should be ripe for the preventive action proposed. Timing is also an important consideration in peacemaking and peace-keeping. The prevention, control and resolution of a conflict is like the prevention, control and cure of disease. If treatment is prescribed at the wrong moment in the evolution of a disease, the patient does not improve, and the credibility of both the treatment and the physician who prescribed it is compromised.

The term "peacemaking", as used by the United Nations, *593* refers to the use of diplomatic means to persuade parties in conflict to cease hostilities and negotiate a peaceful settlement of their dispute. All the types of action that can be used for preventive purposes, such as diplomatic peace-keeping, humanitarian aid and peace-building, have their role in creating conditions for successful peacemaking, and implementing and consolidating the negotiated settlement for peace.

The primary responsibility for preventive action and *594* peacemaking rests with the Department of Political Affairs, headed by Under-Secretary-General Marrack Goulding. The Department was created in 1992 to consolidate the political work of the Secretariat in a single department. There is, however, a distinction to be made between the Department's roles in these two fields. In the preventive field, its role is to identify the action required, with execution being entrusted to the specialist department or other agency concerned. In the peacemaking field, its role generally includes execution as well.

595   The Department of Political Affairs has five main responsibilities in support of preventive action and peacemaking. First, it must monitor, analyse and assess political developments throughout the world. Next, the Department identifies potential or actual conflicts in whose control and resolution the United Nations can play a useful role. It then prepares recommendations to the Secretary-General about appropriate actions in such cases. Fourth, the Department executes the approved policy when it is of a diplomatic nature. Finally, it assists the Secretary-General in carrying out political activities decided by him and/or mandated by the General Assembly and the Security Council in the areas of preventive diplomacy, peacemaking, peace-keeping and peace-building, including arms control and disarmament.

596   The Centre for Disarmament Affairs, an integral part of the Department of Political Affairs, provides advice, analysis and assessment on all disarmament matters and carries out the responsibilities entrusted to the Secretariat in this field. The Electoral Assistance Division, another integral part of the Department, provides services requested by Member States in the electoral field. The Department also provides secretariat services to the General Assembly, the Security Council and their various subsidiary organs.

C. PEACE-KEEPING IN A CHANGING CONTEXT

597   United Nations peace-keeping is the responsibility of the Department of Peace-keeping Operations, headed by Mr. Kofi Annan. It remained a dynamic and demanding activity, responding to continuing turbulence in relations between States as well as to armed conflict within State borders. Certain peace-keeping missions were brought to a successful conclusion and new missions

were established by the Security Council, while the status of existing operations ranged from relative stability to high danger. In the face of these challenges, the Organization continued to encounter grave difficulties in obtaining resources from Member States, in both specialized and properly equipped military units and adequate financing. At the end of July 1995, approximately 65,000 military personnel, 1,700 civilian police and 6,000 civilian personnel were deployed in 16 United Nations peace-keeping operations, with an aggregate annual budget of approximately $3.6 billion (see table 2).

In Haiti, the suspended United Nations Mission was re- *598* deployed after a multinational force established stable and secure conditions. Likewise, in Angola, an effectively suspended United Nations peace-keeping operation, the United Nations Angola Verification Mission, has been newly deployed after the Angolan parties, following prolonged negotiations under

TABLE 2

Peace-keeping toops, military observers and civilian police in peace-keeping operations on 31 July 1995

	Troops	Observers	Police	Total
UNTSO	—	220	—	220
UNMOGIP	—	40	—	40
UNFICYP	1 165	—	35	1 200
UNDOF	1 036	—	—	1 036
UNIFIL	4 963	—	—	4 963
UNIKOM	859	243	—	1 102
UNAVEM	3 014	333	207	3 554
MINURSO	48	236	113	397
UNCRO	13 683	347	435	14 465
UNPROFOR	27 738	288	18	28 044
UNPREDEP	1 107	25	26	1 158
UNOMIG	—	134	—	134
UNMIH	5 850	—	841	6 691
UNOMIL	7	62	—	69
UNAMIR	3 792	306	59	4 157
UNMOT	—	39	—	39
Total	63 262	2 273	1 734	67 269

United Nations auspices, finalized an agreement to bring the interrupted peace process back on course. In Tajikistan, a small United Nations Mission of Observers was deployed in support of a negotiating process under United Nations auspices, with the goal of national reconciliation and the promotion of democracy. Two major missions, in Mozambique and in El Salvador, were steered to a commendably successful conclusion, both culminating in elections monitored by the United Nations and the establishment of elected Governments, with the promise of the consolidation of stability in both countries. In contrast, the United Nations Operation in Somalia II, long plagued by interminable hostility between clan leaders who often turned upon the mission itself, was terminated, with a residual good offices mission being maintained to assist in the search for political compromise. Although the ambitious goal of reconstructing a stable Somali State was not achieved, the mission's principal objectives of ending the dire conditions of famine and of restoring some stability to most of the country were secured.

599   In recent years, the practice of peace-keeping, developed during the cold war and based on the consent and cooperation of the parties and impartiality of United Nations forces, with resort to arms only in self-defence, has proved most effective in multidimensional operations where the parties not only entered into negotiated agreements but demonstrated the political will to achieve the goals established. However, where the climate was one of hostility and obstruction instead of cooperation and political will, peace-keeping came under heavy strains and pressures. This has been the experience in Bosnia and Herzegovina, where the United Nations itself came under armed attack. While efforts to achieve a political agreement between the parties remained futile, the determination to press for military advantage undermined laboriously negotiated cease-fires, and

the force of events on the ground drove the United Nations into situations in which mandates assigning peace-keeping tasks simultaneously with limited enforcement actions proved contradictory and ineffective. The Bosnian Serbs' use of military force to obtain their objectives demonstrated the perilous balance to be maintained by the international community between the limits of a mandate defined in response to a particular situation and the larger objective of realizing the purposes of the Charter. This has compelled renewed reflection on the instruments available to the international community in its efforts to maintain international peace and security.

The limits of peace-keeping in ongoing hostilities starkly *600* highlighted by the distressing course of events in the former Yugoslavia have become clearer, as the Organization has come to realize that a mix of peace-keeping and enforcement is not the answer to a lack of consent and cooperation by the parties to the conflict. The United Nations can be only as effective as its Member States may allow it to be. The option of withdrawal raises the question of whether the international community can simply leave the afflicted populations to their fate. The Organization has been confronted with this issue with increasing frequency, not only in Bosnia and Herzegovina, but also in Somalia, Rwanda, Liberia, Angola and elsewhere.

The international community's response to these situations *601* was varied. In some cases, it became necessary to rethink and readjust the measures taken. Such, often difficult, readjustment can be minimized if mandates given the Organization establish well-defined, achievable objectives and have the necessary political and material backing of Member States. Especially in instances where the Security Council authorizes the use of force even to a limited extent, under Chapter VII of the Charter, the composition, equipment and logistic support of such an operation must be commensurate with the task.

602   Peace-keeping missions have multiplied in number and complexity in recent years (see fig. 16). United Nations personnel in much larger numbers are now involved in a wider spectrum of operations ranging from the monitoring of tradi-

FIGURE 16

Civilian personnel in peace-keeping missions, 1994 and 1995

1994

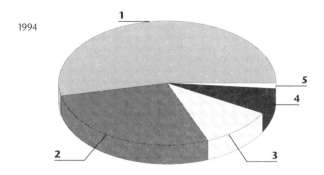

1995

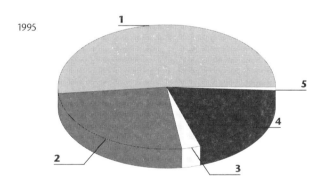

1 Local (1994 - 4715, 1995 - 4288)
2 International (1994 - 2459, 1995 - 2124)
3 Temporary (1994 - 941, 1995 - 228)
4 Contractual (1994 - 601, 1995 - 1572)
5 United Nations Volunteers (1994 - 120, 1995 - 79)

tional cease-fires to the task of armed protection of humanitarian convoys, and from the control of buffer zones to assistance in the implementation of peace settlements. As expectations rise and more missions are deployed, the United Nations is finding it increasingly difficult to keep up with fast-moving situations. Delays resulting from factors such as procedures and readiness have meant that local situations could get worse while the Organization prepares forces for deployment.

The Stand-by Forces Planning Team, established by the *603* Secretary-General, developed the stand-by arrangements system in 1993, and the process to institutionalize it in the Secretariat began in May 1994. The mandate of the Secretariat *vis-à-vis* stand-by arrangements is to maintain a system of stand-by resources, able to be deployed as a whole or in parts, anywhere in the world, at the Secretary-General's request, with agreed response times, for United Nations duties, as mandated by the Security Council. The system calls for Member States to provide the Secretariat with detailed information regarding probable contributions (military, civilian police and civilian specialists) to peace-keeping operations. The information provided by participating Member States includes such data as response times, capabilities, air and sealift volumetrics as well as indications regarding equipment requirements.

The aim of the initiative is to reduce mounting times for *604* new or expanding peace-keeping and enhancing efficiency and coordination at the Secretariat and mission levels. The stand-by arrangements system is based on conditional offers by Member States of specified resources which could be made available within agreed response times for United Nations peace-keeping operations. These resources can be military individuals or formations, civilian police, specialized personnel (civilian and military) and services, as well as material and equipment.

605   The resources remain on "stand-by" in their home country, where training prepares them to fulfil specific tasks or functions in accordance with United Nations guidelines. Stand-by resources would be used for peace-keeping operations mandated by the Security Council and should not be confused with peace-enforcement units, which are described in "An Agenda for Peace" (A/47/277-S/24111) as forces meant to respond to "outright aggression, imminent or actual". In these arrangements, Member States retain full responsibility for stand-by resources as long as they remain in their home country. During the period of their assignment to peace-keeping operations, personnel made available by participating Member States would remain in their national service but would be under command of the United Nations.

606   To ensure its effectiveness, the stand-by arrangements system relies on detailed volumetric information on resources specified in each of the stand-by arrangements. By maintaining a comprehensive database of the volumetrics, the Secretariat will be in a better position to assess detailed requirements. Secretariat planners will know well in advance what movement provisions are required and what items should be procured if deficiencies exist. In addition, procurement activities can be pre-planned, thereby reducing costs.

607   So far 46 Member States have confirmed their participation in stand-by arrangements and 13 are in the process of finalizing their offers. The commitments made to date do not, however, cover the whole spectrum of resources required to mount and execute future peace-keeping operations adequately. Deficiencies still exist in critical areas such as communications, multi-role logistics, health services, supply, engineering and transportation.

608   The Stand-by Arrangements Management Team is currently manned by one United Nations–contracted military officer and three others on loan from Governments. In addition, the team is temporarily assisted by four officers from other teams within the Mission Planning Service of the Department of Peace-keeping Operations.

Potentially, the stand-by arrangements system will offer *609* an effective means of rapidly deploying needed resources to new or current peace-keeping missions. If these arrangements are fully built up, the Secretariat would be in a better position to meet current challenges. The system's success is totally dependent on the support and participation of Member States, since even under the stand-by arrangements Member States will retain the right to deploy the agreed units in a particular operation.

The daunting experiences in United Nations peace-keeping *610* in the turbulence following the end of the cold war also have confronted the Organization with problems on a more practical level. The difficulties in securing resources have led to unacceptable delays in deployment of peace-keeping forces in emergency situations that cannot afford delay. In the Supplement to "An Agenda for Peace", I urged that serious thought be given to the idea of a rapid reaction force to provide the Security Council with a strategic reserve for deployment in emergencies requiring the immediate presence of peace-keeping troops. The system of stand-by arrangements does not so far ensure the reliability and speed of response which is required in such emergencies. It is essential that the necessary capabilities are reliably available when they are needed and can be deployed with the speed dictated by the situation. It is evident that Member States possess such capabilities; what is needed is the will to make them available for the execution of Security Council mandates.

The work of peace has never been without risk, but today *611* United Nations personnel are routinely required to face dangers to their life and health in the course of unpredictable and risky operations in hostile environments. This is demonstrated by the

FIGURE 17

Total fatalities in peace-keeping operations, 1988-1995

Military, civilian police and observers

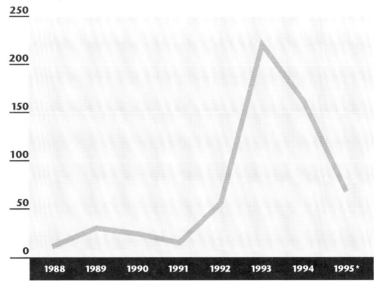

Local and United Nations staff

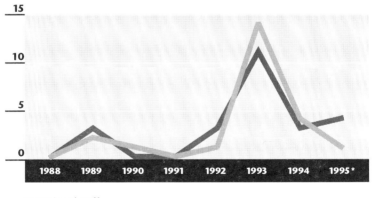

 Local staff
UN staff

* As at 17 August 1995

unfortunate fact that there have been 456 fatalities in peace-keeping missions between 1991 and 1995 as compared to 398 between 1948 and 1990. Particularly disturbing is the tendency by some to ignore the international status of United Nations personnel and to attack peace-keepers as they carry out their duties mandated by the Security Council (see figs. 17 and 18). The Convention on the Safety of United Nations and Associated Personnel adopted by the General Assembly at its forty-ninth session is of crucial importance, and I urge Governments to take the necessary action to ensure that the Convention enters into force as soon as possible.

There is an increasing awareness among Member States *612* that public information, both internationally and in the mission area, is critical to the success of peace-keeping operations. In

FIGURE 18

Fatalities of United Nations civilian personnel, 1992-1994

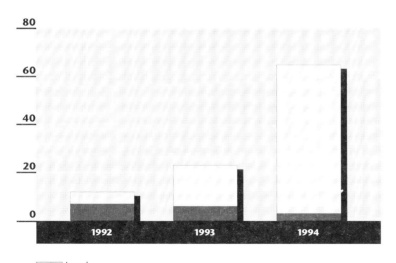

the planning of recent major operations, therefore, the requirements for an information capacity were examined at an early stage and the resources required were included in the proposed budget.

D. CURRENT ACTIVITIES IN PREVENTIVE DIPLOMACY, PEACEMAKING AND PEACE-KEEPING

1. *Afghanistan*

613   During the period under review the Special Mission established in accordance with General Assembly resolution 48/208 continued its work under the leadership of Mr. Mahmoud Mestiri. Also in January 1995, the Office of the Secretary-General in Afghanistan (OSGA) was established in Jalalabad, until conditions could permit it to return to Kabul.

614   I visited Pakistan from 6 to 8 September 1994 and was briefed by Mr. Mestiri on his intensive consultations in previous weeks about transitional arrangements which would lead to a cease-fire and the convening of a *Loya Jirga* (Grand National Assembly). I also met separately with various representatives of the party leaders and with independent Afghans. Mindful of the strong desire of the Afghan people for peace, I instructed Mr. Mestiri to continue his endeavours.

615   On Mr. Mestiri's initiative, an advisory group of recognized and respected independent Afghan personalities from within and outside the country met at Quetta for 19 days starting on 29 September 1994 to advise the United Nations in its efforts to achieve progress. Their recommendations for an early transfer of power to a fully representative Authoritative Council, a country-wide cease-fire, a security force for Kabul and the subsequent establishment of a transitional government or the convening of a *Loya Jirga* were endorsed by the Security Council

Peace-keeping Operations as of 31 July 1995

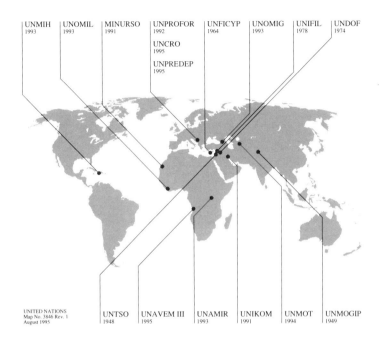

in November and subsequently by the General Assembly in December. In October, President Burhanuddin Rabbani had made a conditional offer to transfer power and Afghanistan gave its support to the United Nations peace proposals in a statement issued by the Ministry for Foreign Affairs (S/1994/1227, annex).

Mr. Mestiri returned to the region on 29 December 1994 *616* and focused his efforts on the early transfer of power to the Authoritative Council. During January 1995, negotiations on its membership were held with all the major leaders, including

President Rabbani, who reiterated his readiness to step down on 20 February when the Council was to be set up.

617 The military successes of the Taliban, a newly established armed force, delayed the setting up of the Council in Kabul. Efforts were made to include this group in the Council but it declined to participate in the process directly. The convening of the Authoritative Council was postponed to 21 March while a committee of four personalities worked to reconcile the areas of divergence. Its proposal that the Council be composed of two representatives from each of Afghanistan's 32 provinces, plus 15 or 20 representatives nominated by the United Nations to achieve the necessary ethnic and political balance, was accepted by some, but not all, of the parties.

618 As the date for the transfer of power drew closer, changes in the political and military situation began to accelerate. On 6 March, intensive fighting erupted in Kabul and adjacent areas between the forces of General Massoud and those of Mr. Mazari (Hezb-i-Wahdat), and then between those of General Massoud and the Taliban. The renewed fighting resulted in a virtual stalemate in the peace process. No nomination for the Authoritative Council had been received by mid-April, when Mr. Mestiri departed from the area.

619 In June, I called Mr. Mestiri to New York and, after discussing the new situation with him, decided that the United Nations should immediately resume its efforts towards peace in Afghanistan. On my instructions, Mr. Mestiri visited the region between 18 July and 1 August in order to reassess the prevailing situation. During his visit, he exchanged views with key Afghan leaders and senior officials of the neighbouring countries on ways in which the United Nations could assist the peace process. His interlocutors included President Rabbani, General Dostum, Mr. Ismael Khan and leaders of the Taliban.

I received Mr. Mestiri's report on the latest round of his   *620*
activities in early August and agreed with him that he should
assume residence inside Afghanistan and pursue his efforts to
obtain the agreement of all concerned to the modalities for
the transition to a broad-based and widely accepted Government. I also decided to enhance the Special Mission and OSGA
by stationing additional political affairs officers in the country.

The United Nations Office for the Coordination of Humani-   *621*
tarian Assistance to Afghanistan (UNOCHA) continued to coordinate the humanitarian programme throughout the country.
A consolidated appeal, seeking $106 million to cover humani-
tarian needs for a 12-month period, was issued in October 1994.
The main targets of the appeal were the emergency in Kabul,
the needs of the internally displaced and support for voluntary
repatriation of refugees from neighbouring countries. The total
cash and in-kind contributions received during 1994 by United
Nations agencies and non-governmental organizations for activities outlined in the approach are estimated at $85 million. As
a result of a mid-term review that was carried out early in 1995,
a general consensus has emerged among all humanitarian partners concerned over the need for a new consolidated appeal
covering the period from October 1995 to September 1996. The
appeal will include projects covering the provision of emergency relief to vulnerable groups in urban and rural areas, including internally displaced persons and returnees. Emergency
rehabilitation projects targeting communities made vulnerable
by loss of livelihood, basic services or shelter will also be incor-
porated.

When I met the leaders of all the main Afghan factions in   *622*
Islamabad in September 1994, I urged them to lift the blockade
of Kabul, which had prevented the delivery of humanitarian aid
to the city since late June. As a result, convoys carrying over
1,500 tons of urgently needed supplies reached Kabul in

December. After fighting ended in the city, regular United Nations convoys carrying relief supplies reached the city as of mid-March. Refugees and displaced people also began to return. However, much of the southern part of the city is completely devastated. Mines and unexploded ordnance present a constant danger, and little clean water is available. United Nations agencies and non-governmental organizations are working together to address these most urgent humanitarian needs, providing food, shelter, sanitation and health care.

623   Throughout 1994, internally displaced persons from Kabul continued to arrive in Jalalabad. By January 1995, almost 300,000 persons were living in camps assisted by the United Nations, the International Committee of the Red Cross (ICRC) and non-governmental organizations. As a result of coordinated efforts, the health and nutritional status of camp residents improved dramatically.

624   Joint United Nations interventions in the humanitarian field include a mass immunization campaign, organized by the World Health Organization and the United Nations Children's Fund, in collaboration with the Ministry of Public Health and non-governmental organizations. The first round took place in November 1994. Following an appeal by the United Nations, a complete cease-fire prevailed for the week of the campaign. The second and third rounds took place in April and May 1995.

2.   *Armenia and Azerbaijan*

625 The conflict over the region of Nagorny Karabakh, which involves Armenia and Azerbaijan, remains unresolved, but the situation on the ground in and around Nagorny Karabakh has not deteriorated in the past 12 months. The cease-fire agreed to on 12 May 1994 through the mediation of the Russian Federation has been observed to a large extent and no additional territory has been occupied.

The members of the Security Council have continued to *626* support the peacemaking efforts of OSCE, which decided at its summit meeting at Budapest on 6 December 1994 to establish a co-chairmanship for its OSCE Minsk Conference and, *inter alia*, to conduct speedy negotiations for the conclusion of a political agreement on the cessation of the armed conflict that would permit the convening of the Minsk Conference and make it possible to deploy a multinational OSCE peace-keeping force in the region.

In its presidential statement of 26 April 1995 (S/PRST/ *627* 1995/21), the Security Council reiterated its support for the efforts of the Co-Chairmen of the OSCE Minsk Conference and, *inter alia*, strongly urged the parties to conduct negotiations constructively without preconditions or procedural obstacles and to refrain from any actions that might undermine the peace process. Furthermore, the Council stressed that the parties to the conflict themselves bore the main responsibility for reaching a peaceful settlement.

I remain prepared to provide my full support for the efforts *628* of OSCE. To that end, the United Nations Secretariat has had a number of consultations with the OSCE High-level Planning Group to extend technical advice and expertise in the field of peace-keeping. I am also fully prepared, if so requested, to lend my good offices to the OSCE-led political process towards reaching a comprehensive settlement of the conflict.

During my visit to Baku and Yerevan in October/November *629* last year, the first such visit of a Secretary-General to the newly independent transcaucasian nations, I was able to obtain a first-hand assessment of the very serious effects of this conflict, in particular in its humanitarian dimension, on both Armenia and Azerbaijan.

Active humanitarian programmes coordinated by the *630* Department of Humanitarian Affairs are being implemented in both countries. Activities of the 1995-1996 humanitarian programmes, as presented in the United Nations consolidated inter-agency appeal for the Caucasus (1 April 1995–31 March 1996), include relief projects in the food, non-food, shelter, education and health sectors, as well as capacity-building and projects addressing the transition from emergency assistance to development. As at 31 July 1995, 37.4 per cent ($10.5 million) of funding had been received for the Armenia component of the appeal and only 37 per cent ($12.8 million) of requirements pledged for humanitarian activities in Azerbaijan. It is anticipated that the majority of refugees and internally displaced persons in both Azerbaijan and Armenia, who are among the most vulnerable members of the population, will continue to require humanitarian assistance in the foreseeable future. I requested Under-Secretary-General Aldo Ajello to undertake a mission of goodwill to Armenia and Azerbaijan.

3.   *Baltic States*

631 In accordance with the agreements between the parties concerned, the Russian Federation withdrew its troops from the territory of Estonia and Latvia by 31 August 1994. In a letter addressed to me on 26 August 1994 (A/49/344-S/1994/1008), the Permanent Representative of the Russian Federation confirmed the guarantees that the Russian Federation gave to the Latvian side that the Agreement concerning the legal status of the Skrunda radar station during the period of its temporary operation and dismantling would not be used to carry out acts directed against the sovereignty and security interests of Latvia.

632   At the forty-ninth session of the General Assembly, it was generally recognized that completion of the withdrawal of foreign armed forces from the territory of the Baltic States would contribute to enhancing stability in Europe and developing

better relations between the Baltic States and the Russian Federation. The General Assembly thus concluded its consideration of this item.

4.   *Bougainville*

I welcomed the establishment of a Bougainville Transitional   *633*
Government in April of this year. I am pleased to note that, following the signing of the agreement reached at the Bougainville Peace Conference at Arawa last October, and following the talks held by my Special Envoy in August 1994 and January 1995 with the leaders of Papua New Guinea and Solomon Islands, and with representatives of all Bougainvillian groups in pursuance of Commission on Human Rights resolution 1994/81 of 9 March 1994, there has been a marked improvement in the political and human rights situation on the island.

Convinced that reconstruction and rehabilitation are es-   *634*
sential for the strengthening of the peace process, I dispatched a United Nations inter-agency mission to Papua New Guinea in April-May 1995. The Mission has prepared a development programme for the reconstruction and rehabilitation of Bougainville.

In accordance with the mandate entrusted to me by Com-   *635*
mission on Human Rights resolution 1995/65, I will continue to lend my good offices to the peace process now under way in Bougainville.

5.   *Burundi*

The threatening situation in Burundi has been a major preoccu-   *636*
pation throughout the period under review. I visited the country on 16 and 17 July 1995. Since his appointment in November 1993, my Special Representative for Burundi, Mr. Ahmedou Ould-Abdallah, has actively promoted national reconciliation in the country through his contacts with all parties concerned.

637   On 10 September 1994, all the parties reached agreement on a system of power-sharing and later signed a Convention of Government, with the sole exception of the Parti pour le redressement national (PARENA), headed by former President Jean-Baptiste Bagaza. On 30 September 1994, the National Assembly elected Mr. Sylvestre Ntibantunganya, a Hutu, as the new President of the Republic of Burundi. Mr. Anatole Kanyenkiko, a Tutsi, was reconfirmed as Prime Minister on 3 October 1994, and five days later a new coalition Government, representing 7 of the 13 political parties, was sworn in.

638   In my report to the Security Council of 11 October 1994 (S/1994/1152), I noted that although the situation had stabilized somewhat with the election of a new President, it still remained precarious. The international community should therefore continue to encourage the moderate forces in Burundi.

639   Throughout the period under review, the Security Council repeatedly deplored the attempts of extremist elements to destabilize the situation further and called upon all parties to respect and implement fully the provisions of the Convention of Government. The Council dispatched a fact-finding mission, the second in six months, to Bujumbura on 10 and 11 February 1995. The mission recommended, *inter alia,* the establishment of an international commission of inquiry into the October 1993 coup attempt and the massacres that followed, a substantial increase in the number of Organization of African Unity military observers, the strengthening of the office of my Special Representative and the deployment of United Nations human rights monitors throughout the country (S/1995/163).

640   In a presidential statement of 29 March 1995 (S/PRST/1995/13), the Security Council requested me to report on the steps to be taken to establish the commission of inquiry recommended by its mission which had visited Burundi the previous month. After considering various options, I concluded that it was necessary to explore the possibility of establishing a commission on the truth for Burundi similar to the one that had worked in El Salvador. I appointed a Special Envoy, Mr. Pedro Nikken, to visit Burundi for two weeks starting 26 June 1995. His mission was to determine whether the appropriate national entities in Burundi were prepared to set up a commission on the truth. The Council also reaffirmed its support for a regional conference on peace, stability and security and called with great urgency upon the countries of the region to convene such a conference. My Special Envoy visited Bujumbura from 28 June to 9 July 1995. In his report, he concluded that neither a commission on the truth nor an international commission of judicial inquiry would be an adequate response to the need to put an end to impunity in Burundi. However, an international commission of inquiry could be viable and useful. I reported to the Council on 28 July (S/1995/631) with recommendations for the establishment of such a commission.

The Conference on Assistance to Refugees, Returnees and *641* Displaced Persons in the Great Lakes Region, organized by the Organization of African Unity and UNHCR, took place as scheduled at Bujumbura from 12 to 17 February 1995, in pursuance of General Assembly resolution 49/7 of 25 October 1994. The Conference adopted a plan of action and decided to ask UNDP to organize a round table to assist the countries affected by the Rwandan and Burundian refugees. Preparatory meetings for holding the round table are scheduled to take place from September to December 1995.

On 15 February, the Union pour le progrès national *642* (UPRONA), the main opposition party, forced the resignation of Prime Minister Kanyenkiko. Five days later, Mr. Antoine Nduwayo was appointed Prime Minister. On 10 March, a new 25-member coalition Government was appointed. The security situation nevertheless remained fragile. Violence did not subside, despite a reconciliation and pacification campaign launched by the Government in April 1995, and it continued to affect parts of the country. Two problems, in particular, were potentially explosive: the sudden influx of Hutu refugees who left the Kibeho camp for displaced persons in Rwanda and crossed the northern border of Burundi (27,000 as of 12 May 1995) and the question of a shipment of small arms and ammunition ordered by Burundi from China in 1992, but blocked in Dar es Salaam by the authorities of the United Republic of Tanzania.

643   A fresh outbreak of violence in Bujumbura in June 1995 led to the announcement by President Ntibantunganya of new security measures, but they were rejected by the Parliament with the Front pour la démocratie au Burundi (FRODEBU) majority voting against them. The same month, arrest warrants were issued against two Hutu extremist leaders — former Minister of the Interior Leonard Nyagoma and his top adviser, Mr. Christian Sendegeya, who had sought refuge in Zaire. The situation was further aggravated by the unexpected resignation of the Tutsi Minister for Foreign Affairs. On 6 July 1995, Mr. Paul Munyambari, a Hutu (FRODEBU), was appointed Foreign Minister in his place. Preparations for the national debate, which is tentatively scheduled for November or December 1995, are under way.

644   During his visit to Burundi from 29 to 31 March 1995, the United Nations High Commissioner for Human Rights received support from the President of Burundi for the expansion of the office of the High Commissioner in Bujumbura, opened since 15 June 1994. On 4 May, the Economic and Social Council appointed Mr. Paulo Pinheiro (Brazil) Special Rapporteur on the situation of human rights in Burundi. Mr. Pinheiro paid his first visit to the country from 21 June to 2 July.

645   On the humanitarian front, the violence in Burundi severely affected the northern provinces. Populations have continued to flee to the United Republic of Tanzania and Zaire. The reduction in the availability of food resources to meet regional needs has forced the World Food Programme to cease distributions among the displaced populations while continuing to serve refugees. This has led to the exacerbation of ethnic tensions within the northern regions.

The fact that the humanitarian needs which surfaced after the events in October 1993 in Burundi were largely met by September/October 1994 seems to account for the general consensus within the relief community in Burundi that the humanitarian crisis is past. However, although an emergency does not exist at present, there remain reasons for concern about the future. Health and educational services are continuously perturbed by ethnic turmoil, forcing the international community to set up parallel administrative structures. Dwindling international emergency resources and the absence of follow-up development assistance pose questions about the Government's capacity to take over the provision of basic services. *646*

The United Nations Development Programme is actively involved in assisting the Government in its transition from a relief-assisted State to one which may lead a recovery effort. A 15-month continuum programme of close to $3.4 million was initiated to help elaborate sectoral strategies. In addition, a number of conferences attract donor support. *647*

The World Health Organization is implementing a four-pronged assistance effort, totalling nearly $3.9 million. The efforts are focused on strengthening the National Epidemiological Surveillance Network, assisting in the prevention and control of communicable diseases and epidemics, supporting the provision of health services to the most affected provinces, and aiding in the prevention and control of sexually transmitted diseases. *648*

The efforts of UNICEF are geared towards reinforcing the existing health network as well as the integration of preventive *649* and curative services of health and nutrition, the provision of water supply and environmental sanitation, supporting basic education and peace education, and giving assistance to 8,000 unaccompanied children. Over $10 million has been contributed for these efforts.

650   The Food and Agriculture Organization of the United Nations has concentrated its efforts on providing displaced persons, returnees and refugees with agricultural tool kits and seeds. In addition, the organization is involved in reforestation and stockbreeding. A total of $12 million has been allocated for these tasks.

651   In addition to providing assistance to approximately 200,000 refugees, UNHCR has been assisting 220,000 returnees and displaced persons and 5,000 urban poor. UNHCR also provides secondary-school and higher education, and implements repatriation operations of former refugees from and to Rwanda. Approximately $30 million has been raised for the accomplishment of these tasks.

652   WFP continues to assist the internally displaced persons and returnees as well as 200,000 Rwandan refugees in Burundi, and 150,000 Rwandan and Burundian refugees in Zaire. The reduction in regional food availability has led WFP to implement an accelerated reintegration programme for the internally displaced.

6.   *Cambodia*

653   In April 1995, the Royal Government of Cambodia agreed to my decision that the term of my Representative in Cambodia, whom I had appointed following the termination of the mandate of the United Nations Military Liaison Team in May 1994, be extended by six months and that he should be assisted during this period by one military adviser. In accordance with his mandate, my Representative has maintained close liaison with the host

Government, as well as with United Nations programmes and agencies operating in the country.

The broad cooperation between the Government, the *654* United Nations and the international community has brought further progress to the country during the past year. The generous pledges made at the third meeting of the International Committee on the Reconstruction of Cambodia (ICORC) are clear evidence of the sustained commitment of the international community to assist the Government in its endeavours to establish a peaceful, democratic and prosperous State.

Discussions in May 1995 between my Special Envoy, *655* Under-Secretary-General Marrack Goulding, and the Cambodian Government led to an agreement to introduce measures to improve communication between the United Nations Centre for Human Rights in Phnom Penh and the Government, and for the office to continue to function with its existing mandate. At that time I issued a personal appeal to Member States for contributions to the Trust Fund for a Human Rights Education Programme in Cambodia. I repeat this appeal now.

7. *Cyprus*

During the past year, my mission of good offices proceeded *656* within the overall framework set out by the Security Council in resolution 939 (1994): to continue to work for progress on both the substance of the Cyprus problem and the implementation of the package of confidence-building measures that had been the focus of efforts during the previous period.

After my Special Representative, Mr. Joe Clark, visited the *657* region in September 1994 for meetings with the Cypriot parties and the Governments of Greece and Turkey, he reported to me that matters were close to an impasse. The Greek Cypriot leader continued to insist on progress on an overall solution, while the Turkish Cypriot leader placed priority on the early implementation of the confidence-building measures. In response, I wrote to each of the community leaders on 10 October 1994, informing them that I had requested my Deputy Special Representative to invite them to join him for a number of informal consultations. These consultations were to explore, in a concrete manner, ways in which the implementation of the confidence-building measures and the long-contemplated overall settlement of the Cyprus problem might be advanced.

658　　Both leaders accepted this invitation, meeting five times between 18 and 31 October 1994. They discussed the essential elements of a federation in Cyprus as well as the implementation of the confidence-building measures, exploring a broad range of ideas pertaining to political equality, sovereignty, membership in the European Union, aspects of the federal constitutional arrangements, security and demilitarization, displaced persons, property claims and territorial adjustments, as well as modalities for the early establishment of the federation and implementation of the confidence-building measures. The ideas broached under these headings offered ways of satisfying in an equitable manner what have consistently been the most deeply held concerns and interests of each community.

659　　In November and December 1994, I met separately with each of the Cypriot leaders to hear their views on the informal meetings. I told them that given the necessary political will, the elements discussed during their meetings offered the possibility of a significant step forward both on the substance of the Cyprus question and on the confidence-building measures. I also strongly encouraged the Turkish Cypriot leader to respond in a commensurate manner to the ideas that had been broached. I instructed my Representatives to pursue their contacts with the parties in order to establish the basis for a further discussion of these issues. To this end, Mr. Clark travelled to the region in March and May 1995.

The continuing support of the members of the Security *660* Council for the efforts of my mission of good offices has been particularly encouraging. But I regret that, in spite of the presence on the negotiating table of almost all elements required for a just and lasting settlement, the negotiating process again appears to be blocked.

The United Nations Peace-keeping Force in Cyprus *661* (UNFICYP) has continued to carry out effectively its mandate despite the reduction of its strength by nearly half over the past couple of years. The two sides have generally exercised restraint in the past year. However, the continuing quiet should not obscure the fact that there is merely a cease-fire — not peace — on the island. I continue to be concerned by the excessive level of foreign troops and of armament in Cyprus, and the rate at which these are being strengthened. The two sides have not yet agreed, in accordance with the proposed package of confidence-building measures, to extend without delay the 1989 unmanning agreement to all parts of the buffer zone where their forces remain in close proximity to each other. The Security Council's repeated call for a significant reduction in the number of foreign troops and in defence spending should be heeded by all concerned. I again urge both sides to take reciprocal measures to lower the tension, including mutual commitments, through UNFICYP, not to deploy along the cease-fire lines live ammunition or weapons other than those that are hand-held and to prohibit firing of weapons within sight or hearing of the buffer zone.

8. *East Timor*

I have continued to provide my good offices in the search for a *662* just, comprehensive and internationally acceptable solution to the question of East Timor. During the period under review, I held two more rounds of talks at Geneva, on 9 January and 8 July

1995, with the Foreign Ministers of Indonesia and Portugal. These talks identified a number of substantive issues for further discussions and explored possible avenues towards a solution.

663   During my visit to Indonesia in April, I had very useful discussions with President Suharto. I have had equally valuable meetings with President Mario Soares when I visited Portugal at the end of August. I also dispatched a mission to Portugal, Indonesia and East Timor in December 1994 to consult with the two Governments and a broad range of East Timorese personalities on a series of ideas to help move the process forward.

664   With the support of the two Ministers, I took the initiative to facilitate and offer necessary arrangements for the convening of an all-inclusive intra–East Timorese dialogue. The dialogue does not address the political status of East Timor or represent a second negotiating track. Instead, it is intended to be a forum for free and informal discussions among the East Timorese on practical ideas aimed at creating an atmosphere conducive to the achievement of a solution to the question. The first meeting of the dialogue was convened at Burg Schlaining, Austria, from 2 to 5 June 1995, and was attended by 30 East Timorese of all shades of political opinion. In a positive atmosphere, the delegates reached a declaration by consensus and produced a number of useful ideas that I examined in July with the Foreign Ministers of Indonesia and Portugal. The participants voiced their desire to have further meetings of this kind in the future. I share this view and intend to pursue this matter with the two parties.

665   While deep differences remain between the two sides on the core issue of the status of the Territory, I am convinced that a solution can be found through patient dialogue. I am encouraged in this belief by the willingness of the two sides to continue the dialogue and to seek a lasting solution. I am also heartened by the desire expressed by the East Timorese, recently manifested at the first session of the dialogue, to contribute to the

peace process. The next ministerial meeting will take place in London in January 1996.

9. *El Salvador*

With the assistance of the United Nations, El Salvador contin-   *666* ued its progress from a violent and closed society towards one in which democratic order, the rule of law and respect for human rights are being established. However, as in previous years, significant progress in the implementation of outstanding elements of the peace accords was not without problems or delay. These included the full deployment of the National Civil Police and the completion of the demobilization of the National Police; the reform of the judicial and electoral systems; the transfer of land to former combatants; and the conclusion of reintegration programmes for them. On 31 October 1994, I reported to the Security Council that I deemed it necessary to recommend that the mandate of the United Nations Observer Mission in El Salvador (ONUSAL) be extended until 30 April 1995.

The Government of President Armando Calderón Sol and   *667* the Frente Farabundo Martí para la Liberación Nacional (FMLN) have continued to express their determination, e.g., in a joint declaration signed on 4 October 1994, to see the peace accords promptly implemented for the benefit of all Salvadorans. Specifically in the latter part of the year, implementation of the outstanding points assumed a more rapid pace. For example, the long-delayed demobilization of the National Police was formally effected on 31 December 1994. In the early months of 1995, however, the land programme slowed and some worrisome indicators emerged.

In the light of these developments, I informed the President   *668* of the Security Council on 6 February 1995 of my intention to set up in El Salvador, following the expiration of the mandate of ONUSAL, a small team of United Nations officials to provide good offices and verify implementation of the outstanding provisions of the peace accords. The team, which would be established for an initial period of six months, would also provide me with a continuing flow of information, thus allowing me to keep the Council informed of further developments. On 17 February, the Council welcomed my proposal, and preparations began for the team's deployment.

669   At the beginning of April 1995, I made a visit to El Salvador, the third occasion on which I had done so as Secretary-General. Although I stressed that the primary responsibility for the process lay with Salvadorans, I assured the Government and people of El Salvador that the commitment of the United Nations remained, despite the withdrawal of ONUSAL.

670   On 27 April 1995, the parties to the Chapultepec Peace Agreement signed a programme of work for the completion of all outstanding points in the peace accords. On the following day the Security Council adopted resolution 991 (1995), formally marking the end of the mandate of ONUSAL. The new United Nations Mission in El Salvador (MINUSAL), led by Mr. Enrique ter Horst, my Special Representative, began its work as planned on 1 May 1995. With its staff partly funded by voluntary contributions, MINUSAL represents a much reduced United Nations presence, but one that confirms the Organization's ongoing support for peace-building in El Salvador.

671   The Programme of Work had divided the remaining accords into six areas (public security, land transfer, human settlements, reinsertion programmes, Fund for the Protection of the Wounded and Disabled and legislative reforms) and established dates by which specific provisions in each area must be completed. Monthly updates on its progress, which I circulated informally to members of the Security Council, revealed the continuing determination of the parties to the peace accords to bring them to completion. Progress was made in all areas, with the Government's deposit of ratification of international human rights instruments with the United Nations Secretariat and the secretariat of the Organization of American States and its recognition of the jurisdiction of the Inter-American Court of Human Rights particularly to be welcomed.

However, by early August 1995 it was clear that significant 672 delays had occurred in the land transfer programme (which reached the 60 per cent target set for 30 April 1995 only in the first week of July), in the design of a "special regime" for rural human settlements, in the strengthening of the National Civil Police and in the implementation of the judicial reforms recommended by the Commission on the Truth. With a little under three months before the expiration of its term, MINUSAL continued to exercise its good offices and verification responsibilities in favour of one final effort to bring these outstanding elements of the peace accords to conclusion.

10. *Georgia/Abkhazia*

My Special Envoy for Georgia, Mr. Edouard Brunner, sup- 673 ported by the Russian Federation as facilitator and the Organization for Security and Cooperation in Europe as participant, has continued his efforts to achieve a comprehensive settlement of the conflict, particularly in identifying a political status for Abkhazia acceptable to both the Georgian and Abkhaz sides. He has visited the region and chaired several rounds of negotiations and expert talks. I visited the Republic of Georgia from 31 October to 2 November 1994 in order to explore with the Head of State, Mr. Eduard Shevardnadze, and other Georgian Government officials how the political process could be advanced. I have also offered to assist by meeting either separately or jointly with the leaders of the two sides. The Russian Federation, acting in its capacity as facilitator, made intensive efforts in 1995 to reach agreement on a draft protocol that might provide the basis for a Georgian-Abkhaz settlement. Unfortunately, all these efforts have resulted in little political progress to date.

674　A significant gap remains between the two sides regarding the political status of Abkhazia within the territorial integrity of Georgia. Abkhazia's Constitution, which was promulgated by the Supreme Soviet of Abkhazia on 26 November 1994, declares Abkhazia to be a "sovereign democratic State . . .". Such constitutional arrangements are unacceptable to the Georgian side, which insists on preserving its territorial integrity. The Government of Georgia proposes to establish a federation for Georgia within which Abkhazia would be granted a wide degree of autonomy.

675　Assuming that it is possible to find agreement on a draft protocol now under discussion, a prolonged period of detailed negotiations will have to follow in order to agree on ways to implement a settlement. Such negotiations will require continuous attention *in situ*. I have therefore decided to appoint a deputy to my Special Envoy, who will be resident in the area and thus able to provide a continuous presence at a senior political level. Following the precedent of other operations, such as those in Cyprus and Tajikistan, the Deputy will also be the head of the United Nations Observer Mission in Georgia (UNOMIG). In carrying out the tasks of political contact and negotiation, the Deputy will divide his time between Tbilisi and Sukhumi and will travel as necessary to Moscow for direct consultations with the Russian authorities.

676　UNOMIG has been fulfilling the tasks mandated by the Security Council in resolution 937 (1994) of 21 July 1994. It maintains its headquarters at Sukhumi, but because of the unavailability of suitable accommodation in that city, part of the Mission's headquarters staff is now stationed in Pitsunda. The Mission also has a liaison office in Tbilisi and three sector headquarters — at Sukhimi, Gali and Zugdidi. In addition,

UNOMIG has six team site bases: three in the Gali region, two in the Zugdidi region and one in the Kodori Valley.

The Government of Georgia and the Abkhaz authorities *677* have largely complied with the agreement of 14 May 1994 on a cease-fire and separation of forces. All armed forces have been withdrawn from the security zone, although a few pieces of non-operational heavy military equipment remain in the restricted weapons zone.

The situation in the security and restricted weapons zones, *678* especially in the Gali region, has been tense. One of the most pressing problems in the security zone has been the presence on both sides of unauthorized weapons among the population, and among some of the Abkhaz militia, as well as the Georgian police. In addition, armed elements beyond the control of either the Government of Georgia or the Abkhaz authorities have been responsible for criminal activities in the Gali region. The situation in the Kodori Valley, which had been tense towards the end of 1994, has now calmed down. The relations on the ground between the Abkhaz and the Svan have been satisfactory, with a slow but steady build-up of mutual confidence.

UNOMIG has reported that the Commonwealth of Inde- *679* pendent States (CIS) peace-keeping force has been conducting its operations within the framework of the agreement of May 1994, and any variation from the tasks set out in the agreement has been made in consultation with the parties. Cooperation between UNOMIG and the CIS peace-keeping force has been very productive. Cooperation between UNOMIG and the Government of Georgia and the Abkhaz authorities has also been satisfactory. Through its liaison office in Tbilisi, UNOMIG has been cooperating with OSCE.

In pursuance of paragraph 10 of Security Council resolu- *680* tion 937 (1994), I have established a voluntary fund for contributions in support of the implementation of the agreement of

14 May 1994 for humanitarian aspects including demining, as specified by the donors, which will facilitate the implementation of UNOMIG's mandate. One pledge has been made so far.

681 At independence, the people of Georgia had one of the highest standards of living among the republics of the former Soviet Union. Today, the country is racked by political instability, civil strife on two fronts and the displacement of some 270,000 people. Lack of foreign exchange for essential inputs, such as fuel, and hyper-inflation have devastated the economy. Agricultural production contracted in 1994 for the fourth year in succession. In the break-away region of Abkhazia, some 75 per cent of the original inhabitants have reportedly fled civil conflict into other parts of Georgia and the area remains the scene of extensive destruction. In some areas, large numbers of mines have been laid and roads are impassable.

682 Of all the difficulties currently facing Georgia, the most immediate are the scarcity of basic foods and the critical energy supply situation. After several years of huge budget deficits, the Government lacks the resources to ensure the continued provision of basic social services. Many primary health-care units and hospitals are unable to function because of shortages of medicines and equipment. Health care is now almost entirely dependent on international humanitarian assistance.

683 In addition, large numbers of orphans, abandoned children and people in need of special education are currently living in extremely poor circumstances because of reduced government spending. Most lack adequate food, bedding, warm clothes and learning materials. As in the neighbouring Caucasus republics, textbooks and school materials are in short supply and many school buildings urgently need rehabilitation.

684 There has also been little progress in the return of refugees and displaced persons to Abkhazia. Though voluntary repatriation under UNHCR auspices commenced in mid-October

1994, movement as at December 1994 of a mere 311 persons out of an estimated total 250,000 refugees and displaced persons has been very disappointing. Since the end of November 1994, formal repatriation has virtually halted, and the Quadripartite Commission has not met since 16 February 1995. About 20,000 persons have returned spontaneously to the Gali district.

The Abkhaz side continues to object to the large-scale and *685* speedy return of refugees and displaced persons. Its offer of 17 April 1995 to repatriate 200 persons a week and to be more flexible with regard to those refugees and displaced persons returning spontaneously does not meet UNHCR requirements for a meaningful timetable. The continued delay in resettling internally displaced persons to Abkhazia has placed a heavy burden on the economy of Georgia, weakening its capacity to recover and exacerbating social and political tensions. The Abkhaz side continues to link progress on the question of refugees to progress on political issues. The authorities are withholding thousands of other applications and have refused to process further requests owing to a stalling of the peace negotiations on both sides.

As part of its efforts to move from a centrally planned to a *686* market economy, the Georgian Government is taking steps towards economic reform. The task of transferring the State-run economy into private hands is daunting and has, in itself, inflicted severe social and economic hardship. In 1994, subsidies for important staples were progressively removed, resulting in price increases. Further liberalization of prices for most commodities will be progressively instituted during 1995. Although the minimum wage and pensions have also been increased, these reforms cannot keep pace with rising inflation.

In the light of these problems, the Department of Humani- *687* tarian Affairs led an inter-agency mission to Georgia in February 1995, for the second consecutive year, to assess the needs of the country and formulate an inter-agency consolidated appeal for the Caucasus, including Georgia, and covering the period from 1 April 1995 to 31 March 1996. That appeal was launched at Geneva on 23 March 1995. Activities covered in the appeal include relief projects to be undertaken by United Nations agencies/programmes and non-governmental organizations in the food, non-food, shelter and health sectors, as well as projects aimed at strengthening the country's self-reliance in a post-emergency phase.

688   On 19 May 1995, the Quadripartite Commission convened in Moscow to explore once again the possibilities for resuming the voluntary repatriation programme under the auspices of the Office of the United Nations High Commissioner for Refugees. Representatives of UNHCR presented a concrete timetable for such returns, under which the displaced population from the Gali district would have returned before the end of 1995. Despite strenuous efforts to obtain a more flexible response, the Abkhaz side maintained its previous position of April 1995 of allowing only 200 persons per week to return. This continues to be unacceptable to the other parties.

689   Minor improvements to security conditions in the Gali district have resulted in increased daily movements back and forth across the Inguri River by displaced persons, primarily to the lower security zone, to work in the fields, trade or repair houses. Some of these persons have decided to stay in the Gali district as long as security does not again deteriorate. The size of the semi-resident population is estimated at 25,000 to 35,000 persons. However, large numbers continue to live in difficult circumstances, placing great strain on the Georgian economy, on human relations and on local services. In these circumstances, the level of frustration and distress is very high, leading to calls for mass spontaneous repatriation.

As of July 1995, $9.4 million, representing 25.7 per cent of *690* funding requirements for Georgia, had been contributed to the appeal, as reported to the Department of Humanitarian Affairs by agencies making the appeal. A mid-term review of the appeal will be launched in late August 1995, to review both the implementation of the projects presented in the appeal and the funding situation, and to present plans for the continuation of activities until the end of the appeal period.

11. *Guatemala*

During the reporting period, negotiations between the Govern- *691* ment of Guatemala and the Unidad Revolucionaria Nacional Guatemalteca (URNG) have continued under the auspices of the United Nations. While advances in the process have been uneven, the establishment of the United Nations Mission for the Verification of Human Rights and of Compliance with the Commitments of the Comprehensive Agreement on Human Rights in Guatemala (MINUGUA) and the signing of the Agreement on Identity and Rights of Indigenous Peoples are encouraging developments.

Taking into account progress made during the first half of *692* 1994 as well as Commission on Human Rights resolution 1994/58, I recommended to the General Assembly in my report of 18 August 1994 (A/48/985) the earliest establishment of a human rights verification mission in Guatemala. On 19 September 1994, by resolution 48/267, the Assembly established MINUGUA for an initial period of six months, and I appointed Mr. Leonardo Franco as the Mission's Director. MINUGUA was officially inaugurated in November 1994. With eight regional offices, five subregional offices and an authorized strength of 245 international staff, the Mission represents a significant effort by the United Nations in human rights verification and institution-building. It is also the most tangible result so far of the talks between the Government of Guatemala and URNG.

693   After the signing of five agreements between January and June 1994, the pace of the negotiations slowed down during the last six months of the year. On 28 December 1994, I expressed my concern to the General Assembly and the Security Council and stated that the time-frame originally foreseen for the conclusion of a peace agreement would have to be revised. In addition, I wrote to the parties to ask them to renew their commitment to the process and to indicate the steps they would be prepared to take to allow it to regain momentum.

694   As a result of initiatives by the Secretariat, the parties agreed in February 1995 to several proposals aimed at facilitating the continuation of the talks, including a new time-frame. On that basis, I informed the General Assembly and the Security Council that conditions existed for further United Nations involvement in the peace process. Negotiations were resumed soon thereafter and the landmark Agreement on Identity and Rights of Indigenous Peoples was signed at Mexico City on 31 March 1995. Immediately afterwards, preparatory work began for the negotiation of the next item of the agenda — socio-economic aspects and the agrarian situation.

695   On 1 March 1995, I transmitted to the General Assembly the first report of the Director of MINUGUA (A/49/856 and Corr.1, annex), in which he acknowledged the cooperation received from the parties, the international community and the agencies of the United Nations system. With regard to MINUGUA's verification mandate, the Director confirmed the existence of a pattern of serious human rights abuses and widespread impunity in Guatemala. He also summarized MINUGUA's institution-building activities, aimed at strengthening those national institutions responsible for the protection

of human rights. On 31 March 1995, the Assembly renewed MINUGUA's mandate for a further six months.

In April, I visited Guatemala to review the work of MINUGUA and progress in the peace process. I congratulated the parties on their achievements so far, in particular the Agreement on Identity and Rights of Indigenous Peoples, but I stressed that their continued commitment, perseverance and political will were essential if the process was to succeed. I emphasized that the efforts of the Guatemalans towards national reconciliation would be backed by the international community with the United Nations as its instrument. As a follow-up to my visit, I appointed Mr. Gilberto Schlittler as my Special Envoy for the Guatemala Peace Process. *696*

On 29 June, I transmitted to the General Assembly the second report of the Director of MINUGUA on human rights (A/49/929). The Director concluded that progress achieved since the installation of the Mission, while insufficient, demonstrated that with political will from the parties and commitment on the part of society as a whole, it was possible to improve the situation of human rights in Guatemala. *697*

Currently, the parties are negotiating on several items, including the socio-economic aspects and the agrarian situation. Several items remain to be considered, namely, the strengthening of civilian power and the role of the army in a democratic society, the reintegration of URNG into political life, a definitive cease-fire, constitutional reforms and the electoral regime and, lastly, a schedule for implementation, enforcement and verification. *698*

Guatemala is now in the first stages of an electoral campaign leading to presidential elections scheduled for November 1995. The timetable I proposed in February 1995 partly intended to ensure that electoral considerations would not affect the negotiations. It now appears, however, that the negotiations *699* and the electoral process will overlap in time. This complex situation notwithstanding, I hope that the parties will be able to proceed steadily towards the signing of a final peace agreement, as early as possible in 1996.

12. *India and Pakistan*

700   Since 1949, the United Nations Military Observer Group in India and Pakistan (UNMOGIP) has been deployed to monitor the cease-fire in Jammu and Kashmir. India and Pakistan have affirmed their commitment to respect the cease-fire line and to resolve the issue peacefully in accordance with the Simla Agreement of 1972. The increasing reports of incidents of violence in Jammu and Kashmir have further aggravated relations between the two countries. These developments highlight the urgency of seeking a political solution through a meaningful dialogue. In this connection, I have maintained contacts with both Governments and visited the two countries in September 1994. I reiterated to them my readiness, should they so wish, to render whatever assistance may be needed to facilitate their search for a lasting solution.

13. *Iraq-Kuwait*

701   During the past year, I have continued to stress to Iraqi representatives the importance of Iraq's cooperation in implementing all of its obligations as expressed in the resolutions of the Security Council.

702   Further significant progress was made by the United Nations Special Commission (UNSCOM), headed by Mr. Rolf Ekeus, and the International Atomic Energy Agency (IAEA) Action Team in the implementation of section C of Security Council resolution 687 (1991), concerning the elimination of Iraq's weapons of mass destruction and long-range missile capabilities. They completed the process of establishing a system to monitor Iraq's dual-purpose industries (i.e., those that have non-proscribed uses but which could be used to acquire banned weapons capabilities), aimed at monitoring Iraq's compliance with its obligations not to reacquire such banned capabilities. This system became operational in April 1995.

Further refining of the system will continue as UNSCOM and IAEA gain experience in operating it, but all the elements of the system are now in place. Some 120 remote-controlled monitoring cameras have been installed at over 28 sites and linked in real time to the Baghdad Monitoring and Verification Centre. Twenty or so automated chemical air samplers have been installed at sites, and a highly sensitive chemical laboratory has been installed in the Centre to analyse these samples. The Centre also has a biological preparation room to prepare and package biological samples for shipment to laboratories in other countries. Communications have been upgraded to perform the new tasks associated with ongoing monitoring and verification. *703*

Resident teams of inspectors in each of the weapons disciplines are now operating full-time out of the Centre. Their activities are supplemented by aerial inspection and surveys conducted using a high-altitude surveillance aircraft provided by the United States. These aerial assets remain key to the ability of UNSCOM and IAEA to fulfil their mandates as they provide the initial survey capability to identify sites which might need to be inspected and ensure the ability to conduct short-notice inspections of sites as necessary. *704*

Efforts continue to elucidate and hence account for all elements of Iraq's past banned weapons capabilities. Much progress has been made in this regard but major issues remain in the biological area. *705*

UNSCOM and IAEA also, in accordance with paragraph 7 of resolution 715 (1991), submitted in May 1994 a proposal for *706* an export/import monitoring mechanism which would require that all exports be notified by both Iraq and the Governments of the exporters to a joint unit to be established in New York by UNSCOM and the IAEA Action Team.

707   I wish to express my appreciation to those Governments that contributed to UNSCOM operations, and in particular to the Government of Germany, which generously provided the Special Commission with air support in the form of both C-160 transport aircraft and CH-53G helicopters.

708   In November 1994, the Government of Iraq took an important step forward by affirming its recognition of the sovereignty, territorial integrity and political independence of Kuwait. The United Nations Iraq-Kuwait Observation Mission (UNIKOM) has continued to operate within the demilitarized zone established on both sides of the border between Iraq and Kuwait. In December 1994, Iraq formally recognized the international border demarcated by the United Nations in 1993. The situation has been calm in the Mission's area of responsibility.

709   The United Nations Coordinator for the return of property from Iraq to Kuwait has continued to facilitate the hand-over of property. In September 1994, Iraq informed me that once a damaged C-130 aircraft had been dismantled and returned, it would have "nothing else whatever to return". Kuwait responded by transmitting to me what it described as "an indicative but far from exhaustive list" of Kuwaiti property that had yet to be returned. It has also stressed the importance it attaches to the return of irreplaceable archives.

710   In January 1995, Kuwait transmitted a list of military equipment belonging to the Ministry of Defence that it claimed was still in the possession of Iraq. Arrangements were made for the hand-over, which began on 22 April 1995 and continued into July 1995. On many of the hand-over documents signed by the parties, Kuwait complained of the state of disrepair of the

items returned while Iraq, for its part, noted that the vehicles had been "brought as is from Kuwait". Kuwait also noted that of 120 armoured personnel carriers handed over, only 33 were found to belong to Kuwait.

Among a number of urgent humanitarian issues to which   *711* the situation between Iraq and Kuwait has given rise is the fate of over 600 Kuwaiti and third-country nationals who are still missing in Iraq. I have urged Iraq to cooperate with the International Committee of the Red Cross so that a full accounting may be achieved.

The suffering of the Iraqi civilian population is also of con-   *712* siderable concern to me. On a number of occasions I have urged Iraqi officials to accept the Security Council's "oil for food" formula described in resolutions 706 (1991) and 712 (1991). I believe the Council's latest offer in resolution 986 (1995) addresses the humanitarian needs of the Iraqi people while taking into account a number of concerns Iraq had previously expressed over resolutions 706 (1991) and 712 (1991). I can only regret that Iraq has not yet accepted this temporary humanitarian measure, which would indeed be an important step towards overcoming the crisis which exists between Iraq and the international community.

I have made every effort to comply with Security Council   *713* resolution 778 (1992), of 2 October 1992, in which the Council requested me to ascertain the whereabouts and amounts of assets related to Iraqi petroleum and petroleum products which could be deposited to the escrow account, as well as the existence of any Iraqi petroleum and petroleum products that could be sold. I regret to note that no further funds have been deposited into the account as a result of my effort to seek information on such assets directly from Governments with jurisdiction over relevant petroleum companies and their subsidiaries. As at 1 August 1995, $365.5 million, representing voluntary contributions and Iraqi petroleum assets, had been deposited into the escrow account since the adoption of resolution 778 (1992).

714   The United Nations recognizes Iraq's obligation to pay compensation to the victims of its aggression. The Commission established to administer the United Nations Compensation Fund, provided for in paragraph 18 of Security Council resolution 687 (1991), has held four regular sessions since August 1994. During that period, its Governing Council has approved the reports and recommendations of Panels of Commissioners and issued decisions for three instalments of category "A" (departure) claims; two instalments of category "B" (serious personal injury and death) claims; and one instalment of category "C" (individual losses up to $100,000) claims. In issuing its decisions, the Governing Council awarded over $1.3 billion in compensation to 354,920 successful claimants.

715   Unfortunately, with the exception of approximately $2.7 million paid to the first 670 successful claimants in category "B" in May 1994, and approximately $8.1 million to be paid to 2,562 category "B" claimants in 1995, depending on the availability of funds, the remaining awards of the Compensation Commission have gone unpaid owing to the lack of sufficient resources in the Compensation Fund.

716   During 1994, the lack of adequate funding affected all sectors covered by the United Nations Inter-Agency Humanitarian Programme. In terms of food assistance, the bulk of donations was earmarked for the "Autonomous Region" (Governorates of Erbil, Dohuk and Suleimaniyah). According to reports of the World Food Programme, approximately 70 per cent of food requirements had been met in the north and only 40 per cent in the centre and south. As a result of lack of resources, a substantial amount of the food destined for the centre and south was covered by counterpart matching funds from the United Nations escrow account.

Health conditions have continued to deteriorate through-   *717*
out the country because of shortages of essential drugs and
medical supplies. The situation is further aggravated by the inadequate supply of potable water and poor sanitation facilities,
as essential equipment and spare parts are lacking to rehabilitate the water, sewage and electricity supply systems.

With respect to security, since early December 1994,   *718*
armed conflicts between members of the two major political
parties have been reported in the northern governorates of Erbil
and Suleimaniyah. Moreover, the recent Turkish military operations on the Turkish/Iraq border, and in particular near Zakho
(Dohuk Governorate), resulted in restrictions on the movements of humanitarian aid workers and relief commodities.

By the end of April 1995, the strength of the United   *719*
Nations Guards Contingent in Iraq had been reduced from a
high of over 500 in 1991 to 50 guards, the majority deployed in
the "Autonomous Region" for the protection of humanitarian
personnel. As a result of recent donor contributions received in
support of the Guards Contingent, arrangements are under way
for the assignment of an additional 100 guards during the
summer of 1995. In a tense and volatile environment such
as Northern Iraq, the continued presence of the Guards
Contingent is required to protect United Nations and non-
governmental organization personnel as well as assets and
operations linked with the United Nations Inter-Agency Humanitarian Programme.

Under the previous appeal (covering the period from 1 April   *720*
1994 to 31 March 1995), the United Nations Inter-Agency
Humanitarian Programme continued to provide humanitarian
assistance to vulnerable population groups throughout the
country. Projects implemented by United Nations agencies and
programmes and humanitarian non-governmental organizations covered all the priority sectors included in the appeal, with

particular emphasis on food, health, water and sanitation, agriculture, shelter and rural integration, and education. Response to the previous appeal was inadequate, with approximately 51 per cent ($146 million) of overall Programme requirements ($288.5 million) covered by allocations of voluntary contributions, "matching" funds from the United Nations escrow account and carry-over from the previous phase. From this amount, funding for United Nations–directed humanitarian activities amounted to $92.5 million, while contributions made available to humanitarian non-governmental organizations and other direct/bilateral programmes amounted to $53.5 million.

721　　On 21 March 1995 at Geneva, during a donor consultation meeting for Iraq, the United Nations launched a consolidated inter-agency humanitarian appeal for Iraq covering the period from April 1995 to March 1996. The Programme, which calls for a total of $183.3 million, is designed to address only the most essential needs to sustain relief and rehabilitation activities as well as to prevent a further deterioration of the conditions affecting the most vulnerable population groups throughout the country. Since April 1995, approximately $27 million (representing voluntary contributions and "matching" funds from the United Nations escrow account) has been pledged/received in support of United Nations–directed activities in Iraq. In addition, a number of direct contributions have been made in support of humanitarian non-governmental organizations and bilateral programmes in northern Iraq.

722　　Under the current appeal, humanitarian needs continue to increase in practically all sectors covered by the Programme, in particular in the nutrition and health sectors. By all accounts, children are increasingly dying of ailments linked to malnutrition and lack of adequate medical care. The World Health Organization reports a rise in tuberculosis and an acute shortage of essential drugs and medical equipment in hospitals. At least 4 million people are in need of food assistance and hunger threatens the lives of over 1 million among them. As of June 1995, because of rapidly depleted food stocks in the "Autonomous Region", the World Food Programme decided to reduce food distributions from 350,000 to only 300,000 people. In the Centre and south, from a targeted 550,000 caseload, WFP was able to continue feeding only some 60,000 vulnerable people in social institutions. The support of the international community is urgently required to cover outstanding needs for the procurement and warehousing of food, medicines and shelter materials before the onset of winter.

14. *Korean peninsula*

I have continued to follow closely developments in the Korean *723* peninsula. I am pleased to note that, in implementation of the October 1994 Framework Agreement between the Democratic People's Republic of Korea and the United States of America, the two countries reached agreement in June on the provision of two light-water reactors to the Democratic People's Republic of Korea and that discussions are in progress on the question of safe storage of the spent fuel removed from that country's reactors. In addition, trade and communications barriers between the two countries have been lowered, and liaison offices in the respective capitals are expected to open in the near future.

Hopefully, progress in these areas will contribute to steady *724* improvement of the situation on the Korean peninsula, especially through the re-establishment of the North-South dialogue. I remain ready to provide any good offices which the parties might find useful. I plan to visit the Republic of Korea in September 1995 and intend to go to the Democratic People's Republic of Korea in the first half of 1996 on a mission of goodwill.

15. *Liberia*

725   The United Nations Observer Mission in Liberia (UNOMIL) was established under Security Council resolution 856 (1993) of 10 August 1993 to work with the Monitoring Group (ECOMOG) of the Economic Community of West African States (ECOWAS) in the implementation of the Cotonou Peace Agreement signed between the Liberian parties on 25 July 1993. However, delays and obstacles created by different Liberian factions with respect to the Agreement necessitated a range of subsequent agreements between the factions, and the work of UNOMIL had to continue far beyond the original time-frame of the Security Council resolution.

726   Initial progress was made under the Cotonou Peace Agreement and this encouraged the Security Council, by its resolution 911 (1994) of 21 April 1994, to extend the mandate of UNOMIL until 22 October 1994, with the expectation that the Mission would be terminated in December 1994. Subsequently, the situation in Liberia took a negative turn as fighting intensified between factions and the whole peace process came to a standstill.

727   My Special Envoy, Mr. Lakhdar Brahimi, visited Liberia from 16 to 26 August 1994 in order to assist me in determining options for the United Nations in facilitating the peace process. Shortly thereafter, the Chairman of ECOWAS, President Jerry Rawlings of Ghana, convened a meeting of the factions at Akosombo, Ghana, on 7 September to review the delays in implementing the peace process. This meeting resulted in the signing at Akosombo, on 12 September, of a supplementary agreement to the Cotonou Peace Agreement.

728   The conclusion of the Akosombo Agreement coincided with an upsurge of fighting in Liberia and, on 9 September, 43 unarmed United Nations military observers and six non-governmental organization personnel were detained. By 18 Sep-

tember, they had all been released or otherwise found their way to safety. In September 1994, with the breakdown in the cease-fire, and the fact that the security of unarmed military observers could not be assured, I restricted UNOMIL military operations to the greater Monrovia area and reduced the Mission's military component from its authorized strength of 368 to approximately 90 observers.

In mid-November, I sent a high-level mission, led by the *729* Assistant Secretary-General for Political Affairs, to the region to consult with the Chairman of ECOWAS and the heads of ECOWAS States on how best to revive the peace process. Soon thereafter, the Chairman of ECOWAS carried out further consultations with the Liberian parties and interest groups, which led to the signing of a further agreement at Accra on 21 December 1994.

The Accra Agreement, unlike the Akosombo Agreement, *730* was signed by all the Liberian factions and attempted to clarify the Akosombo Agreement. Other than a new cease-fire which came into effect on 28 December 1994, the factions failed to implement all the other major elements of the Accra Agreement, including the decision to form a new Council of State. The cease-fire, while re-established on 28 December, again broke down in early February 1995.

On 28 December, my new Special Representative for *731* Liberia, Mr. Anthony Nyakyi (United Republic of Tanzania), took up his office in Monrovia. Since then Mr. Nyakyi has been consulting the Liberian factions, the Chairman of ECOWAS, as well as the Heads of State of ECOWAS, with a view to facilitating the search for a peaceful solution to the continuing hostilities.

In its resolution 972 (1995) of 13 January 1995, the Secu- *732* rity Council expressed deep concern over the Liberian situation. It also expressed the hope that a summit of the ECOWAS

States would be convened to harmonize their policies on Liberia, in particular the application of the arms embargo imposed by the Security Council in resolution 788 (1992). On 11 March 1995, President Rawlings of Ghana and I agreed at a meeting in Copenhagen that, subject to the concurrence of the Nigerian Head of State, a summit of the ECOWAS Committee of Nine would be held at Abuja.

733   In my ninth progress report to the Security Council of 24 February 1995 (S/1995/158), I conveyed specific options to the Council, including the provision of necessary resources to ECOMOG if the Liberian factions would demonstrate readiness to implement the Accra Agreement. I express my appreciation to the countries contributing troops to ECOMOG; they have made enormous sacrifices since the operation was launched in 1990.

734   On 13 April 1995, the Security Council adopted resolution 985 (1995) extending the mandate of UNOMIL until 30 June 1995. Following extensive consultations between the Chairman of ECOWAS and the West African Heads of State and several contacts between the Chairman and myself, the third meeting of Heads of State and Government of the ECOWAS Committee of Nine on Liberia was held at Abuja from 17 to 20 May 1995. The Heads of State of Côte d'Ivoire, the Gambia, Ghana, Liberia, Mali, Nigeria, Sierra Leone and Togo attended the meeting. Burkina Faso and Guinea were represented by their Foreign Ministers. The Senior Minister at the Presidency for Governmental Affairs and National Defence of Benin and the Minister of African Economic Integration of Senegal also attended. My Special Envoy, Mr. Vladimir Petrovsky, and my Special Representative for Liberia, Mr. Anthony Nyakyi, were also present, as were the Eminent Person for Liberia of the Organization of African Unity, Reverend Canaan Banana, and the Special Envoy for Liberia of the United States of America, Mr. Dane Smith.

Delegations were sent by the following Liberian parties: *735* the Armed Forces of Liberia (AFL), the Lofa Defense Force (LDF), the Liberia National Conference (LNC), the Liberian Peace Council (LPC), the National Patriotic Front of Liberia (NPFL), the Central Revolutionary Council of the National Patriotic Front of Liberia (CRC-NPFL), Alhaji Kromah's wing of the United Liberation Movement of Liberia for Democracy (ULIMO-K) and General Roosevelt Johnson's wing of ULIMO (ULIMO-J). Mr. David Kpomakpor, the current Chairman of the Council of State, participated in the meeting. Delegations of all the Liberian factions except NPFL were headed by their respective leaders. At the invitation of the Government of Nigeria, Mr. Charles Taylor, the leader of NPFL and the only Liberian faction leader who did not attend the ECOWAS summit, travelled to Abuja on 2 June for consultations with Nigerian officials. On 10 June 1995, I submitted my eleventh progress report on UNOMIL to the Security Council (S/1995/473). By unanimously adopting resolution 1001 (1995) on 30 June 1995, the Council extended the mandate of UNOMIL until 15 September 1995 and declared that unless serious and substantial progress was made towards a peaceful settlement, the Mission would not be renewed after that date. The Council urged the Liberian parties to use the Mission's extension to implement the peace process envisaged in the Akosombo and Accra agreements of 1994, particularly their provisions on the installation of the Council of State; the re-establishment of a comprehensive and effective cease-fire; the disengagement of all forces; and the creation of a timetable for the implementation of disarmament agreements.

My Special Representative conveyed to the Liberian fac- *736* tions the contents of Security Council resolution 1001 (1995) and urged them to abandon their selfish, narrow interests and agree on positive urgent steps to bring peace to their country.

The Liberian factions also held a consultative meeting, with the exception of NPFL, on 19 July which was attended by my Special Representative and the representatives of OAU and ECOWAS.

737   The eighteenth summit meeting of ECOWAS was held at Accra on 28 and 29 July 1995, and was attended by the Heads of State of Benin, Côte d'Ivoire, Ghana, Guinea, Liberia and the Niger. In his report to the Committee of Nine, the Chairman of ECOWAS (the President of Ghana) pointed out that positive developments, which he characterized as confidence-building measures, had taken place since the last Abuja summit. He also referred to the recent Monrovia consultative meetings and deplored the fact that, despite all efforts made, some of the outstanding issues remained unresolved. He referred to Security Council resolution 1001 (1995) and explained the final deadline set by the Council. He called on the United Nations to continue assisting the peace process.

738   The Liberian factional leaders agreed on 19 August 1995 to end hostilities and to hold elections within a year. The ceasefire in Liberia came into force on 26 August 1995.

739   In the context of Security Council resolution 1001 (1995), if serious and substantial progress is achieved by 15 September, it was agreed that the Council would consider restoring UNOMIL to its full strength, with appropriate adjustment of its mandate and its relationship with ECOMOG, including matters relating to post-conflict peace-building in Liberia. In this regard, the swearing in of a Council of State for Liberia on 1 September 1995 gives rise to hopes for a new momentum for peace. The assistance of the international community will be crucial in this regard.

740   On 15 January 1995, I launched the United Nations consolidated inter-agency appeal for Liberia. The appeal sought $65 million required by United Nations agencies and pro-

grammes to meet the life-saving needs of the 1.8 million Liberians affected by the war. As at 10 August, the international donors' community had contributed 71 per cent of the funds requested.

United Nations humanitarian agencies and programmes, *741* in cooperation with non-governmental organizations, have developed agreed protocols for carrying out relief work in Liberia. Guided by these principles, the humanitarian assistance community will continue to work with my Special Representative to gain access to as many war-affected civilians as possible.

16. *The Middle East*

In the course of the past year, significant results were achieved *742* in the Middle East peace process, signalling the parties' continued commitment to proceed on the road to peace. An outstanding achievement was the conclusion, on 26 October 1994, of the historic Treaty of Peace between the State of Israel and the Hashemite Kingdom of Jordan. I warmly welcome this momentous agreement, which ended a decades-long state of war.

Israel and the Palestine Liberation Organization (PLO) *743* continued the implementation of their Declaration of Principles on Interim Self-Government Arrangements, signed on 13 September 1993. By December 1994, the Palestinian Authority, which had been established in May in most of the Gaza Strip and the Jericho area, was given responsibility for health, education, social welfare, tourism and direct taxation in the other areas of the West Bank. Israel and the PLO are at present negotiating the redeployment of Israeli military forces in the West Bank and the holding of elections for the Palestinian Council; interim understandings on an agreement have been reached by leaders on both sides.

744   Meanwhile, multilateral negotiations on Middle East regional issues have proceeded, creating a network of common projects among countries in the region. The United Nations participates actively in the multilateral negotiations as a full extraregional participant.

745   Hope has been generated by these encouraging signs that progress can be accelerated in the Israeli-Lebanese and Israeli-Syrian negotiations leading to a comprehensive, just and lasting peace in the Middle East, based on Security Council resolutions 242 (1967), 338 (1973) and 425 (1978).

746   The Israeli-Palestinian peace talks have been complicated and set back, on more than one occasion, by terrorist attacks from enemies of peace in which dozens of civilians have been killed and wounded. I have condemned these incidents and I am encouraged by the determination of Israeli and Palestinian leaders to continue the peace process.

747   In addition, concern in the international community has been generated by the Government of Israel's decisions to expropriate land and expand settlements in the occupied territories. The subject was taken up in deliberations in the Security Council at its formal meetings on 28 February 1995 and 12 May 1995.

748   The peace process needs broad public support and without a visible improvement in the living conditions of the Palestinians this support will remain fragile. In this connection, I have to draw attention to the damaging effects which closures of the occupied territories by Israel have had on the nascent Palestinian economy.

749   In its efforts to support the Arab-Israeli peace process, the United Nations has placed special emphasis on sustainable economic and social development in the occupied territories. The United Nations Special Coordinator, Mr. Terje Rod Larsen, has been active in strengthening local coordination between agencies and programmes of the United Nations system, the Bretton Woods institutions and the donor community. He works in close cooperation with the Palestinian Authority and the Palestinian Economic Council for Development and Reconstruction. The first results of the international assistance efforts are already visible, especially in institution-building and the infrastructure.

In southern Lebanon hostilities have continued at a high *750* level between Israeli forces and armed elements that have proclaimed their resistance to Israeli occupation. On several occasions civilian targets on both sides came under attack. I have called for restraint and urged the parties to refrain from attacking civilians.

The United Nations Interim Force in Lebanon (UNIFIL) *751* has sought to limit the conflict and to protect inhabitants from violence. In resolution 1006 (1995) of 28 July 1995, the Security Council reaffirmed the mandate of UNIFIL as defined in its resolution 425 (1978) and subsequent resolutions, to confirm the withdrawal of Israeli forces, restore international peace and security, and assist the Government of Lebanon in ensuring the return of its effective authority in the area. Although UNIFIL has not been able to make visible progress towards these objectives, it has contributed to stability in the area and afforded a measure of protection to the population of southern Lebanon. On the basis of the request for my good offices regarding the detainees held in Khiam jail in the area controlled by the Israel Defence Forces in southern Lebanon, I have authorized the appropriate contacts in that regard.

In July 1994, I initiated a study to determine how UNIFIL *752* could perform its essential functions with reduced strength in view of the long-term problem of the shortfall in its assessed contributions. By its resolution 1006 (1995), the Security Council approved my proposal for a streamlining, which will result in a 10 per cent reduction of the Force's strength and direct savings of $10 million a year. This will not affect UNIFIL's operational capacity.

753   The United Nations Disengagement Observer Force (UNDOF) continued to supervise the area of separation between the Israeli and Syrian forces and the areas of limitation of armaments and forces provided for in the disengagement agreement of 1974. With the cooperation of both sides, UNDOF has discharged its tasks effectively and its area of operation has been quiet.

754   The United Nations Truce Supervision Organization (UNTSO), which is the oldest existing peace-keeping operation, has continued to assist UNDOF and UNIFIL in carrying out their tasks and has maintained its presence in Egypt. A streamlining undertaken by UNTSO is under way and will result in a 20 per cent reduction of its strength and corresponding savings in expenditures.

17. *Mozambique*

755 Over a three-day period from 27 to 29 October 1994, Mozambique conducted, with the assistance and support of the United Nations, the first free and fair multi-party elections in the country's history. The elections brought together in an open democratic contest the ruling Frente de Libertação de Moçambique (FRELIMO) and the Resistência Nacional Moçambicana (RENAMO), the country's two major political parties and former foes. Immediately after the results of the election were announced, my Special Representative declared the elections free and fair, based on reports from United Nations observers. This was fully supported by the Security Council. This was a welcome change from a long-running conflict that had claimed the lives of tens of thousands of people, driven millions from their homes and destroyed much of Mozambique's economic and social infrastructure. The elections were the culmination of a major success story in United Nations peacemaking, peace-keeping, and humanitarian and electoral assistance.

The mandate entrusted to the United Nations Operation in 756 Mozambique (ONUMOZ) by the Security Council in resolution 797 (1992) of 16 December 1992 was to verify and monitor the implementation of the General Peace Agreement, signed by the Government of Mozambique and RENAMO at Rome on 4 October 1992. The peace accords required the United Nations to supervise the cease-fire between the two parties, provide security for key transport corridors, monitor a comprehensive disarmament and demobilization programme, coordinate and monitor humanitarian assistance operations throughout the country, and provide assistance and verification for national elections. ONUMOZ subsequently undertook a number of additional tasks at the request of the parties.

One of the most important aspects of the operation was the 757 emphasis it placed on peace-building. ONUMOZ's unprecedented endeavours in this regard were concentrated not only in its oversight of the electoral process but also in the channelling of special trust funds to strengthen the organizational capacity of parties contesting the election. This was particularly important in regard to RENAMO. The transformation of a guerrilla force into a political entity with a stake in the democratic process is one of the most significant legacies of the United Nations operation.

The final meeting of the Supervisory and Monitoring 758 Commission established under the Rome Agreement was held on 6 December 1994. At that meeting, final reports were submitted by the Chairmen of the Cease-fire Commission, the Commission for the Formation of the Mozambican Defence Force, the Commission for Reintegration, the National Police Affairs Commission and the National Information Commission. My Special Representative, Mr. Aldo Ajello, handed these reports over to Mr. Joaquim Alberto Chissano, the President-elect. Subsequently, the new Assembly of the Republic was installed on 8 December, and the newly-elected President of Mozambique was inaugurated the next day; he appointed his Government on 16 December. In accordance with paragraph 4 of Security Council resolution 797 (1992), these events marked the expiry of the political mandate of ONUMOZ, and my Special Representative left Mozambique on 13 December 1994.

759   The withdrawal of the military, police and civilian components of the Mission proceeded according to plan, beginning on 15 November 1994. A limited force of four infantry companies and medical personnel, a skeleton headquarters staff, demining personnel and a small number of military observers were retained to assist in residual operations and the liquidation phase of the Mission. With the official closure of ONUMOZ at the end of January 1995, a small number of United Nations civilian logisticians remained in Mozambique to deal with outstanding financial, legal and logistic issues.

760   When the last ONUMOZ contingents departed from Mozambique in January 1995, they had overseen a remarkable transformation in the country, from the ravages of civil war to the implementation of democratic government and the creation of a peaceful environment in which economic activity could once again flourish. The strong commitment of the major participants to peace, along with firm support from the international community, were important prerequisites that enabled the United Nations to help bring about this transition. In this regard, neighbouring States played a vital role; first, in bringing the major participants to the negotiating table, and then in helping to sustain the peace process under ONUMOZ.

761   Although both the General Peace Agreement and the ONUMOZ mandate were successfully implemented, a number of concerns requiring further action remained at the time of the

Mission's withdrawal. These included, on the security front, the continuing need to train and equip the new integrated armed forces and to upgrade the police in accordance with Security Council resolution 898 (1994) of 23 February 1994, while attending to the collection and disposal of outstanding caches of weapons. Mozambique also needed to strengthen its democratic institutions and to promote economic and social reconstruction so that peace, democracy and development could be sustained. While the last United Nations peace-keeping forces left Mozambique in January 1995, their colleagues from the development arm of the Organization remained behind to assist Mozambique in consolidating a peaceful and stable future.

I should like to express my appreciation to the international 762 community and to those programmes and organizations whose financial and technical assistance to the Mozambican authorities made it possible to hold the elections in an exemplary manner. There is agreement among the international community that ONUMOZ was a success. Key factors that contributed to this result include: the political will of the Mozambican people and their leaders, demonstrated by their strong commitment to peace and national reconciliation; the clarity of the ONUMOZ mandate and the consistent support provided by the Security Council; and the international community's strong political, financial and technical support of the peace process.

The United Nations Office for Humanitarian Assistance 763 Coordination (UNOHAC) was made the humanitarian component of ONUMOZ by the Security Council in resolution 797 (1992). In the transition from war to reconciliation to peace, UNOHAC and its humanitarian assistance partners addressed the emergency needs of between 4 and 5 million internally displaced persons, 1.5 million returning refugees and some 90,000 demobilized soldiers. Effective and coordinated humanitarian assistance activities helped to create conditions that allowed civilians affected by the war to begin rebuilding their lives. The success of the Consolidated Humanitarian Programme, developed by UNOHAC and its partners, received tremendous support from the international community, which contributed more than 82 per cent of the approximately $775 million required for execution of the Programme.

764   As the mandate of ONUMOZ neared termination in late 1994, UNOHAC focused its activities on ensuring completion of projects where possible, and on finalizing arrangements with humanitarian assistance partners in-country for the transfer of a number of responsibilities that would continue beyond the life of the peace-keeping operation.

765   One such hand-over involved the Trust Fund for Humanitarian Activities in Mozambique, established by the Department of Humanitarian Affairs to provide financial support for the implementation of 26 projects which were to be fully implemented only after the expiration of the ONUMOZ mandate on 15 November 1994. The Trust Fund financed a variety of critical activities within the Programme, including demobilization and reintegration of demobilized soldiers, emergency supply of non-food relief items, provision of seeds for the family sector, multisectoral area-based activities, and demining. In order to ensure effective continuation of these projects, the Department has passed responsibilities for trust fund project-monitoring and coordination to the office of the United Nations Development Programme in Maputo.

766   The area of demining also required carefully planned transition arrangements. The accelerated demining programme was designed by the Department of Humanitarian Affairs and UNOHAC to ensure that Mozambique would be provided with an indigenous demining capacity. The Department and UNDP agreed that at the expiration of the ONUMOZ mandate, UNDP would assume responsibility for the financial management of

resources that are or will be made available for the implementation of the programme, while policy guidance and technical support for the programme would continue to be provided by the Department of Humanitarian Affairs.

The accelerated demining programme has established a 767 Mozambican demining organization of 10 platoons (450 deminers), 15 supervisors, four survey teams, an Explosive Ordnance Disposal team, demining instructors, and the headquarters and support staff to manage the instructors and the organization. In total, 500 Mozambicans are employed by the programme. Since the commencement of demining operations in September 1994, 5,000 anti-personnel mines and some 400,000 square metres of land have been cleared. The emphasis of the programme is on training in order fully to develop local mine-clearance capability, resulting in a sustainable Mozambican entity able to address Mozambique's long-term mine-clearance problems.

18. *Myanmar*

In keeping with the good offices mandate I received from the 768 General Assembly and from the Commission on Human Rights, I have established a dialogue with the Government of Myanmar in order to address various issues of concern to the international community, in particular with respect to the process of democratization and national reconciliation in that country. During the period under review, my Representatives have held several rounds of talks in New York and Yangon with Secretary 1 of the State Law and Order Restoration Council, the Minister for Foreign Affairs and other authorities of the Government. In the talks, a series of ideas were discussed, which, if implemented, would assist in moving the process forward.

I welcome the Government's decision to lift the restrictions 769 imposed on Daw Aung San Suu Kyi and to release a number of other political prisoners, including several leading members of the National League for Democracy. I look forward to further steps to speed up the return of multi-party democracy in Myanmar. I will report to the General Assembly at its fiftieth session on the progress of those discussions, which are being continued on my behalf at Yangon in August by the Assistant Secretary-General for Political Affairs.

19. *Republic of Moldova*

770   I visited the Republic of Moldova on 4 November 1994 to discuss rehabilitation efforts in the aftermath of the severe droughts, hurricanes and floods that hit the country in mid-1994. At its forty-eighth session, the General Assembly, upon appeal by President Mircea Ion Snegur, adopted a resolution on 14 September calling upon the Secretary-General, in cooperation with the relevant organs and organizations of the United Nations system, to assist in the rehabilitation efforts of the Government.

771   On 21 October 1994, the Republic of Moldova and the Russian Federation signed the agreement on the withdrawal of the Russian Federation's 14th army from the Trans-Dnestr region. Both countries have agreed that the withdrawal should be synchronized with a political settlement of the Dnestr conflict. The withdrawal is anticipated to take place within three years.

772   Following an earlier parliamentary decision, a large majority of ethnically-mixed districts taking part in the referendum held on 5 March 1995 decided to join the Gagauz autonomous region within the Republic of Moldova.

773   The Organization for Security and Cooperation in Europe (OSCE) has been taking the leading role on issues concerning the Republic of Moldova since the OSCE mission was established in that country on 27 April 1993.

20. *Sierra Leone*

In December 1994, in response to a formal request from Captain   *774*
Valentine Strasser, Head of State of the Republic of Sierra
Leone, I dispatched an exploratory mission to that country to facilitate negotiations between the Government and the forces
known as the Revolutionary United Front. That mission reported to me on the serious consequences of the three-year conflict in Sierra Leone. A significant percentage of the population
had taken refuge in neighbouring countries or been internally
displaced and most of the country's infrastructure had been destroyed. If the conflict continued, it would further complicate
the problem of bringing peace to Liberia and could have a more
general destabilizing effect in the region. On the basis of the
mission's findings, I decided to appoint a Special Envoy for
Sierra Leone, Mr. Berhanu Dinka, to help the parties to work
towards a negotiated settlement.

In April and May 1995, Captain Strasser announced that to   *775*
restore democracy he would set up a national reconciliation
conference to prepare for a return to civilian rule in 1996 and
that a three-year ban on political parties was being rescinded.
He called on the Revolutionary United Front to renounce its
armed struggle and to join the electoral process, declaring that
the Government was ready to enter into a cease-fire in order to
negotiate peace without preconditions. However, the Front
spurned the offer to end the armed struggle, stressing that dialogue was conditional on the withdrawal of foreign troops
fighting alongside Sierra Leonean armed forces. Notwithstanding these difficulties, my Special Envoy is continuing his
efforts to help bring about a settlement of the conflict.

On 26 May, I congratulated the Head of State of Sierra   *776*
Leone on the democratic initiatives announced on 27 April, in
particular the lifting of the ban on political parties. On 22 June,
the National Provisional Ruling Council issued a decree bar-

ring for the next 10 years 57 persons, including presidents, vice-presidents, ministers, ministers of State and deputy ministers, from holding any public office or holding office in any corporation in which the State held a financial interest, from being elected president of the Republic or member of parliament, or from being elected to or holding office in any local body. According to the Government, the ban was based on the findings of two commissions of inquiry.

777   On 20 July, seven prospective political parties jointly petitioned the Head of State to repeal restrictive elements of the decree lifting the ban on political parties. Further complicating matters, on 25 July the Sierra Leone Bar Association refused to attend the National Consultative Conference on Elections (15-17 August), linking its refusal to participate to the decree banning 57 persons from holding political office and restrictions placed on political parties by the Government.

778   It is widely recognized that the conflict in Sierra Leone cannot be resolved through military means. It is important therefore for the Revolutionary United Front to respond positively to the Government's offer to negotiate a settlement of the conflict. The sixty-second ordinary session of the Council of Ministers of OAU adopted a resolution expressing concern over the worsening conflict. I call upon the international community to support the United Nations efforts to ensure that peace and democracy prevail in Sierra Leone.

779   Following a series of rebel attacks that began late in 1994, thousands of Sierra Leoneans were forced to leave their homes and thousands more sought asylum in neighbouring States. As a result, the total number of internally displaced persons in Sierra Leone is estimated at over 500,000 persons. They are concentrated in and around Freetown, as well as in a number of towns in eastern and central Sierra Leone, including Bo, Kenema, Makeni, Segbwema and Daru. In Freetown, it is estimated that

the influx has swollen the population threefold, to 1.5 million persons. The overall result of these developments is characterized by, among other things, overcrowding in a small number of areas, acute shortages of basic survival requirements and the breakdown of overburdened infrastructure.

In response to these developments, the Inter-Agency *780* Standing Committee (IASC) took up the question of Sierra Leone at a meeting in February. The Standing Committee is composed of the executive heads of the United Nations humanitarian organizations as well as ICRC, the International Federation of the Red Cross and the Red Crescent Societies, the International Organization for Migration and the non-governmental consortia International Council of Voluntary Agencies, Interaction and the Steering Committee for Humanitarian Response. As a result of the discussions held, the working group of the Inter-Agency Standing Committee was charged with developing the terms of reference for an inter-agency appeal for resources required by United Nations organizations to meet emergency needs. The result was the United Nations interagency appeal for new refugee flows and populations affected by the humanitarian situation in Sierra Leone. From March to December 1995, the appeal sought $14.6 million to respond to the unmet needs of internally displaced persons within Sierra Leone, as well as those of the new outflow of Sierra Leonean refugees who had recently fled to the Forecariah region of Guinea. There has not yet been any response to the appeal.

As well as being limited by resource mobilization difficul- *781* ties, humanitarian assistance efforts have been hindered by the prevailing security situation, which led to a withdrawal of United Nations international staff to Freetown in late January 1995. However, humanitarian activities continue on a smaller scale, with the involvement of national staff and the utilization of innovative implementation methods.

782   The office of the United Nations Resident Coordinator has developed an emergency information management system to ensure that United Nations organizations respond to the humanitarian crisis in Sierra Leone in a coordinated and complementary manner. The system will gather and analyse data required by the relief community to develop and target programmes for affected populations.

783   At its meeting on 2 June, the Inter-Agency Standing Committee further decided to pursue these efforts by dispatching an inter-agency mission to assess the coordination of humanitarian assistance activities in Sierra Leone. The mission, led by a representative of the Department of Humanitarian Affairs, recommended a strengthening of the capacity of the United Nations to support the Government's efforts to coordinate the emergency relief response in Sierra Leone. Actions have been taken to implement this recommendation through the placement of experienced personnel within the office of the Resident Coordinator.

21. *Somalia*

784   During the 12 months since my last report, it has become evident that the humanitarian tragedy in Somalia has been overcome, thanks to the international humanitarian assistance supported by the United Nations Operation in Somalia (UNOSOM II). This achievement contrasts sharply with the lack of tangible progress in national political reconciliation, for which the responsibility must be borne by the Somali leaders and people. Because of the deteriorating security situation in the country, including attacks and harassment directed against UNOSOM II and other international personnel, and because of the lack of cooperation from the Somali leaders concerned, the continued presence of UNOSOM II became increasingly questioned.

On 14 October 1994, I reported to the Security Council *785* (S/1994/1166) that the Somali leaders still had not carried out commitments entered into under the Addis Ababa Agreement and the Nairobi Declaration. The UNOSOM goal of assisting the process of political reconciliation was becoming ever more elusive, while the burden and cost of maintaining a high level of troops were proving increasingly difficult for Member States to justify. The presence of UNOSOM II troops was having a limited impact on the peace process and on security in the face of continuing inter-clan fighting and banditry.

I therefore recommended that if the Security Council *786* maintained its previous decision to end the mission in March 1995 and to withdraw all UNOSOM II forces and assets, it should extend the mission's mandate until 31 March 1995 to allow the time required to ensure a secure and orderly withdrawal. At the same time, I stressed that the withdrawal of UNOSOM II would not mean United Nations abandonment of Somalia. However, although humanitarian organizations were committed to continuing their work in Somalia, they could continue doing so only in a secure environment for which Somali leaders would bear the ultimate responsibility. The United Nations would also remain ready to assist the Somali parties in the process of national reconciliation.

On 26 and 27 October 1994, before taking a decision on *787* the withdrawal of UNOSOM II, the Council sent a mission to Somalia to convey its views directly to the Somali leaders. The mission concluded that 31 March 1995 was the appropriate date for the end of the mandate of UNOSOM II. None of the Somali factions, humanitarian agencies or non-governmental organizations had requested a longer extension.

On 1 November, the United Somali Congress/Somali *788* National Alliance (USC/SNA), led by General Mohamed Farah Aidid, and other factions convened a unilateral national reconciliation conference in south Mogadishu. This was against the advice and warning of the Security Council mission and my Special Representative, Mr. Victor Gbeho, who had warned that the convening of such a conference before the question of participation in it was resolved would be a recipe for continued strife.

789   On 4 November, by its resolution 954 (1994), the Council extended the mandate of UNOSOM II for a final period until 31 March 1995. On 10 November, I transmitted to the Council a statement by the Inter-Agency Standing Committee reaffirming the commitment of the humanitarian agencies to continue their emergency and rehabilitation work in Somalia after the expiration of the UNOSOM mandate. The President of the Security Council, on behalf of the Council's members, wrote to me on 7 December welcoming the commitment of the agencies. The Council also encouraged me to play a facilitating or moderating role in Somalia after March 1995 if the Somali parties were willing to cooperate.

790   Prior to the withdrawal of UNOSOM II, General Aidid and Mr. Ali Mahdi signed a peace agreement on behalf of the SNA and the Somali Salvation Alliance (SSA), respectively. In February they also signed three other agreements to manage the operations of the Mogadishu airport and seaport by a joint committee. The Mogadishu seaport was reopened to civilian traffic on 9 March. I was encouraged by the signing of these agreements, which helped to avert fighting over the facilities.

791   The withdrawal of the 15,000 United Nations troops, as well as civilian personnel, facilities and property from Somalia, began in November 1994. In response to my request, seven Member States joined forces in providing support and security for the withdrawal. To that end they established a combined task force, "United Shield", composed of France, India, Italy, Malaysia, Pakistan, the United Kingdom of Great Britain and Northern Ireland and the United States of America, under

U.S. command. I announced on 2 March that the withdrawal had been completed in a safe and orderly manner, ahead of schedule and virtually without a problem. I again emphasized that the United Nations effort could continue and that the United Nations would not abandon Somalia.

On 28 March, I submitted to the Security Council a general *792* assessment of the United Nations achievements in political, humanitarian, military and security matters and the police and justice programme. I recalled that, in late 1992, some 3,000 Somalis had been dying daily of starvation; that tragedy had been ended by the international relief effort. However, the endeavour to achieve political reconciliation had not succeeded because of the lack of political will among the Somali leaders. The international community could only facilitate, encourage and assist the process; it could neither impose peace nor coerce unwilling parties into accepting it.

In a presidential statement of 6 April (S/PRST/1995/15), *793* the Council supported my view that Somalia should not be abandoned by the United Nations and welcomed my intention to maintain a small political mission, should the Somali parties so wish, to assist them in achieving national reconciliation. However, the SNA, then headed by General Aidid, expressed objection to a United Nations political presence and role in Somalia, although a wide range of Somali leaders representing the main factions, including a wing of the USC/SNA, had called for such a presence. In view of these divisions among the Somali parties, I have concluded that, for the time being, a political office, headed by Mr. Abdul Hamid Kabia, should monitor the situation from Nairobi. It is my intention to relocate the political office to Mogadishu when the necessary conditions exist, including adequate security. The President of the Security Council conveyed to me in his letter of 2 June (S/1995/452) the agreement of the members of the Council with my decision.

794   On 15 June, General Aidid was named "interim president" by his supporters. Following his announcement of a unilateral "government", General Aidid made an attempt to claim Somalia's seat at the OAU summit meeting, but OAU refused to recognize his "government" and decided to keep Somalia's seat open until a generally accepted government was formed. OAU urged the Somali leaders urgently to promote dialogue to ensure the formation of a broad-based national authority.

795   I remain convinced that a durable political settlement through national reconciliation is an indispensable prerequisite for the re-establishment of government, restoration of law and order, and rehabilitation and reconstruction in Somalia, and that the attainment of national reconciliation for the sake of the common good is well within the power of the Somali leaders. It is my hope that they will find the strength and the courage to pursue a more productive peace process in the coming weeks.

796   Coordination of the United Nations humanitarian assistance programme was, until December 1994, the sole responsibility of the Division for Coordination of Humanitarian Affairs of UNOSOM, which was headed by a Humanitarian Coordinator. The Division's tasks included fielding humanitarian affairs officers throughout the country, coordinating inter-agency assessment missions, providing funding for small-scale projects, assisting with emergencies, building essential structures such as schools and clinics, digging wells, facilitating the protection of humanitarian relief convoys, providing logistical support to humanitarian partners, holding security briefings and information-sharing meetings with United Nations agencies and non-governmental organizations, and providing support to local bodies such as district and regional councils.

797   In October 1994, when it became apparent that the UNOSOM mandate would not be extended and the Division would be dismantled, the agencies established a United Nations

Coordination Team, chaired by the Resident Representative of UNDP (who was later appointed United Nations Humanitarian Coordinator) and composed of representatives of United Nations agencies and IOM, to manage the transition to a post-UNOSOM period and to ensure the continued coordination of the United Nations humanitarian assistance programme. The Coordination Team works in close cooperation with both international and Somalia non-governmental organization consortia. It also works to support the coordination efforts of the Somalia Aid Coordination Body, a consortium of donor Governments, United Nations agencies and organizations, and international non-governmental organizations.

In 1994, no consolidated inter-agency appeal for Somalia *798* was issued. Instead, United Nations agencies presented their requirements and plans for that year through a document prepared for the Fourth Humanitarian Coordination Meeting, held at Addis Ababa from 29 November to 1 December 1993. Consequently, in 1994 there was no systematic tracking of contributions received by various agencies for Somalia as is ordinarily done by the Department of Humanitarian Affairs under the procedures adopted for consolidated inter-agency appeals. The agencies nevertheless reported that their programmes were relatively well funded, although implementation was hindered by security conditions in the country.

Despite the absence of political progress in Somalia, sig- *799* nificant gains have been made on the humanitarian front over the past year. Agencies and organizations have focused their efforts on community-based community initiatives, providing support to capacity-building programmes while assisting local non-governmental and community-based organizations in the areas of relief and initial rehabilitation. Direct support was provided in the form of supplies, training and management services. Food-for-work schemes replaced free food distributions as the preferred mode of delivering food assistance, while agricultural assistance took the form of targeted initiatives rather than the large-scale distributions of seeds and tools undertaken in previous years.

800   It was possible in 1994 to undertake modest rehabilitation activities in areas where relative security existed. In other areas, however, incidences of kidnapping of humanitarian aid workers occurred, while operations continued to be vulnerable to frequent labour disputes and subjected to unrealistic demands for the payment of security services. The humanitarian agencies expect that for the foreseeable future they will continue to operate against a background of uncertainty. The United Nations agencies nevertheless believe that they can, with the direct support of the Somali people and their leaders, collectively assist Somalia to progress into a new era of rehabilitation, recovery and development.

801   In view of this, the Department of Humanitarian Affairs launched a consolidated inter-agency appeal for Somalia, covering a period of six months beginning in January 1995. The organizations participating in the appeal requested a total of $70.3 million for their activities during the first half of 1995.

802   To date the consolidated inter-agency appeal for Somalia has received under 20 per cent of the resources requested. It is essential that funding for the humanitarian relief and rehabilitation programmes be provided to ensure that progress made by the United Nations agencies, international organizations and national and international non-governmental organizations over the past three years is not reversed.

22. *Tajikistan*

803 The situation in Tajikistan, particularly on its border with Afghanistan, has remained unstable during the past year. My Special Envoy, Mr. Ramiro Píriz-Ballón, continues his efforts to

mediate a political dialogue between the Government of Tajikistan and the opposition to achieve progress towards national
reconciliation.

High-level inter-Tajik consultations, held at Teheran in *804*
September 1994, resulted in the signing of an Agreement on a
Temporary Cease-fire and the Cessation of Other Hostile Acts
on the Tajik-Afghan Border and within the Country. The two parties also agreed on important confidence-building measures,
including the exchange of prisoners and prisoners of war. The
parties also agreed to establish a joint commission consisting of
representatives of the Government and the opposition. They requested the Security Council to assist the work of the Joint
Commission by providing political good offices and dispatching United Nations military observers.

In my report to the Security Council dated 27 September *805*
1994 (S/1994/1102), I recommended, as a provisional measure, the strengthening of the group of United Nations officials
in Tajikistan with up to 15 military observers drawn from existing peace-keeping operations, pending a decision by the Council
to establish a new United Nations observer mission in Tajikistan. The cease-fire came into effect on 20 October following the
deployment of 15 military observers. A technical survey mission was immediately sent to the country to assess the modalities for establishing a future observer mission.

The third round of inter-Tajik talks took place at Islamabad *806*
from 20 October to 1 November. The parties succeeded in extending the Agreement for another three months, until 6 February 1995, and also signed the protocol on the Joint Commission
to monitor the implementation of the 17 September cease-fire
agreement. On 30 November, I submitted a report to the Security Council recommending a possible United Nations peace-
keeping operation in that country (S/1994/1363). On 16 December, the Council, by its resolution 968 (1994), welcomed

the extension of the cease-fire agreement by the Tajik parties and decided to establish the United Nations Mission of Observers in Tajikistan (UNMOT) in accordance with the plan outlined in my report.

807　　　Despite the agreement reached in Islamabad to hold the fourth round of inter-Tajik talks in Moscow in December 1994, the negotiating process was at a stalemate. In order to revitalize it, my Special Envoy undertook consultations with the Government of Tajikistan, leaders of the opposition and certain Governments in the region in December. In January 1995, a United Nations team held consultations at Teheran with the Tajik opposition leaders and high-ranking officials of the Islamic Republic of Iran.

808　　　The fourth round of inter-Tajik talks remained blocked as a result of conditions put forward by the opposition and by the plans of the Government to hold parliamentary elections in February. However, at the end of January, President Emomali Rakhmonov and Mr. Akhbar Turajonzodah, of the Tajik opposition delegation, informed me of their decision to extend the cease-fire agreement until 6 March 1995. In a report dated 4 February (S/1995/105), I informed the Security Council that the Tajik parties had complied only in part with the provisions of Security Council resolution 968 (1994).

809　　　At the end of February, I asked Under-Secretary-General Aldo Ajello to hold consultations with the Tajik parties and some Governments in the region in order to reach agreement on the agenda, time and venue for the fourth round of inter-Tajik talks. He obtained the agreement of the parties to extend the cease-fire agreement until 26 April 1995 and made some progress in addressing the conditions stipulated by the opposition for the resumption of inter-Tajik talks.

810　　　My Special Envoy held new consultations with the Tajik parties and the Governments in the region, which resulted in high-level inter-Tajik consultations in Moscow from 19 to 26 April. The two sides agreed on the agenda and dates for the fourth round of inter-Tajik talks at Almaty, the extension of the cease-fire for another month and important additions to the cease-fire agreement and the protocol on the Joint Commission.

The fourth round of talks took place at Almaty from 22 May   *811* to 1 June. They followed the high-level consultations at Kabul from 17 to 19 May between the President of the Republic of Tajikistan and Mr. Abdullo Nuri, leader of the opposition Islamic Revival Movement of Tajikistan, under Afghan auspices, where it was decided to extend the cease-fire agreement for a further three months, until 26 August.

As I reported to the Security Council on 10 June   *812* (S/1995/472), at the Almaty talks the parties for the first time held an in-depth discussion of the fundamental institutional issues and the consolidation of the statehood of Tajikistan, as set forth in the first round of talks in Moscow in April 1994; however, they were unable to reach any decisions on those issues. The parties welcomed the decision of the Kabul summit meeting to extend the Teheran cease-fire agreement until 26 August and decided to implement a number of confidence-building measures by 20 July and to request the continuation of the good offices of my Special Envoy.

In its resolution 999 (1995), the Security Council wel-   *813* comed these decisions, called for the achievement of substantive progress on the fundamental political and institutional issues, and sought the convening of a further round of talks. It encouraged the dialogue between the President of Tajikistan and the leader of the Islamic Revival Movement of Tajikistan, and urged the substantial extension of the cease-fire agreement. The Council also called for discussions with the Afghan authorities on the possible deployment of a number of United Nations personnel inside Afghanistan.

814   In accordance with this, I dispatched my Special Envoy on 31 July to hold consultations in the region with the Tajik parties and with some Governments in order to create the conditions for a second summit meeting between President Rakhmonov and Mr. Nuri. At that meeting, to be held as soon as possible, it is hoped to obtain agreement on a set of general principles for a comprehensive political solution to be negotiated during the next stage.

815   The small United Nations Mission of Observers in Tajikistan has played an important role in containing the conflict. It has provided essential support to the Joint Commission set up by the parties as the main instrument for maintaining the cease-fire and it has been instrumental in containing local conflicts.

816   The establishment of UNMOT and the extension of its mandate last June for another six months were subject to the proviso that the Teheran cease-fire agreement of 17 September 1994 remain in force and the parties continue to be committed to an effective cease-fire, national reconciliation and the promotion of democracy. The Security Council thus underlined the primary responsibility of the parties themselves for composing their differences. It is to be hoped that they will use well the goodwill and support of interested Governments and the international community as a whole in order to make decisive progress towards that goal.

817   While improvements in the overall stability of conflict-affected areas of Tajikistan in 1994 led to the return of more than 90 per cent of former refugees and internally displaced persons and to substantial progress in their reintegration, the country continues to face critical difficulties in conditions of tremendous economic hardship, especially in the most affected communities of the Khatlon region in the south-west, Gorno-Badakshan in the east and parts of the Garm Valley. Emergency food aid is a major source of nutrition for many of the most

vulnerable. Many health centres have been destroyed; functioning ones lack basic equipment and drugs are often unavailable. Schools and hospitals lack water and sanitation facilities and many schools are not operating, which threatens to erode the high levels of literacy of past decades. Shortages of fuel have severely affected the country's production capacity. Inadequate employment opportunities compound the existing deep clan and regional divisions.

During 1994, the humanitarian community endeavoured *818* to address the most pressing needs. Over 60 per cent of funding requested in the Department of Humanitarian Affairs' 1994 consolidated inter-agency appeal for Tajikistan ($42.5 million) was pledged or contributed. Humanitarian assistance also included capacity- and confidence-building activities, targeting areas of return of former refugees and internally displaced people.

The last mission to the country led by the Department of *819* Humanitarian Affairs took place in October 1994. The mission held extensive consultations with the United Nations and non-governmental organization community to prepare proposals for humanitarian activities in 1995. The subsequent consolidated inter-agency appeal for Tajikistan (1 January-31 December 1995) was launched on 6 December 1994 and officially presented to donors on 23 March 1995 at Geneva. The appeal seeks to meet the most urgent humanitarian needs in-country (estimated at some $37.3 million) of some 600,000 people, who have been most affected by conflict, population movements and the deterioration of the economic, health and social infrastructures. By 31 March, $9.9 million, representing 53.4 per cent of funding requirements, had been contributed, as reported to the Department of Humanitarian Affairs by agencies making the appeal.

The current appeal aims to provide emergency food aid, *820* as well as assistance in the health and education sectors. This assistance, provided in consultation with the humanitarian community, national and district authorities, targets the most vulnerable, including pensioners, invalids and widows with children, and returned and displaced people. Emphasis in the 1995 humanitarian programme is also on information management and capacity-building, with programmes aiming to assist in the training of health workers, community development, capacity- and confidence-building, and self-reliance activities. The appeal also covers a number of non-governmental organization initiatives in addition to United Nations agencies and programmes, and is the result of efforts to enhance coordination and cooperation among humanitarian partners in the field. While substantial humanitarian needs remain, support to Tajikistan will focus increasingly on rehabilitation and economic development. United Nations agencies and programmes are thus phasing down relief activities and promoting development-oriented projects.

23. *Western Sahara*

821 The referendum for the self-determination of the people of Western Sahara, to be conducted by the United Nations in co-operation with OAU, should have taken place in January 1992. However, major differences in the interpretation of the main provisions of the settlement plan resulted in delays. None the less, agreement was reached on the interpretation of the criteria for eligibility to vote, which enabled the United Nations Mission for the Referendum in Western Sahara (MINURSO) to commence the identification and registration of potential voters on 28 August 1994. Also according to the plan, the cease-fire has been in effect since 6 September 1991.

822 During my visit to the mission area in late November 1994, the parties — Morocco and the Frente Popular para la Liberación de Saguia el-Hamra y de Río de Oro (Frente POLISARIO) —

assured me of their commitment to the settlement plan. The two neighbouring countries, Algeria and Mauritania, also continued to support it firmly.

In my report to the Security Council of 14 December *823* (S/1994/1420), I noted that, given the large number of applications received, the only way to complete the identification and registration process within a reasonable time-frame would be through a major reinforcement of personnel and other resources. In its resolution 973 (1995) of 13 January, the Council approved my recommendation to expand MINURSO and requested me to report by 31 March to confirm 1 June 1995 as the date for the start of the transitional period. The Council also decided to extend the mandate of MINURSO until 31 May 1995.

On 30 March, I informed the Council that, while the rate *824* of identification and registration was increasing steadily, the progress achieved as at that date did not permit me to recommend 1 June 1995 as the start of the transitional period. I explained that problems relating, in particular, to the timely availability of tribal leaders had caused interruptions in the identification operation. At the same time, some progress had been achieved in the implementation of other aspects of the Settlement Plan. I concluded that, if the parties made it possible to raise the rate of identification to 25,000 per month, and if they cooperated in resolving expeditiously the remaining issues in the Settlement Plan, it might be possible for the transitional period to begin in August 1995 and to hold the referendum in January 1996.

In a presidential statement of 12 April (S/PRST/1995/17), *825* the Security Council called upon both parties to cooperate fully with the United Nations to ensure prompt and full implementation of all aspects of the Settlement Plan. The Council hoped to see continuous and rapid progress by the time of my next report, in May 1995.

826   In that report (S/1995/404), I recommended that the mandate of MINURSO be extended for a period of four months. Following my report, the Security Council decided by its resolution 995 (1995) of 26 May to extend the mandate of MINURSO for only one month and to send a mission to the region in order to accelerate the implementation of the Settlement Plan. The Mission held consultations with senior government officials at Rabat, Algiers and Nouakchott and with the POLISARIO leadership at Tindouf, and visited MINURSO headquarters at Laayoune.

827   In its report presented to the Council on 20 June (S/1995/498), the Mission indicated that, given the complexity of the tasks to be performed, the continuing delays caused by the two parties and the constraints imposed by the limited resources and local conditions, there was a real risk that the identification process might be extended beyond the time previously envisaged and that the referendum might not be held in January 1996.

828   On 23 June, the Frente POLISARIO announced its decision to suspend its participation in the identification operation, because of the sentencing to 15-20 years in prison, by a Moroccan military tribunal, of eight Saharan civilians who had participated in a demonstration at Laayoune and because of the Moroccan authorities' declared intention to have 100,000 applicants residing in Morocco take part in the voter identification operation. Following POLISARIO's decision, the Prime Minister and Minister for Foreign Affairs of Morocco addressed a letter dated 26 June to the President of the Security Council. In the letter, he claimed that the Frente POLISARIO was displaying bad faith, said that its decision could have most serious consequences and requested the Security Council to take all the necessary steps to ensure the resumption of the process with a view to holding the referendum on schedule.

On 12 July, the Frente POLISARIO informed the President *829* of the Security Council that it had decided to continue to participate in the identification process. In announcing its decision, POLISARIO cited efforts made by certain States Members of the Security Council to induce Morocco to reconsider the sentences imposed on the Saharan civilians, the adoption of Security Council resolution 1002 (1995) and the positive discussion at the thirty-first session of the Assembly of Heads of State and Government of OAU. On 27 July, the identification process resumed in the identification centres in Western Sahara and the Tindouf area. As at mid-August 1995, some 50,000 persons had been identified by MINURSO.

On 30 June, the Security Council adopted resolution 1002 *830* (1995), by which it extended the mandate of MINURSO until 30 September 1995. The Council also expected, based on the report I would present by 10 September on the progress achieved, to confirm 15 November as the start of the transitional period, to allow the referendum to take place in early 1996.

24. *Yemen*

Over the past year, Yemen has continued its efforts to recover *831* from the devastation of the civil war. In its resolution 931 (1994), the Security Council requested me and my Special Envoy to examine appropriate ways to facilitate the aim of political dialogue directed towards the restoration of peace and stability in the country. I continue to believe that political reconciliation is an indispensable step to ensure the stability of Yemen. I thus applaud the amnesty granted by the Government to most of those who fled the country at the conclusion of the war.

The continued implementation of the commitments *832* pledged by the Government — to ensure democratic order, political pluralism, freedom of opinion and the press and respect for human rights, and to develop close cooperative relations with its neighbours — will indeed contribute to the restoration of stability. Earlier this year, the Foreign Minister reiterated to me that Yemen was willing to reach a negotiated settlement of its territorial dispute with Saudi Arabia on the basis of the norms and principles of international law and in accordance with the Charter of the United Nations. Progress in this area will testify to the strength of that commitment and will add to security and stability in the area.

833   In August 1994, the Department of Humanitarian Affairs launched a consolidated inter-agency appeal focusing on the most urgent humanitarian requirements through February 1995, totalling some $21.7 million. The priority sectors covered in the appeal were health, water and sanitation, emergency food aid, agriculture and fisheries, education and limited mine clearance. Response from the donor community has been extremely disappointing, with only $3.3 million (15 per cent of the overall requirements) received to date, mainly for health and food supply projects.

834   Land-mines pose a continuing threat to the lives and the livelihood of civilians in the south and have hampered efforts of health rehabilitation and restoration of agricultural production in affected areas. The Department of Humanitarian Affairs, however, received limited funding ($150,000) from a mine-clearance trust fund to undertake a land-mine assistance project in the Aden region. The project began in late February 1995 and aims to provide technical advice to the government authorities. Two international land-mine specialists were recruited by the Department of Humanitarian Affairs for the purpose.

E. MAJOR COMPREHENSIVE EFFORTS

1. *Angola*

During the past year, significant progress has been achieved in *835*
the search for peace in Angola. After protracted negotiations,
the Lusaka Protocol was signed and the United Nations Angola
Verification Mission (UNAVEM III) was established to facilitate the implementation of its provisions. A cease-fire has been
generally holding throughout the country and has opened access
to all regions for the delivery of humanitarian relief assistance.

At the Lusaka peace talks, the most contentious issue was *836*
the question of national reconciliation, which included the allocation of posts at the national, provincial and local levels to the
members of the União Nacional para a Independência Total de
Angola (UNITA). In May 1994, the Government accepted a set
of proposals on this issue put forward by the United Nations
and the three observer States to the Angolan peace process —
Portugal, the Russian Federation and the United States of
America. After lengthy discussions and the intervention of a
number of African leaders, including President Nelson Man-
dela of South Africa, UNITA finally accepted the proposals in
September.

The way was thus paved for the signing of the Lusaka Pro- *837*
tocol in the Zambian capital on 20 November 1994 and for the
cease-fire that came into force two days later. President José
Eduardo dos Santos and several other Heads of State, foreign
ministers and dignitaries attended the ceremony.

In my report to the Security Council of 1 February *838*
(S/1995/97), I recommended the establishment of a new United
Nations peace-keeping operation in Angola to assist the Government and UNITA in implementing the Lusaka Protocol. In
particular, I recommended that UNAVEM III be composed of
political, military, police and, in future, electoral components.

The Humanitarian Assistance Coordination Unit, which has been operational since March 1993, would continue to serve as a coordinating body for all humanitarian operations under the authority of my Special Representative. The main features of the new United Nations mandate would include: to assist in the implementation of the Lusaka Protocol by providing good offices and mediation to the parties; to supervise, verify and, if necessary, control the disengagement of forces and to monitor the cease-fire; to assist in the establishment of quartering areas and to verify and monitor the withdrawal, quartering and demobilization of UNITA forces; to verify the movement of the Angolan Armed Forces to barracks; to verify and monitor the completion of the formation of a new armed force and the free circulation of people and goods. Other aspects of the proposed mandate were to monitor the activities of the Angolan National Police and the quartering of the Rapid Reaction Police, and to coordinate and support humanitarian activities linked directly to the peace process.

839   Having considered my report, the Security Council adopted resolution 976 (1995) on 8 February, authorizing the establishment of UNAVEM III with an initial mandate until 8 August 1995 and with an authorized strength of 7,000 military personnel, in addition to 350 military observers and 260 police observers, as well as an appropriate number of international and local staff. The Council decided that the deployment of the infantry units would take place gradually and only if the parties complied with the provisions of the Lusaka Protocol.

840   The Joint Commission, chaired by my Special Representative for Angola, Mr. Alioune Blondin Beye, and comprising the representatives of both parties and the three observer States, was established at Luanda soon after the signing of the Lusaka Protocol. It is the body responsible for the implementation of the Protocol and has met in regular and extraordinary sessions on numerous occasions at Luanda and outside the Angolan capital.

Owing to some initial difficulties and delays in implemen-   *841* tation of the Protocol, I dispatched my Special Adviser, Mr. Ismat Kittani, to register my concern with the parties and to assess conditions for the deployment of peace-keepers. The peace process subsequently regained momentum in mid-April. Although a number of incidents, unauthorized movements of troops and other cease-fire violations have occurred, the general trend has been towards a progressive decrease of such violations. Two meetings between the Chiefs of General Staff from the Government and UNITA, held in January and in February, also helped to consolidate the cease-fire and strengthen the peace process. Under the supervision of UNAVEM III, progress has been achieved in the disengagement of forces. In an especially positive development, the President of the Republic of Angola, Mr. José Eduardo dos Santos, and Mr. Jonas Savimbi, President of UNITA, met at Lusaka on 6 May in the presence of my Special Representative. This meeting gave a new and important impetus to the peace process and the parties took further concrete steps to consolidate the progress achieved. In June and July, the parties reached agreement on several important issues and approved an accelerated timetable for the implementation of the Lusaka Protocol.

Following this encouraging development, I visited Angola   *842* from 14 to 16 July to give additional impetus to the peace process. I had extensive meetings with President dos Santos, and met with Mr. Savimbi in his headquarters in the central part of Angola. Both the Government and UNITA emphasized the crucial role of the United Nations in the settlement of the Angolan conflict and stressed their commitment to the implementation of the Lusaka Protocol. I also reviewed the performance of United Nations troops in several regions of Angola. Several issues were resolved following my visit. The National Assembly created two vice-presidential posts, one of which is to be filled by Mr. Savimbi. The parties have decided that the future strength of the Angolan Armed Forces would be 90,000 soldiers and they have made progress on the modalities for the incorporation of UNITA troops, 74,000 of whom would be ground troops. The national armed forces would also comprise air and naval forces of 11,000 and 5,000 personnel, respectively. President dos Santos and Mr. Savimbi held a second meeting, on 10 August in Gabon, to address outstanding questions.

843   United Nations military and police observers have been deployed to nearly 60 locations throughout the country and their presence has increased United Nations verification capabilities, as well as its ability to provide good offices on the ground.

844   The deployment of UNAVEM infantry and support units has reached an advanced stage, with some 3,500 troops present in the country, including three infantry battalions. Full deployment of the contingents is expected in September/October. The United Nations has made strenuous efforts to ensure that mine verification and clearance of major deployment routes and quartering sites is carried out in order to begin early preparations for the quartering of UNITA troops and for the withdrawal of the Angolan Rapid Reaction Police and regular troops to barracks.

845   The civilian police component of UNAVEM has proved to be indispensable in enabling the United Nations to monitor and verify the neutrality of the national police. In addition, a United Nations human rights unit has contributed to the civil education campaign and to confidence-building among the Angolan population. The Government of Angola and the United Nations have agreed to establish an independent United Nations radio station in Angola, as recommended in my report of 1 February

and endorsed by the Security Council in its resolution 976 (1995), which would broadcast information programmes on the role of the United Nations in Angola and on the peace process. Equipment for the United Nations radio station is expected to arrive in Angola in September and UNAVEM is holding discussions with the Angolan authorities regarding the allocation of broadcasting frequencies. In the meantime, UNAVEM has been given access to the government radio and is broadcasting its programmes on it.

On 8 August, the Security Council extended the mandate *846* of UNAVEM for an additional six months, but expressed concern at the pace of implementation of the Lusaka Protocol and strongly urged the parties to accelerate the peace process. In the meantime, the General Assembly approved some $150 million for the UNAVEM budget for 1995.

Improvements in the security situation and the consolida- *847* tion of the cease-fire have enabled the United Nations and international and local non-governmental organizations to extend their humanitarian relief activities to all regions of the country. Since the signing of the Lusaka Protocol, humanitarian agencies have reoriented their programmes to support the peace process in three realms of activity: relief and resettlement; demobilization and reintegration of former combatants; and action related to land-mines. It is estimated that over 3 million Angolans are receiving food aid or other types of relief assistance. These activities are directed inside Angola by the Humanitarian Assistance Coordination Unit, affiliated with the Department of Humanitarian Affairs.

The long-term prospects for peace depend in large part on *848* the successful demobilization and reintegration into civilian life of those combatants who are not retained in the Angolan armed forces. Preparations are under way for the quartering and disarmament of UNITA soldiers under United Nations supervision and control. Humanitarian agencies will provide basic services to the soldiers in the quartering sites and organize programmes to facilitate their return to civilian society. The Department of Humanitarian Affairs has appealed to the international community for $102 million to support the demobilization and reintegration process over a period of approximately two years.

849   The intensive mine pollution in Angola seriously hinders the movement of goods and people as well as the resumption of economic activity. The problem is being addressed through a coordinated programme of mine survey and clearance, mine-awareness training for civilians and the training of Angolan technicians and managers.

850   Despite some progress on the humanitarian front, the economic and social situation in Angola continues to be extremely precarious. As in other peace-keeping operations, I have attached particular importance to these aspects of the situation in Angola. As the peace process advances, the focus of United Nations assistance is gradually shifting from emergency relief activities to rehabilitation of the country's war-wracked economic and social infrastructure, and to development. With support from UNDP and the Secretariat, the Government of Angola has organized a round table for rehabilitation and community development to be held in September.

851   By providing humanitarian and development assistance, the international community can ease Angola's transition from war to sustainable peace. The Angolan people and their institutions, however, remain the primary agents of the necessary social, psychological and economic transformations.

2. Haiti

Restoration of democracy

The goal of restoring democracy in Haiti was significantly ad-   *852*
vanced by the return, in October 1994, of the legally and demo-
cratically elected President of the Republic of Haiti, Reverend
Jean-Bertrand Aristide, who had been forced into exile by a
military coup in September 1991.

Pursuant to Security Council resolution 940 (1994) of   *853*
31 July 1994, the Multinational Force, led by the United States
of America, started operation in Haiti on 19 September 1994.
After the departure from the country of the military leadership,
President Aristide returned to Port-au-Prince on 15 October.
On the same day, the Security Council adopted resolution 948
(1994), effectively lifting all sanctions imposed against Haiti.

On 23 September, I appointed Mr. Lakhdar Brahimi as my   *854*
new Special Representative for Haiti to replace Mr. Dante
Caputo, whose resignation I had received with regret four days
earlier. I also sent a small advance team to Haiti to assess
requirements and prepare for the deployment of the United
Nations Mission in Haiti (UNMIH), as well as to monitor the
operations of the Multinational Force.

On 25 October, President Aristide designated Mr. Smarck   *855*
Michel as Prime Minister. The new Government took office on
8 November. Seven days later, I paid a visit to Haiti and assured
President Aristide that the United Nations, in collaboration
with OAS, would continue to assist the Government of Haiti in
achieving a lasting transition to democracy.

Upon my return to Headquarters on 21 November, I re-   *856*
ported to the Security Council. Responding to my recommendation, by its resolution 964 (1994) the Council authorized an
expansion of the advance team to up to 500 members for the
transition period.

857   In my report to the Security Council on 17 January 1995, I noted that, following the arrival of the Multinational Force and the subsequent disintegration of the Haitian Armed Forces (FADH), politically motivated violence and human rights abuses had decreased and Haitians were enjoying fundamental rights. At the same time, however, the collapse of the FADH had created a security void that contributed to an increased level of crime in the country.

858   The Security Council considered my report, the statement of 15 January by the commander of the Multinational Force and the accompanying recommendations of the States participating in the Force regarding the establishment of a secure and stable environment in Haiti. The Council determined that, as required by resolution 940 (1994), a secure and stable environment appropriate to the deployment of UNMIH existed in Haiti and it authorized me to recruit and deploy military contingents, civilian police and other personnel sufficient to allow UNMIH to assume the full range of its functions. The full transfer of responsibility from the Multinational Force to UNMIH was to be completed by 31 March and the mandate of UNMIH was extended for a period of six months until 31 July 1995. The Council also authorized the deployment of up to 6,000 troops and 900 civilian police observers.

859   On 13 April, I submitted a progress report on the deployment of UNMIH, informing the Council that the official ceremony of transfer of responsibilities from the Multinational Force to UNMIH had successfully taken place, as scheduled, on 31 March. My second visit to Haiti, on that occasion, provided a good opportunity to observe the beginning of the operation of UNMIH and to exchange views with the President of Haiti on the political and security situation in the country. The issue of security remained central to the entire United Nations operation, in particular at the time of elections. Legislative and local

elections were held on 25 June under generally secure conditions. However, the elections were marked by organizational
flaws and a partial rerun was held on 13 August. The second
phase of the election is scheduled to be held in September.

    On 31 July, the Security Council extended the mandate of   *860*
UNMIH to the end of February 1996. The Mission continues to
assist the Haitian authorities in maintaining a stable and secure
environment and in protecting humanitarian convoys. UNMIH
also provides the Haitian Provisional Electoral Council with
logistical and financial assistance and its civilian police component guides the work of the Interim Public Security Force
and trains the Haitian National Police on the job.

Human rights

A core group of the International Civilian Mission in Haiti   *861*
(MICIVIH) had returned to Haiti on 22 October 1994. In my report to the General Assembly on the situation of democracy and
human rights in Haiti of 23 November 1994 (A/49/689), I proposed that MICIVIH should also contribute to the strengthening
of democratic institutions.

    The General Assembly, in its resolution 49/27 of 5 Decem-   *862*
ber 1994 on the situation of democracy and human rights in
Haiti, requested the speedy return of all members of MICIVIH
to Haiti. At present, the United Nations component has approximately 110 members. The Mission made a major contribution
to the improvement of respect for human rights in Haiti, both
during the military rule and since the restoration of the constitutional order last October. On 12 July, following my report of
29 June (A/49/926) and consultations with the Government of
Haiti and the Secretary-General of OAS, the General Assembly
extended the mandate of the United Nations component of
MICIVIH until 7 February 1996.

863   MICIVIH continued to give priority to the monitoring and promotion of respect for human rights in Haiti. During the preparation of elections, the Mission facilitated and monitored respect for the freedom of expression and association as well as investigating allegations of intimidation and violence. Both UNMIH and MICIVIH worked closely with an OAS electoral observation mission set up in May 1995. UNMIH helped to ensure that the legislative and local elections on 25 June, while marred by organizational problems, took place in a secure environment, and MICIVIH staff assisted the electoral observation mission in the performance of its tasks. In its report on the 25 June elections, released by the Secretary-General of OAS on 13 July, the observation mission concluded that the elections had established a foundation that, although shaky, provided the basis for further positive progress towards the continuing evolution of an increasingly peaceful democracy in Haiti.

Development

864 After the events of September 1991, United Nations agencies and the international community provided humanitarian assistance to Haiti to address the most pressing basic needs. The main sectors targeted for intervention under the humanitarian assistance programme to alleviate the situation of the poorest sectors of the population were health care, nutrition, water supply and sanitation, and agriculture. To allow for the continuation of the humanitarian programmes during the embargo, a humanitarian fuel supply programme was undertaken. A total of 3,632,277 gallons of fuel was distributed among the non-governmental organizations and other institutions involved in humanitarian aid.

865   With the return of constitutional government in October 1994 and the restoration of democracy after years of political instability and deteriorated socio-economic conditions, reorienting Haiti towards the path of economic development will be a daunting task. After a thorough review of the ongoing humanitarian activities, it was deemed necessary to find a new approach in order gradually to phase out the emphasis on strictly humanitarian relief, while facilitating the initiation of longer-term reconstruction initiatives.

An appeal for a six-month transitional period was 866 launched on 6 December 1994 simultaneously in Port-au-Prince and Washington, D.C., by the Government of Haiti, the United Nations and OAS. The activities presented in the appeal reflected urgent needs that could be implemented rapidly and be of immediate positive impact. They were also intended to be sustainable in order to facilitate a smooth transition to medium- and long-term reconstruction and development efforts. The appeal requested $78 million to meet the needs for continued humanitarian and reconstruction assistance during Haiti's critical transition periods. As at 10 August, 54.1 per cent of the appeal target, or some $50.8 million, had been either received or pledged.

In 1995, cooperation between the Government and its de- 867 velopment partners has moved from emergency and ad hoc initiatives to more strategically planned public works and employment-creation projects, leading, in particular, to major agreements with EU, the United States Agency for International Development (USAID) and the World Bank in July 1995. UNDP activities centre on governance, economic growth and poverty eradication, and the Programme has also provided seed money for certain initiatives by donor countries. In order to coordinate development activities with the peace-keeping mission of UNMIH in a manner consistent with its mandate, my Deputy Special Representative has been concurrently appointed Resident Representative of UNDP.

Natural disasters

868　On 13 November 1994, Tropical Storm Gordon caused heavy rains and floods that devastated sections of Port-au-Prince as well as the southern part of the country. The death toll was estimated at 1,122, and some 1.5 million people were affected. Altogether, 8,600 families became homeless and 61,500 were in need of emergency relief. Destruction of infrastructure, agricultural land and property was extensive and included 11,402 houses partially damaged and 3,905 completely destroyed.

869　Following the appeal for international assistance by the Government of Haiti, the United Nations Humanitarian Coordinator called on the United Nations Management Disaster Team to join the relief effort undertaken in support of the affected populations. The Department of Humanitarian Affairs sent a three-person team from United Nations Disaster Assessment and Coordination to strengthen the Humanitarian Coordinator's efforts to bolster the capacity of the special task force established by the Prime Minister.

870　In response to the emergency situation, the international community's cash contributions amounted to $8.6 million, of which United Nations contributions amounted to some $500,000. Relief items were received from the Department of Humanitarian Affairs warehouse at Pisa, Italy, as well as from the Governments of France, Japan and Mexico.

3.　*Rwanda*

871　Since my last annual report on the work of the Organization, the situation in Rwanda has shown signs of gradual normalization, continuing a process that started with the end of the genocide and civil war and the establishment of the present Government on 19 July 1994. With the completion of the withdrawal of the French-led Operation Turquoise from south-west Rwanda on 21 August 1994, the United Nations Assistance Mission for

Rwanda (UNAMIR) assumed full responsibility for the former humanitarian protection zone prior to a gradual take-over by the new Rwandan civilian administration.

In my reports to the Security Council on UNAMIR, I have *872* emphasized that while the situation in Rwanda has to some extent stabilized, a number of serious obstacles remain to be overcome. Continued problems in repatriation, reconciliation and reconstruction efforts have triggered frustration in Rwanda, which, in turn, has contributed to the deterioration of security and affected relations between UNAMIR and the Rwandan authorities. The Government of Rwanda expressed the wish that, at an appropriate time, UNAMIR's mandate and its possible phase-out from Rwanda should be discussed. However, I urged the Government to continue to extend the necessary cooperation without which the Mission could not carry out its tasks, while requesting my Special Representative, Mr. Shahryar Khan, to consider, in consultation with the Government, adjustments to UNAMIR's mandate.

Following those consultations, I recommended that the *873* mandate of UNAMIR, which was due to expire on 9 June 1995, be renewed for another period of six months and its focus shifted from a peace-keeping to a confidence-building role. In its resolution 997 (1995), the Security Council extended the mandate and authorized a reduction of its force level to 2,330 troops within three months and to 1,800 troops within four months. The mandate is to end in December 1995, with all troops withdrawn. Since the adoption of UNAMIR's new mandate, relations between UNAMIR and the Rwandan authorities have improved. UNAMIR is helping them to promote national reconciliation, the return of refugees and the setting up of a national police force. It is also responsible for the protection of humanitarian organizations, human rights observers and members of the International Criminal Tribunal for Rwanda. In my report of 4 June, I described Rwanda as relatively stable and largely at peace, with some utility services back in operation, schools reopened and the economy and agriculture showing signs of revival.

874   Three major factors have nevertheless complicated international efforts to help the Government to restore normal conditions in Rwanda. Firstly, there has been the delay in bringing to justice individuals implicated in the 1994 genocide. In October 1994, the Independent Commission of Experts concluded that acts of mass extermination against Tutsi groups had been perpetrated in a planned and systematic way by certain Hutu elements and that this constituted genocide under the United Nations Convention on Genocide.

875   On 8 November, the Security Council, in its resolution 955 (1994), decided to establish a tribunal to prosecute persons responsible for genocide and other such violations committed between 1 January and 31 December 1994. Mr. Richard J. Goldstone was appointed Prosecutor and the Prosecutor's Office, headed by the Deputy Prosecutor, Mr. Honoré Rakotomana, was to be established at Kigali. Under his supervision, the investigation of some 400 identified suspects, among them leaders of the former regime and principal planners of the genocide, who sought refuge in neighbouring countries, is being conducted in and outside Rwanda.

876   In its resolution 977 (1995), the Security Council determined that the seat of the Tribunal should be established at Arusha, United Republic of Tanzania. Since the Tribunal shares a common appeals chamber with the International Criminal Tribunal for the Former Yugoslavia, the General Assembly has appointed only six judges for the Tribunal: Mr. Lennart Aspegren (Sweden), Mr. Laïty Kama (Senegal), Mr. T. H. Khan (Bangladesh), Mr. Yakov A. Ostrovsky (Russian Federation), Ms. Navanethem Pillay (South Africa) and Mr. Willam H. Sekule (United Repub-

lic of Tanzania). Their first plenary session was held at The Hague from 26 to 30 June 1995. During the session, the judges adopted the rules of procedure and evidence of the Tribunal and elected a President (Mr. Kama) and a Vice-President (Mr. Ostrovsky). The judges will assume their functions with the commencement of trial proceedings. The Tribunal is expected to process the first indictments in the second half of this year; however, the justice system as a whole is not yet operational and is in urgent need of support. It will be difficult to achieve national reconciliation and a meaningful political dialogue if justice in the wake of the horrific events of the summer of 1994 is not seen to be done.

In July 1994, an estimated 1.2 million Rwandan refugees *877* arrived in the Kivu provinces of Zaire following the April-July civil war in Rwanda. The presence of such a large number of refugees in Zaire, and its impact on the security and economy of the country, was one of the main subjects of the discussion I held with Prime Minister Kengo Wa Dondo during his visit to Headquarters on 15 December. At that time, the Prime Minister requested me to appoint a "special representative for Rwanda in Zaire". It was agreed that a civilian UNAMIR liaison office should be established at Kinshasa to facilitate communication between my Special Representative for Rwanda and the Government of Zaire. The Prime Minister offered to provide 1,500 troops for a proposed United Nations force to ensure security in the refugee camps. The Government of Zaire cited the presence of the Rwandan refugees as one of the factors that had contributed to the postponement of the first multi-party parliamentary and presidential elections and to the extension for two more years of the transitional period in Zaire until 10 July 1997.

On 27 January 1995, the Government of Zaire and the *878* United Nations High Commissioner for Refugees signed an *aide-mémoire* outlining specific measures to improve security in the camps. Under the agreement, the Government of Zaire agreed to deploy a contingent of 1,500 military and police personnel — the Zairian Camp Security Contingent — to provide security in the camps. The measures included the prevention of violence, escort of repatriation convoys and maintenance of law and order, especially at food distribution centres.

879 Some 1,513 Zairian Camp Security troops and more than 38 members of the UNHCR civilian Security Liaison Group are now deployed in refugee camps. Their deployment has greatly improved security conditions. However, rumours about military training of elements of the former Government's army have persisted in some camps. Thus, in furtherance of Security Council resolution 997 (1995), I sent a Special Envoy, Mr. Aldo Ajello, to the region to discuss the issue with all countries concerned and to explore the possibility of deploying military observers, in particular in the airfield of eastern Zaire, to monitor the alleged flow of arms. From 20 to 28 June, my Envoy visited Rwanda, Burundi, Zaire, Uganda and the United Republic of Tanzania. On 9 July, I reported to the Security Council that some countries of the region were opposed to the deployment of United Nations military observers on their territory. However, Zaire reiterated that it would welcome an international commission of inquiry, under United Nations auspices, to investigate allegations of arms deliveries to the former Rwandese Government Forces. For its part, the Government of Rwanda has reiterated its determination to promote the earliest return of the refugees and has stated its readiness for dialogue with those of them who were implicated in the genocide.

880 The second complicating factor is that national reconciliation can hardly become a reality without the safe return of the refugees and internally displaced persons not implicated in acts of genocide. For that purpose, the assistance of the international community will be needed to build up structures for the reset-

tlement of the refugees and internally displaced persons and their reintegration into society. However, efforts in this direction have been jeopardized by the continuing military activities of members of the former Rwandese Government Forces in refugee camps in neighbouring countries, including the launching of organized incursions into Rwanda. The Government is concerned that the elements abroad of the former Rwandese Government Forces receive training and arms deliveries, whereas Rwanda is still subject to an arms embargo.

Given the serious lack of security in the refugee camps out- *881* side Rwanda, I authorized United Nations participation in a joint working group with Zairian authorities to improve the situation. Following consultations with the Secretariat and UNHCR, I emphasized in a report to the Security Council (S/1994/1308) that any operation to achieve the repatriation of refugees and the improvement of security in the camps was futile without parallel efforts to promote national reconciliation and reconstruction. On 1 February 1995, I informed the Security Council that on 27 January UNHCR had concluded an agreement with the Government of Zaire for the deployment of 1,500 security personnel, as well as a UNHCR liaison support group, to camps in eastern Zaire to maintain law and order, to prevent intimidation of refugees by elements opposed to their repatriation and to protect returnees and relief workers. However, while the situation has improved, the problem is far from solved.

The Government made it clear that it wished to close down *882* the camps of internally displaced persons for reasons of security, in particular those in Kibeho, Ndago, Kamana and Munini. At the insistence of UNAMIR, which opposed the closing of the camps by force, the Government agreed to postpone such action. However, on 18 April the Government decided to close Kibeho camp, an action that led to panic, a stampede and indiscriminate firing at displaced persons, resulting in the killing of a large number. I immediately expressed my horror at this deplorable incident and sent a Special Envoy to Kigali. In the aftermath, most displaced persons were repatriated to their communes with the help of UNAMIR and UNHCR. In its report (S/1995/411), the independent International Commission of Inquiry created to investigate the circumstances and causes of the Kibeho tragedy concluded that it was neither premeditated nor an accident that could not have been prevented. The speedy establishment of the Commission and the steps it has taken to penalize the military personnel involved have mitigated some of the tragedy's adverse effects.

883   Thirdly, there has been frustration at the slow pace of delivery of international economic and reconstruction assistance to Rwanda, including aid pledged at the UNDP round table of January 1995. Of $714 million pledged, only $69 million has been disbursed and of this $26 million has been absorbed by debt-servicing costs. With regard to the Rwanda portion of the United Nations consolidated inter-agency appeal for the Rwanda crisis, launched in February this year, out of the $219,490,162 requested for Rwanda, only 50 per cent has been funded. For the subregion, under 60 per cent of the total $586,778,007 required for programmes in the neighbouring countries has so far been received.

884   Although the international donor community made generous pledges to the Government of Rwanda's rehabilitation and reconstruction programme, the slow process in turning them into actual support has frustrated the Government. I have repeatedly invited Member States and other potential donors to contribute to the trust fund for Rwanda, which could serve as a useful channel for contributions to meet the immediate needs of the Government and people of Rwanda. To date, $6,536,911 has been contributed. I also continue to believe that the early implementation of some of the key recommendations of the OAU/UNHCR Regional Conference on Assistance to Refugees, Returnees and Displaced Persons in the Great Lakes Region, held at Bujumbura from 15 to 17 February, would ease the tremendous humanitarian crisis in the region. I appealed to all Member States to act in accordance with the Conference's recommendations.

In this sense, the experience of Rwanda casts a revealing *885* light on some of the problems that a peace-keeping operation is bound to meet when operating in such difficult circumstances. A new integrated approach, enlisting and combining all the resources of the United Nations family, is urgently needed.

Only a small proportion of the Rwandan people who fled *886* their country at different times have returned to Rwanda this year and of those who have the vast majority come from those living in Uganda since the early 1960s. Among the refugees who fled in 1994, enthusiasm for repatriation has waned since March, especially in the Goma area and in northern Burundi. This is a result both of intimidation in the refugee camps and of the high number of security incidents inside Rwanda, including the assassinations of the Prefect of Butare and the head of medical services in the Gisenyi area. The rate of arrests of suspected participants in genocide and strong speeches by some Rwandan authorities have also had a negative impact on repatriation. Despite these set-backs, UNHCR continues to prepare for larger-scale repatriation in the months ahead. In addition to monitoring returnees, UNHCR is trying to organize, in cooperation with the Government of Rwanda, confidence-building visits by refugee groups from camps in Burundi to their home communes.

The Government also has to address the social impact of *887* large numbers of people returning to their homes. In this respect, it should not be forgotten that much of the Rwandan population is still traumatized by the events of 1994. It is thus hardly surprising that serious problems have occurred between the survivors of the genocide and those who are now returning from camps for displaced persons or refugees. Disputes concern the genocide, illegal occupancy of land and property and the settling of old scores and grudges. Since February, commune committees, comprising representatives of local authorities and human rights field officers, are being formed to address issues such as security and arrest procedures.

888   The combination of ethnic polarization in Burundi and Rwanda, massive circulation of arms, porous borders and transborder movements of refugees threaten, at best, to keep the subregion perpetually unstable and, at worst, to ignite a large-scale regional conflict. I will therefore intensify my efforts towards a broader international initiative for a long-term solution to the problems in the Great Lakes region, especially by the early convening of a regional conference on security, stability and development.

889   Food shortages within the region have also occurred and WFP and UNHCR have alerted the international community to the need to cover the shortages, which threaten more than 3 million Rwandan and Burundian refugees and internally displaced persons. Rations in some refugee camps have had to be reduced by as much as half. Inside Rwanda itself, the United Nations and non-governmental organizations have contributed significantly to the present harvest by providing seeds, tools and seed protection programmes. A seed multiplication programme, financed by the World Bank, has been initiated and FAO has been instrumental in the establishment of a consortium of donors for the agricultural sector.

890   UNICEF has reopened a number of nutritional centres, distributed equipment to non-governmental organizations and delivered supplementary food and material to unaccompanied

children centres. With the assistance of UNICEF, ICRC, UNHCR and the Save the Children Fund–UK, 41,800 separated Rwandan children have been registered in Rwanda, Goma, Bukavu and Ngara, out of an estimated total of 95,000. Thanks to these efforts, at least 3,000 children have been reunited with their families. There is evidence that up to one fifth of all unaccompanied minors can be reunited with their families.

UNICEF and the Ministry of Justice have reached an *891* agreement to move an estimated 400 children accused of genocide from prisons to a separate location. In addition, a special division for imprisoned children and women has been created within the Ministry of Justice. Five experienced lawyers have been recruited to act as defence counsels for the children. Regarding the demobilization of child soldiers, UNICEF and the Ministry of Defence have identified a location where the education and skills training of up to 4,000 child soldiers will soon begin.

Much progress has been made in the health conditions of *892* the Rwandan population. WHO has assisted the Ministry of Health with training programmes to enable the national programme of diarrhoeal diseases and acute respiratory infections control to be re-launched and is supporting the Ministry in the production of the national health policy document. Training programmes have also been undertaken on the national health information system, with an emphasis on epidemiological surveillance. With the help of UNICEF and others, more than 100 of the 280 pre-war vaccination centres have reopened in Rwanda; supplies and equipment have been ordered for the remainder. A vaccination campaign against measles has also been launched in Kigali. Some progress has also been made in the rehabilitation of the country's water infrastructure and electric grid line.

Joint UNESCO and UNICEF efforts have continued to *893* improve access to education. Some 1,800 teacher emergency packages, supplying basic classroom resources and an emergency curriculum to over 140,000 primary school children, were distributed inside Rwanda in February. This brings the number of such packages distributed so far to over 7,000, servicing at least 560,000 children.

894   As well as continuing its project for emergency assistance to the national maternal and child health/family planning programme, UNFPA is helping the Government to elaborate an integrated maternal and child health/family planning training programme, which incorporates maternal and child health/family planning, HIV/AIDS prevention and safe motherhood. WHO has also supported the national AIDS programme through the strengthening of managerial capabilities at central and regional levels.

895   In July, I visited Rwanda in order to observe at first hand the progress made and the challenges that remain. In my most recent report on UNAMIR, dated 8 August, I stressed that the achievement of genuine national reconciliation was an essential element in establishing lasting peace in Rwanda. The Government of Rwanda must take determined measures to that end and representatives of all sectors of Rwandan society should begin talks to reach an agreement on a constitutional and political structure necessary to achieve lasting stability. The international community also has an important role to play in the process of Rwanda's reconstruction and reconciliation. While the economic situation has marginally improved, the Government will not be able to cope with the mounting pressures from returning refugees, the rehabilitation of all sectors and tensions from neighbouring countries. The seriousness of the present situation and the growing probability that it will deteriorate further requires urgent and concerted action on the part of the international community. During my visit to the subregion, there was clear consensus among government leaders that instability in any State in the area could have a dramatic effect on all its neighbours. On 16 August, the Security Council unanimously adopted resolution 1011 (1995). In that resolution, the Council, *inter alia,* lifted for the period of one year, until 1 September 1996, the restrictions on the sale or supply of arms and related *matériel* to the Government of Rwanda. Such restrictions remain in force, however, with respect to non-government forces in Rwanda and in neighbouring States. On 1 September 1996, the restrictions imposed by the Council in paragraph 13 of its resolution 918 (1994) shall terminate, unless it decides otherwise after its consideration of the report of the Secretary-General on the matter.

4. *The former Yugoslavia*

The Organization's continuing efforts in the former Yugoslavia *896* remain focused on a multiplicity of mandated responsibilities that span humanitarian, military and political tasks in an environment characterized by vicious cycles of cease-fire violations, human rights infringements, physical destruction and death.

Unceasing conflicts, entrenched hostilities, violation of *897* agreements and a genuine lack of commitment and good faith have become the hallmarks of this crisis. Taken together, these factors give the impression either that not enough is being done to find a peaceful resolution or that fundamental questions and issues that divide the parties are insurmountable. For too long, from the start of military confrontation in 1991 until the time of writing, all efforts aimed at reaching a negotiated and peaceful solution to the conflicts and outstanding issues have been in vain. The Organization and agencies within its common system that have programmes in the area are, however, continuing to devote the highest priority to bringing peace to the region and alleviating the suffering brought about by the conflict.

Preventive diplomacy and preventive deployment

898 The presence of the United Nations Preventive Deployment Force (UNPREDEP) continues to make an important contribution to stability in the former Yugoslav Republic of Macedonia. However, as stated in my report last year, internal differences that could lead to political instability remain a cause for concern. Regarding the dispute between Greece and the former Yugoslav Republic of Macedonia, my Special Envoy, Mr. Cyrus Vance, has continued his efforts pursuant to Security Council resolution 845 (1993).

899 On 7 November 1994, Mr. Vance and I met with President Kiro Gligorov at Geneva following the elections in his country. I urged him to give favourable consideration to a number of proposals for resolving the dispute. On 6 February 1995, Mr. Vance began a series of parallel meetings with the parties with a view to convening direct negotiations. During the meetings both parties took a serious and constructive approach that could in time lead to direct talks. In a subsequent meeting with President Gligorov at Copenhagen on 10 March, I urged him to facilitate a face-to-face meeting with the other side. Between March and June, Mr. Vance continued his meetings with the two sides. When I visited Greece in July, I urged the Greek leaders to respond favourably to his proposals.

Peacemaking and peace-keeping

900 The International Conference on the Former Yugoslavia continues to provide a permanent forum for the negotiation of a comprehensive political solution to the problems in the former Yugoslavia. Its Steering Committee is co-chaired by Mr. Thorvald Stoltenberg, representing the United Nations, and the former Swedish premier Mr. Carl Bildt, who was appointed by EU on 9 June following the resignation of Lord David Owen in May. My Special Representative, Mr. Yasushi Akashi, as well as the

States members of the Contact Group, have continued their efforts to advance the peace process. At an EU summit meeting at Cannes, France, in June, European leaders determined that diplomacy should be the main tool for achieving several primary objectives, including the lifting of the siege of Sarajevo; resumption of a dialogue between the parties on the basis of the Contact Group Plan; establishment of a new four-month cease-fire; re-establishment of a dialogue between the Government of Croatia and the Krajina Serbs; and mutual recognition by the former Yugoslav republics.

Under the auspices of the Co-Chairmen of the International Conference on the Former Yugoslavia and the Ambassadors of the Russian Federation and the United States of America to Croatia, the Government of Croatia and the local Serb authorities in Croatia concluded, on 2 December 1994, an Economic Agreement. That Agreement was seen as a major confidence-building measure towards the restoration of normal economic activities in Croatia. With continued adherence to the cease-fire agreement of 29 March 1994, it seemed that both sides had embarked on a course of normalizing their relationship by pursuing a number of tangible and mutually beneficial economic improvements, such as the opening of the Zagreb-Belgrade highway through Sector West, opening the Adriatic oil pipeline, rehabilitating and reconnecting the electricity grid and exploring the reopening of railway connections. *901*

On 12 January 1995, I received a letter from the President of the Republic of Croatia, Dr. Franjo Tudjman, informing me of his Government's decision not to agree to a further extension of the mandate of the United Nations Protection Force (UNPROFOR) beyond 31 March. While the Government of Croatia's frustration was understandable, its decision to insist on the withdrawal of UNPROFOR from Croatia renewed mis- *902* trust and created new tensions, as a result of which cooperation on further elements of the Economic Agreement petered out.

903   Diplomatic efforts by the international community, Mr. Stoltenberg and my Special Representative eventually won acceptance of the continuation of the United Nations peace-keeping presence in Croatia, albeit with revised tasks and a reduced troop strength of 8,750. At the end of March, the Security Council in its resolution 981 (1995) established the United Nations Confidence Restoration Operation, to be known as UNCRO, which was to implement a number of core tasks that were defined in consultations between Mr. Stoltenberg and the parties. The elements of UNPROFOR stationed in Croatia were to be converted into UNCRO by the end of June 1995. At the same time separate forces were created for Bosnia and Herzegovina (retaining the name UNPROFOR) and the former Yugoslav Republic of Macedonia (UNPREDEP). Overall command and control of all these forces was to be exercised by my Special Representative and the Force Commander from United Nations Peace Forces Headquarters (UNPF-HQ) at Zagreb.

904   On 1 May, the Croatian army and police undertook an offensive against Sector West from both directions on the Zagreb-Belgrade highway with some 2,500 troops, heavy equipment and air support. UNPROFOR, whose mandate was to monitor the cease-fire arrangements agreed in March 1994, was powerless to prevent an offensive on that scale. However, UNPROFOR and other international agencies were able to keep the international community at least partially informed and to discourage violence against the Serb population, though abuses undoubtedly occurred during the early stages of the conflict. More than 10,000 Serb civilians crossed into Serb-controlled areas of Bosnia and Herzegovina. Subsequently, UNPROFOR and UNHCR helped those remaining Serb civilians who so wished to leave Sector West in a protected and

orderly manner. Although the Government of Croatia declared
its intention to respect fully the human rights of the remaining
Serb population, it was not able to create confidence among the
Serbs that it was in their interests to remain in Croatia. The mis-
trust created by the Croatian operation against Sector West further undermined efforts to resume negotiations towards a
peaceful settlement in Croatia.

Following the take-over of Sector West by the Croatian *905*
army, tensions in the UNCRO area of operations remained high,
preventing the deployment of the Operation as originally envisaged in Security Council resolutions 981 (1995), 982 (1995)
and 990 (1995). On 19 July, the Krajina Serb army and the
forces loyal to Mr. Fikaret Abdić launched offensives against the
Bosnian Army V Corps in the Bihać pocket. Croatia almost immediately warned that the displacement of the population of
Bihać would be considered a serious threat to its security and
stability. The Presidents of Croatia and Bosnia and Herzegovina signed the Split Declaration on 22 July, which committed the Government of Croatia to assist Bosnian forces militar-
ily in the Bihać pocket. Within Croatia, the Croatian army
continued a major build-up of troops around Sectors North and
South in apparent preparation for a major military offensive
aimed at re-establishing Croatian control in those areas.

Intensive efforts to defuse the crisis and restart political *906*
negotiations were undertaken by the United Nations as well as
by Member States. My Special Representative met with President Tudjman to forestall a looming military confrontation. He
also met with local Serb leaders at Knin. On 3 August, at Geneva,
Mr. Stoltenberg chaired a meeting of the representatives of the
Government of Croatia and the Croatian Serbs and presented
the two sides with a paper covering seven points of contention.
The Croatian Serb side was inclined to accept the paper as a
useful basis for progress, subject to clearance by its political

leadership, but the Government indicated that the paper did not address its fundamental concern that the Krajina Serbs should be reintegrated under the Croatian Constitution and laws. On the evening of 3 August, I telephoned President Tudjman and urged the utmost restraint.

907   On 4 August, the Croatian army launched a major offensive, which was largely completed a few days later. I immediately issued a statement expressing my regret at the outbreak of hostilities in Croatia, and urged the parties to respect international humanitarian law and the human rights of the affected population. At the start of the action, a significant number of United Nations observation posts were overrun by the Croatian army and some were deliberately fired upon. Some United Nations troops were used as human shields by Croatian army units as they conducted their attacks. Vigorous protests have been launched against these incidents by the United Nations and the troop-contributing Governments concerned. In the period following the Croatian military actions, the United Nations has concentrated on dealing with the humanitarian crisis brought about by the massive displacement of people and on maintaining contacts that would permit political negotiations to be resumed. Thus my Special Representative on 6 August concluded a nine-point agreement with the Croatian authorities allowing the United Nations, and other international organizations, to cope with the major humanitarian difficulties and to monitor the human rights situation on the ground. Mr. Stoltenberg was also in active contact with the authorities at Zagreb and Belgrade. These events had obvious implications for the future role of UNCRO in that, with the collapse of the armed forces of the Krajina Serbs, there was no longer a requirement, except in Sector East, to monitor or control the confrontation line, zone of separation, weapons storage sites and areas of limitations established by the cease-fire agreement of 29 March 1994.

On 23 August, I recommended to the Security Council an immediate start to the repatriation of all UNCRO troops, except the two battalions in Sector East, with the aim of reducing troop strength to below 2,500 by mid-November 1995.

For the most part, developments in Bosnia and Herze- *908*
govina in the past year have been equally discouraging. In the autumn of 1994, military activity assumed unacceptably high levels, in particular in the Bihać area and around Sarajevo. The overall situation reached a crisis point when Bosnian Serb infantry entered the designated safe area of Bihać to repulse an offensive launched from the Bihać pocket in October by the Bosnian army. Following air attacks by Krajina Serbs into the Bihać pocket on 18 and 19 November 1994 and NATO air strikes against the Udbina airfield in Sector South in Croatia and on Bosnian Serb missile sites on 21 and 23 November, respectively, the situation sharply worsened. Some 250 UNPROFOR personnel were confined to the weapon collection points around Sarajevo and 26 United Nations military observers were detained in their quarters. The situation improved when, following former United States President Jimmy Carter's visit in late December, my Special Representative was able to secure a cessation-of-hostilities agreement, which came into effect on 1 January 1995.

Although the cessation of hostilities had been agreed for *909*
four months, fighting in the Bihać area never ceased, and those elements of the agreement which could have secured a more stable cease-fire, such as the creation of buffer zones and the interpositioning of UNPROFOR troops along the confrontation line, could not be implemented for lack of cooperation by the parties. In March 1995, the Government, in the first large-scale violation of the cease-fire agreement outside the Bihać area, launched offensive operations at Mount Vlašić, near Travnik, and the Majevica Hills near Tuzla. When efforts to extend the

cessation-of-hostilities agreement beyond 1 May failed, the situation in and around Sarajevo began to deteriorate rapidly. The humanitarian airlift into Sarajevo airport has been blocked by the Bosnian Serbs from 8 April to the time of writing; sniping and exchanges of artillery fire have increased to levels not experienced since the establishment of the heavy weapons exclusion zone in February 1994.

910   On 25 May, as a result of the failure of the Bosnian Serbs to respect the deadline for the return of heavy weapons, an air strike was launched against an ammunition dump near Pale, with another against the same target the following day as a result of continuing non-compliance. The Bosnian Serbs shelled all safe areas except Žepa, and 70 civilians were killed and over 130 injured as a result of a rocket attack on Tuzla. The Bosnian Serbs surrounded UNPROFOR personnel in weapon collection points and detained 199, many of them under humiliating circumstances.

911   As the crisis heightened, NATO, on 29 June, approved a plan to send up to 60,000 troops to Bosnia and Herzegovina to cover the withdrawal of United Nations peace-keepers, should the need arise. United Nations-designated safe areas came under sustained attack from Bosnian Serb forces and Srebrenica was overrun on 11 July. The Security Council on 12 July demanded the withdrawal of the Bosnian Serb forces from Srebrenica but this demand was ignored. The Bosnian Serb army detained UNPROFOR troops from the Netherlands and by 14 July had evicted thousands of Muslim refugees from Srebrenica, while detaining Muslim men, whose fate is still unknown. The violations of international humanitarian law that appear to have been committed in the wake of the fall of Srebrenica and Žepa are a matter of utmost concern, and it is imperative that access be given to permit full international investigation of these allegations. The degrading and cruel treatment of the

civilian population has been strongly, and justifiably, con-
demned. Žepa then came under attack and also fell to Bosnian
Serb forces. In the Žepa enclave, both sides threatened to kill
UNPROFOR troops from Ukraine — the Bosnian Serbs if
NATO air strikes were used against them, and the Government
of Bosnia and Herzegovina if NATO air assets were not used.
On 20 July, the Security Council adopted a presidential statement condemning humanitarian abuses in Žepa by the Bosnian
Serb army. During this period the United Nations devoted all
energies to dealing with the monumental humanitarian consequences of the fall of the two enclaves. Efforts to account for the
missing and gain access to the detainees are continuing.

These dramatic developments and threats against the re-   *912*
maining safe areas were discussed at a conference in London
on 21 July, which I attended along with leaders of the Contact
Group and representatives of troop-contributing countries. The
London conference considered measures, including air power,
to deter further attacks on the safe areas. On 26 July, NATO approved plans for employing air power should Bosnian Serbs
threaten or attack Goražde. Following intensive discussions between NATO and the United Nations, appropriate procedures
were agreed for this purpose, and I have delegated authority
for launching air strikes in the region to the UNPF Force
Commander.

The crisis situation that began to develop in May once   *913*
again highlighted the vulnerability of UNPROFOR as a lightly
armed, widely dispersed peace-keeping force. I therefore ap-
preciated the offer made by France, the Netherlands and the
United Kingdom of Great Britain and Northern Ireland to make
available to UNPROFOR some 12,500 additional troops as a
rapid reaction capability in order to improve the Force's security
and thus its ability to implement the mandate given to it by the
Security Council. Difficulties raised by the Governments of

Croatia and Bosnia and Herzegovina have delayed the entry into operation of the rapid reaction capability.

914   The five-member Contact Group continued its efforts to arrive at a political solution to the conflict in Bosnia and Herzegovina, but little progress was made in convincing the Bosnian Serb party to accept the territorial map for an overall settlement, despite the support of the Federal Republic of Yugoslavia (Serbia and Montenegro). The latter has continued to minimize its relations with the Bosnian Serb leaders, and the monitor mission of the International Conference on the Former Yugoslavia, established in September 1994, has maintained its monitoring of the closure of the 300-mile border with Bosnian Serb-controlled territory.

915   The dramatic developments that are taking place as this report is being finalized at the end of August provide, at long last, reason to hope that there may be worthwhile progress towards a political settlement. It is regrettable that in order to achieve peace the international community has had to resort to using force, but the warning that was given following the London Conference of 21 July was clear and unmistakable. After so many disappointments in past years of tragedy in Bosnia and Herzegovina, this new opportunity for political negotiation must not be wasted.

916   I am well aware that the patience, resources and will of Member States to resolve the crises in the former Yugoslavia have been sorely tested. Nevertheless, I remain convinced that only a negotiated comprehensive settlement will lead to an enduring peace. Part of that settlement must include arrangements for arms limitations and confidence-building measures that will prevent further outbreaks of conflict in the Balkans. There must also be an extensive plan for reconstruction and rehabilitation in the region as a whole. There will therefore be a continuing need for the international community to remain committed and involved.

Human rights

In August 1992, the United Nations Commission on Human *917*
Rights convened, for the first time ever in its history, in a special
session to consider the human rights situation in the former Yugoslavia. The Commission requested its chairman to appoint a
special rapporteur to investigate the human rights situation in
the former Yugoslavia, in particular within Bosnia and Herzegovina.

The Special Rapporteur, Mr. Tadeusz Mazowiecki (who *918*
resigned on 27 July 1995), submitted regular reports during this
past year to the Commission on Human Rights and to the General Assembly. The Commission requested the Secretary-
General to make those reports available to the Security Council
and to the International Conference on the Former Yugoslavia. In
17 reports, the Special Rapporteur assessed the human rights situation in Croatia, Bosnia and Herzegovina, the former Yugoslav
Republic of Macedonia and the Federal Republic of Yugoslavia
(Serbia and Montenegro). In each of the reports, he presented a
number of recommendations for action by the international
community and various parties in the region.

With regard to the areas under the control of the de facto *919*
Bosnian Serb authorities, the Special Rapporteur drew attention to the ongoing practice of ethnic cleansing and the widespread violation of the human rights of peoples living in those
areas, including Bosnian Serbs who were perceived as disloyal
by the de facto authorities. There has also been a continuation
of military attacks on civilians and interference with the delivery
of humanitarian aid by Bosnian Serb forces in areas throughout
Bosnia and Herzegovina. The Special Rapporteur vigorously
condemned all such violations of human rights and called for
the prosecution of the perpetrators by the International Tribunal.

In addition, the Commission on Human Rights adopted *920*
resolution 1994/75 in which it requested me to report to the

Commission on the situation of human rights in Bosnia and Herzegovina. In my report, I addressed the issue of the actions taken by the Special Rapporteur, the situation concerning the voluntary return of displaced persons, the problem of disappearances and actions taken by the Commission of Experts established pursuant to Security Council resolution 780 (1992), the International Tribunal, the International Conference on the Former Yugoslavia, UNPROFOR and the United Nations High Commissioner for Human Rights.

921   In November 1994, the International Criminal Tribunal for the Former Yugoslavia confirmed the first indictment against a Bosnian Serb, Mr. Dragan Nikolić, on charges of gross violations of the Geneva Conventions, the laws and customs of war and crimes against humanity. Soon thereafter, a formal request was issued to the Government of Germany for the deferral of the *Tadić* case, involving charges of genocide, ethnic cleansing, rape and murder of civilians and prisoners of war. Proceedings for the transfer of the case from the German courts were completed a few months later and the first hearing of the *Tadić* case was held on 26 April 1995.

922   The Tribunal confirmed two more indictments in February 1995, bringing the total number accused to 22. Requests for their arrest and surrender to the Tribunal have been sent to the authorities of Bosnia and Herzegovina and the Serb administration at Pale. Except for Mr. Tadić, however, who was transferred to the Tribunal by Germany, the remaining 21 accused are still at large.

923   In May, the Tribunal issued a formal request to the Government of Bosnia and Herzegovina for the deferral of its investigation and criminal proceedings in respect of crimes committed against the civilian population in the Lašva river valley, where Bosnian Croat forces have allegedly committed mass killings of Bosnian civilians. The Tribunal issued another request for deferral of investigation proceedings to the Government with respect to the Bosnian Serb leadership at Pale. The latter investigation focuses on the question of possible responsibility of the Serb leaders for genocide, murder, rape, torture and forced transfer of population from large parts of Bosnia and Herzegovina. From 21 to 25 July the Tribunal handed down five indictments covering 24 people.

The March 1994 Washington Agreement that led to the *924* establishment of the Federation in Bosnia and Herzegovina, the introduction of the Contact Group Plan in May 1994 and the Agreement on Cessation of Hostilities signed at the end of the year brought a period of stability to Sarajevo and improved freedom of movement. These developments, while not fundamentally changing the situation, made it possible gradually to reduce the number of beneficiaries needing international assistance to some 2.1 million persons, of whom 1.4 million were in Bosnia and Herzegovina. United Nations humanitarian agencies could then concentrate more on displaced persons and the most vulnerable groups.

With the exception of Bihać, overall access for humanita- *925* rian assistance was successful, at least during the period from June 1994 to March 1995, with UNHCR being able to exceed its monthly target in Sarajevo and elsewhere in central Bosnia. It was possible to bring winterization items and fuel to Sarajevo and the eastern enclaves. Arrangements were also made with FAO for the distribution of much-needed seeds and fertilizers throughout Bosnia and Herzegovina.

Overall security rapidly deteriorated in March 1995, making *926* movements of humanitarian assistance increasingly difficult. The airlift to Sarajevo came to a halt on 8 April and with the escalation of the conflict from late May, land convoys became unpredictable and vulnerable. For the first time, signs of malnutrition and exhaustion were visible in Bihać and in the eastern enclaves.

927   The dramatic escalation of the conflict in June, July and August led to the displacement of hundreds of thousands of people throughout the former Yugoslavia. With the Croat authorities regaining control of western Slavonia in June, thousands of Serbs were displaced to north-west Bosnia. Following the fall of Srebrenica in mid-July, some 30,000 people were compelled to flee. At the beginning of August, thousands of men from Srebrenica still remained unaccounted for. Some 4,350 people were evacuated from Žepa in late July. A Bosnian Croat offensive on Glamoc and Grahovo led to the displacement of some 13,000 Serbs in the Banja Luka area.

928   The retaking of the Krajina by the Croat authorities in early August led to an exodus of some 150,000 people to north-west Bosnia and to the Federal Republic of Yugoslavia. UNHCR, in cooperation with other humanitarian partners, mounted a major assistance effort to meet the needs generated by this emergency. The departing Krajina Serbs suffered widespread maltreatment, injuries and some deaths at the hands of Croatian troops and civilians, and UNCRO personnel reported much looting and burning of houses. UNHCR made efforts to monitor the situation of those Krajina Serbs remaining and to ensure the right to return of those who fled. UNHCR and other humanitarian agencies have continued to given assistance in Croatia and in western Bosnia, despite pressures for their departure, all too often through acts of violence. The practice of forced labour, often on front lines, is of great concern, and this situation has been exacerbated by renewed tensions and the recent influx of Serb refugees from western Slavonia and the Krajina, which has resulted in the Banja Luka region in worsening treatment and evictions of Muslims and Croats in retaliation.

929   In general, forced population movements, either associated with ethnic cleansing or leading to the same result, have been of great concern to UNHCR during the period. UNHCR

has actively intervened against forced mobilization of refugees. The United Nations revised consolidated inter-agency appeal for the former Yugoslavia covering January-December 1995 was issued on 2 June by nine United Nations agencies, for a total of $470 million for humanitarian operations. The UNHCR component is $172 million to cover the cost of humanitarian aid for an estimated total of 2,109,500 beneficiaries in Bosnia and Herzegovina, Croatia, the former Yugoslav Republic of Macedonia, Slovenia and the Federal Republic of Yugoslavia (Serbia and Montenegro). Contributions as at 1 August 1995 were $1.36 million.

F.   COOPERATION WITH REGIONAL ORGANIZATIONS

Cooperation between the United Nations and regional organizations must constantly adapt to an ever-changing world situation. The Charter itself anticipated this need for flexibility by not giving a precise definition of regional arrangements and organizations, thus enabling diverse organizations and structures to contribute, together with the United Nations, to the maintenance of peace and security. *930*

The growing interaction between the United Nations and regional organizations has its origins in Chapter VIII of the Charter. With this objective in mind, the Secretary-General met in August 1994 with the heads of several regional organizations with which the United Nations had recently cooperated in peacemaking and peace-keeping efforts. In the January 1995 Supplement to "An Agenda for Peace" (A/50/60-S/1995/1), a typology of current modalities for cooperation between the United Nations and regional organizations was set forth. *931*

Currently, such cooperation takes five different forms. First, there is consultation, which is practised on a regular basis and, in some cases, is governed by formal agreements. *932*

Secondly, there is diplomatic support, by which a regional organization can participate in United Nations peacemaking activities through diplomatic efforts of its own. For instance, OSCE provides technical input on constitutional issues relating to Abkhazia. Conversely, the United Nations can support a regional organization in its efforts, as it does for OSCE over Nagorny Karabakh. Thirdly, the United Nations and regional organizations can engage in operational support. A recent example is the provision by NATO of air support to UNPROFOR in the former Yugoslavia. Fourthly, there is co-deployment: United Nations field missions have been deployed in conjunction with the Economic Community of West African States (ECWAS) in Liberia and with CIS in Georgia. Finally, there can be joint operations, such as the current human rights mission of the United Nations and the OAS in Haiti.

933   However, given the diversification of the forms of cooperation being established between regional organizations and the United Nations, the basic principles of the Charter should be borne in mind. Article 24 confers on the Security Council primary responsibility for the maintenance of peace and Article 52 stipulates that the action of regional organizations must in all cases remain consistent with that principle.

934   The modalities of this cooperation must be refined and adapted to the diversity of local situations. The range of procedures that can be employed is wide and varied, but they all have the same advantage: they facilitate the Security Council's work and delegate responsibility to the concerned States and organizations of the region concerned, thereby promoting the democratization of international relations.

935   In this regard the recent adoption by the General Assembly in its resolution 49/57 of 9 December 1994 of the Declaration on the Enhancement of Cooperation between the United Nations and Regional Arrangements or Agencies in the Maintenance of

International Peace and Security encourages regional arrangements and agencies to consider ways and means to promote closer cooperation and coordination with the United Nations, in particular in the fields of preventive diplomacy, peacemaking and post-conflict peace-building, and, where appropriate, peace-keeping.

1. *Cooperation with the Organization of American States*

Relations between the United Nations and OAS have been *936* strengthened since the adoption of resolution 49/5 on 21 October 1994. OAS Secretary-General César Gaviria visited the United Nations soon after assuming office in October 1994, and as recommended in resolution 49/5, a general meeting between representatives of the two Organizations was held in New York on 17 and 18 April 1995. OAS Secretary-General Gaviria and I opened the meeting and signed an agreement of cooperation between our two secretariats. The agreement provides for regular consultation, participation in each other's meetings when matters of common interest are on the agenda and exchange of information. The agreement also foresees appropriate measures to ensure effective cooperation and liaison between the two Organizations.

The general meeting adopted a set of conclusions and rec- *937* ommendations, mainly on economic and social issues. Reflecting new dimensions in relations between the two Organizations, the meeting adopted recommendations in the areas of preventive diplomacy, promotion of democracy and human rights, and humanitarian issues. It was agreed that the frequency of general meetings should be reviewed and that a more flexible format for consultations on cooperation between the two Organizations should be considered. The United Nations Secretariat was represented at the twenty-fifth regular session of the General Assembly of OAS, held in Haiti from 5 to 9 June

1995, at which two resolutions on cooperation between the United Nations and OAS were adopted.

938   The United Nations and OAS have continued their close cooperation in Haiti within the framework of MICIVIH. On 12 July 1995, the United Nations General Assembly adopted resolution 49/27 B, which extended the mandate of MICIVIH to 7 February 1996. The United Nations has also supported the OAS electoral observer mission in Haiti.

2.   *Cooperation with the Organization of African Unity*

939   The United Nations and OAU have continued their efforts to strengthen and broaden their cooperation. In the economic and social fields, they coordinated their activities and initiatives on the preparation and outcome of international conferences, including those on population, social development and women. They also cooperated on the United Nations New Agenda for the Development of Africa in the 1990s and Agenda 21 to harmonize positions and to facilitate the implementation of programmes on which agreement has been reached.

940   Cooperation between the two Organizations in the areas of preventive diplomacy and peacemaking has made progress. I have maintained close contact with the Secretary-General of OAU to exchange views on how best to contribute to the prevention and resolution of conflicts in Africa. In Burundi, Liberia, Rwanda and Sierra Leone, the two Organizations continue to consult and cooperate in the search for peace and reconciliation. In Western Sahara, OAU is cooperating closely with the United Nations in the process leading to the referendum. I have also met and exchanged views with representatives of the countries that are members of the central organ of the OAU mechanism for conflict prevention, management and resolution. On 17 and 18 July 1995, I met at Addis Ababa with the current Chairman of OAU, President Meles Zenawi of Ethiopia, and the

Secretary-General of OAU, Mr. Salim Ahmed Salim, and discussed with them ways and means of strengthening further the cooperation between the two Organizations.

The secretariats of the United Nations system and OAU are scheduled to meet at Addis Ababa from 6 to 10 November 1995 to work out the details of the programme of cooperation between the two Organizations for 1996 and beyond. High on the agenda of the meeting is cooperation in the prevention and management of conflicts and in democratic transition in Africa. *941*

3.   *Cooperation with the Caribbean Community*

Since 1985, the United Nations has been represented at meetings of Heads of Government of CARICOM. In July 1994, the Heads of Government, meeting at the CARICOM Summit, requested their Secretary-General to pursue efforts to strengthen cooperation with the United Nations. In November 1994, I met in Jamaica with a number of CARICOM Heads of Government and with its Secretary-General on the situation in Haiti and on matters of regional cooperation. I expressed my appreciation for the special role the Community continues to play in the restoration of democracy in Haiti and their contribution of military and police personnel to the United Nations Mission in Haiti (UNMIH), as well as their contributions to the joint United Nations/OAS International Civilian Mission in Haiti (MICIVIH). *942*

On 20 December 1994, the General Assembly adopted resolution 49/141 on cooperation between the United Nations and CARICOM. In January 1995, the Community and ECLAC signed a Memorandum of Understanding for Cooperation. This will offer opportunities to advance cooperation between the two organizations in a number of areas of critical importance. The Secretary-General of CARICOM participated in the Intergovernmental Meeting of Experts on South-South Cooperation at United Nations Headquarters from 31 July to 4 August 1995. *943*

4. *Cooperation in the European area*

944 During the past year, the United Nations has continued to strengthen its cooperation with European regional organizations. In December 1994, I attended the summit meeting of OSCE at Budapest. The United Nations and OSCE had previously agreed upon a practical division of labour concerning activities in the European continent and under this framework each Organization has provided support to the efforts of the other. OSCE has assisted the Special Envoy of the Secretary-General in negotiations he has arranged relating to the situation in Abkhazia, Georgia, while the United Nations has given technical advice and guidance to OSCE regarding an OSCE peace-keeping force being organized for possible deployment in Nagorny Karabakh. Cooperation between the two Organizations has also been extended to a variety of other fields, such as election monitoring. Other Europe-based organizations with which the United Nations has had substantive cooperation in the past year include EU, the Council for Europe, NATO, in the context of military operations in the former Yugoslavia, and CIS, with which the United Nations Observer Mission in Georgia (UNOMIG) works closely in Abkhazia.

5. *Cooperation with the Organization of the Islamic Conference*

945 In the context of ongoing efforts to enhance cooperation with regional organizations, the General Assembly in its resolution 49/15 of 15 November 1994 welcomed the decision of the secretariats of the United Nations and OIC to develop mechanisms of cooperation in the political field. Consultations to that end have been initiated between the two secretariats over the past year. The two Organizations have also had increased consultations during the past year with regard to a number of important regional political issues, such as Afghanistan, Tajikistan,

Somalia and Bosnia and Herzegovina. The recent accordance of observer status to OIC in the United Nations–sponsored inter-Tajik talks reflects the increasing interaction between the two Organizations in the political field. The Coordination Meeting of the focal points of the United Nations system and OIC and its specialized institutions, which took place at Geneva in June, also adopted a number of important decisions to consolidate and rationalize cooperation between the two Organizations in nine mutually agreed priority areas of cooperation.

6. *Cooperation with the League of Arab States*

Areas of cooperation between the United Nations and LAS also   *946* continued to be consolidated, pursuant to General Assembly resolution 49/14 of 15 November 1994. The general meeting on cooperation between the representatives of the secretariats of the two bodies, held at Vienna from 19 to 21 July, on the occasion of the fiftieth anniversary of the United Nations and LAS, provided an opportunity for the follow-up of multilateral proposals aimed at strengthening cooperation to promote social and economic development and the exchange of views in the fields of preventive action and mine clearance. The United Nations continued to cooperate with LAS on the question of Somalia. LAS, jointly with OAU and OIC, held a meeting on Somalia at Cairo on 22 and 23 February 1995 at which the United Nations participated as an observer. The participating organizations agreed to continue to undertake joint efforts to assist national reconciliation in Somalia.

G. DISARMAMENT

Since my previous report on the work of the Organization it has   *947* become increasingly evident that the proliferation of weapons of mass destruction and the availability of their basic components constitute a growing threat to international peace and security. The hypothesis that terrorists, with no territory to defend and unafraid of sacrificing themselves, could develop and use weapons of mass destruction is a frightening prospect, which is already affecting the security perceptions of many people throughout the world. Therefore, a coordinated response of the international community to those threats, and to the destabilizing effects caused by the unrestrained flow of conventional weapons, remains a high priority. Within the context of preventing the proliferation of nuclear weapons, the strengthening of the nuclear non-proliferation regime achieved in 1995 by the Review and Extension Conference of the Parties to the Treaty on the Non-Proliferation of Nuclear Weapons is an appropriate answer and should be accompanied as soon as possible by the entry into force of the Convention on the Prohibition of the Development, Production, Stockpiling and Use of Chemical Weapons, as well as by the establishment of a regime for the verification of compliance with the Convention on the Prohibition of the Development, Production and Stockpiling of Bacteriological (Biological) and Toxin Weapons and on Their Destruction.

948   While the Review and Extension Conference of the Non-Proliferation Treaty was a major focus of disarmament efforts in 1995, the international community has undertaken other disarmament initiatives to deal with the destabilizing effects and unconscionable waste of resources caused by the unrestrained flow of conventional weapons. The progress achieved, as far as the review process of the Convention on Prohibition or Restrictions on the Use of Certain Conventional Weapons Which May Be Deemed to Be Excessively Injurious or to Have Indiscriminate Effects is concerned, in assuring the full protection of civilians from the indiscriminate effects of anti-personnel landmines and working towards their eventual elimination constitutes a step in the right direction. Furthermore, transparency measures, such as the Register of Conventional Arms, must be strengthened, and confidence-building and disarmament initiatives at the regional level should be developed further, in particular with reference to illicit traffic in light conventional weapons.

The Nuclear Non-Proliferation Treaty now has 178 States *949* parties, commanding virtually universal adherence. The indefinite extension of the Treaty, decided upon at the 1995 Review and Extension Conference, as well as the other commitments made by the States parties reflected in the documents of the Conference, have strengthened the nuclear non-proliferation regime and will make a substantial contribution to the maintenance of international peace and security. I expressed gratification at the success of the Conference and recommended that the States parties continue to work in a spirit of cooperation and pursue the elimination of nuclear weapons as the ultimate goal of the non-proliferation process.

There have been advances in other areas of nuclear disarm- *950* ament. The negotiations on a comprehensive test-ban treaty have made progress at the Conference on Disarmament at Geneva and strengthened determination to resolve technical issues could bring the negotiations to a successful conclusion no later than 1996. The negotiating mandate was agreed upon at the Conference on Disarmament on a treaty banning the production of fissile material and this should enable the Conference to begin the negotiations expeditiously and bring them to an early and successful conclusion. Other encouraging steps are Security Council resolution 984 (1995) and the declarations by the nuclear-weapon States concerning both negative and positive security assurances. Proposals aimed at transforming these unilateral declarations into a legally binding treaty obligation would contribute considerably to further progress in this area.

The general strengthening of the nuclear non-proliferation *951* regime is matched and reinforced by the remarkable results achieved so far by the United States of America, the Russian Federation and the other European countries in post-cold-war security arrangements. The elimination of intermediate-range nuclear forces in Europe under the Treaty between the United States of America and the Union of Soviet Socialist Republics on the Elimination of Their Intermediate-Range and Shorter-Range Missiles, the reduction of nuclear strategic warheads in operational deployment resulting from the START process, the continuing successful implementation of the Treaty on Conventional Armed Forces in Europe and the ongoing security dialogue within the OSCE framework form the basis of a cooperative security system that in some measure could transcend the narrow limits of the European region. In Europe, the newly emerging cooperative security system is the product of negotiations based on consensus and cooperation. Significant initiatives for security dialogues are also being promoted in Asia, in Africa and in Latin America. Further enhancement of those initiatives would be an important step towards the strengthening of international peace and security at the regional level.

952   While progress in the dismantlement of nuclear weapons is encouraged, concerns about the safety and security of fissile material have increased. The smuggling of nuclear material is no longer only a fear but a frightening reality. Stronger global and national measures are needed to deal with illicit trafficking and to guarantee the secure disposal and storage of such material. Particularly important is universal recognition that International Atomic Energy Agency (IAEA) safeguards are an integral part of the international non-proliferation regime and that the Agency plays an indispensable role in ensuring the implementation of the Treaty on the Non-Proliferation of Nuclear Weapons.

953   The Treaty for the Prohibition of Nuclear Weapons in Latin America and the Caribbean (Treaty of Tlatelolco) and the

South Pacific Nuclear Free Zone Treaty (Treaty of Rarotonga) are essential building blocks to progress towards nuclear-free regions elsewhere in the world, in particular in the Middle East and Asia, which would include in their scope all weapons of mass destruction. There has also been progress on the treaty establishing a nuclear-weapon-free zone in Africa.

There has been a steady increase in the number of ratifica- 954 tions of the Convention on the Prohibition of the Development, Production, Stockpiling and Use of Chemical Weapons, which has now reached 27 States parties. In discharging my responsibility as depositary to the Convention, I have written to all Member States urging ratification and entry into force of the Convention at the earliest possible date. In connection with the Convention on Biological Weapons, efforts of States parties are under way to strengthen the Convention by developing a legally binding verification protocol. The frightful consequences for humankind of biological warfare, or terrorism, must be avoided at all costs.

Measures to prevent proliferation of weapons should be 955 fashioned to avoid any obstruction to the development process of countries. Developing countries need unimpeded access to technology and agreement is needed on appropriate controls concerning technology transfers, including transparency measures, that would be universal and non-discriminatory in nature.

The urgent problem of the proliferation of conventional 956 weapons also demands the continuing attention of the international community. Unrestrained and illegal arms transfers have resulted in suffering and misery for hundreds of thousands of people particularly in the developing world. At the global level continued support by Member States for the Register of Conventional Arms is essential. Reports to the Register indicate a degree of openness and transparency with regard to legitimate arms transfers for defensive purposes. Such openness will promote confidence and encourage responsible conduct in the transfer of major conventional weapon systems. Initiatives and ideas from regions and subregions, in particular Africa, Asia and Latin America, can enhance the global Register with complementary confidence- and security-building measures.

957   At the regional and subregional level, in particular in the developing world, direct action is needed to deal with the flourishing illicit traffic in light weapons, which is destabilizing the security of a number of countries. With the support of seven Member States in the Sahara-Sahel region, I dispatched an advisory mission with a view to assisting those States in their efforts to combat and stem the illicit flow of light weapons within and across their borders. More resources must be invested if there is to be any prospect of success.

H. POST-CONFLICT PEACE-BUILDING

Strategies

958 An International Colloquium on Post-Conflict Reconstruction Strategies was convened on 23 and 24 June at the Austrian Centre for Peace and Conflict Resolution at Stadt Schlaining, Austria. It was attended by 58 participants from United Nations political, humanitarian and development entities, specialized agencies, the Bretton Woods institutions, donor countries and nongovernmental organizations as well as representatives from wartorn societies. The meeting was organized by the Department for Development Support and Management Services, in cooperation with the Austrian Centre, and supported by the Government of Austria as a contribution to the definition of the role of the United Nations in the next half century as part of the fiftieth anniversary activities. The Department for Development Support and Management Services contributed a paper setting out a strategic programme for reconstruction and development.

The idea for the meeting stemmed from the Supplement to *959* the Secretary-General's "An Agenda for Peace" (A/50/60-S/1995/1), which stresses the need for integrated action between United Nations organizations, the parties to the conflict and other institutions prepared to assist in the reconstruction of a country; its purpose was to identify the practical and institutional issues that must be addressed to bring this concept to reality.

The main topic of post-conflict reconstruction was ad- *960* dressed under four headings: strategic issues, needs and capabilities, an integrated post-conflict reconstruction framework and mobilization of resources. Because of the interrelationship between these four topics, the themes recurred throughout the deliberations and there was considerable cross-fertilization of ideas. The meeting was an example of the coming together of various organizations, within and outside the United Nations system, all with a common interest in a topic that is of increasing concern to the international community. It is hoped that the ideas and recommendations presented in the report will serve as a basis for a clear definition of the role of the United Nations in post-conflict reconstruction, and for establishing arrangements that will ensure a swift, effective and integrated response to such situations by the United Nations system.

Issues falling within the four categories of post-conflict *961* peace-building discussed at the Colloquium have been addressed elsewhere in this report; here I will focus on two specific concerns: electoral assistance and mine clearance.

Electoral assistance

In the period from July 1994 to 10 August 1995, the United Na- *962* tions received 19 new requests for electoral assistance, from Armenia, Azerbaijan, Bangladesh, Benin, Chad, the Congo, Côte d'Ivoire, Fiji, Gabon, the Gambia, Guinea, Haiti, Kyrgyzstan,

Namibia, the Niger, Sao Tome and Principe, the former Yugoslav Republic of Macedonia, Uganda and the United Republic
of Tanzania. In the case of the Congo, assistance could not be
provided owing to lack of lead time. In addition to these new
requests, assistance was also provided in 12 cases, to Brazil,
El Salvador, Equatorial Guinea, Honduras, Lesotho, Liberia,
Malawi, Mexico, Mozambique, the Netherlands Antilles, Sierra
Leone and MINURSO, in response to requests received prior to
July 1994 (see fig. 19).

963   Since July 1994, 30 States and United Nations missions
have received or will soon receive some form of electoral assistance from the United Nations system. The type of electoral assistance provided has varied according to the requests received
and the resources available. Following the guidelines provided
to Member States (see A/49/675 and Corr.1, annex III), verifi-

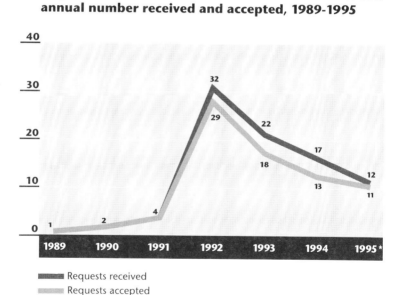

FIGURE 19

**Requests from Member States for electoral assistance:
annual number received and accepted, 1989-1995**

Requests received
Requests accepted
* As at 1 July 1995

cation of electoral processes was conducted in Mozambique and plans for a verification mission in Liberia are currently on hold. The coordination and support approach was used in the cases of Armenia and Benin, and follow-up and report/observation was used in Guinea, Kyrgyzstan, the former Yugoslav Republic of Macedonia and Sao Tome and Principe. Technical assistance, the most frequently provided form of electoral assistance, was given to Brazil, El Salvador, Equatorial Guinea, Haiti, Honduras, Liberia, Malawi, Mexico, Mozambique, Namibia, the Niger, Sierra Leone and Uganda. A total of 11 needs assessment missions were also conducted during this period.

Since the creation of the Electoral Assistance Division in *964* 1992, the United Nations has been involved in the electoral processes of 61 Member States and some States have requested electoral assistance more than once. United Nations electoral assistance this past year in Mozambique and Armenia illustrates the process in action.

In Mozambique, the United Nations provided technical *965* assistance and a verification mission for the first multi-party elections, held in October 1994. In accordance with the terms of the General Peace Agreement signed at Rome on 4 October 1992, ONUMOZ, through its electoral component, monitored the conduct of the entire electoral process. The Electoral Division of ONUMOZ fielded 148 electoral officers throughout the country to monitor voter registration, civic education, political campaigns, political party access to as well as impartiality of the media, polling, vote counting and tabulation of the vote at provincial counting centres. On the election days ONUMOZ deployed 2,300 international observers.

The United Nations also provided technical assistance to *966* Mozambique through a UNDP project implemented by the Department for Development Support and Management Services. The project coordinated international financial and material support and provided technical assistance throughout the entire process in the areas of organization, training, civic education, jurisprudence, social communication and financial management. This assistance entailed management, coordination and monitoring of a $64.5 million budget made up of contributions from 17 countries and international institutions. Technical assistance included the training of 2,600 electoral officers at the national, provincial and district levels, 8,000 census agents, 1,600 civic education agents and 52,000 polling officers. In addition to a 12-person UNDP advisory team to the National Election Commission, 3 to 5 United Nations Volunteers were assigned to each of the 11 electoral constituencies and worked closely with the provincial and district electoral authorities.

967   In addition to the ONUMOZ electoral verification mandate, a United Nations trust fund for assistance to registered political parties was established to assist all political parties not signatories to the General Peace Agreement to prepare for the elections. The electoral component of ONUMOZ also designed a programme to enhance national observation. The programme provided training, transportation and subsidies for nearly 35,000 party agents to monitor the elections. A parallel programme funded by the United Nations trust fund provided computer training to 78 representatives from all political parties to enable them to monitor the processing of the vote at the provincial and national levels.

968   Armenia requested electoral assistance from the United Nations in January 1995 in connection with the elections to the National Assembly to be held in July 1995. In February, an officer from the Electoral Assistance Division conducted a needs assessment mission and returned in April to establish a joint operation coordinating unit together with a representative of OSCE. The purpose of the joint operation was to coordinate and

support the activities of the international observers. Members of the joint operation were stationed in three regional offices for a period of six weeks in order to follow the pre-election process, including the registration of candidates, the electoral campaign, and poll preparations. On election day, 5 July, the joint operation deployed over 90 observers throughout the country to observe the conduct of the elections. Observers visited more than 300 precinct electoral committees, starting from the opening of the polls to the counting of votes at the precinct level. The group of observers represented 18 Governments and several governmental and non-governmental organizations.

Mine clearance

The ever-growing problem of uncleared land-mines continues to pose a humanitarian crisis of enormous proportions, devastating vast amounts of territory, possibly for decades. Despite the increased efforts of the international community, more than 20 times more mines are being laid than removed. Within the United Nations system, the Department of Humanitarian Affairs has intensified its activities as focal point for the coordination of land-mine assistance programmes. Since its establishment in early 1992, the Department has been involved in the formulation and implementation of mine-assistance programmes. Pursuant to General Assembly resolutions 48/7 of 19 October 1993 and 49/215 of 23 December 1994, the Department has been convening interdepartmental/inter-agency consultations on land-mine policy to examine all aspects of United Nations involvement in mine-related activities and to develop standard United Nations policy concerning the institutional aspects that need to be addressed in an integrated United Nations land-mine operation. The United Nations approach has been to focus on the creation of a national indigenous mine-clearance capacity, including appropriate arrangements to enable continuity of national

969

mine-clearance efforts, as normalization of conditions in a country progresses.

970   During the past year, the United Nations engaged in the implementation and/or development of demining activities in nine countries. Programmes differ in structure, size and arrangements for funding and implementation.

971   Afghanistan is the most mature of the United Nations programmes, having been in operation for six years. There are currently almost 3,000 deminers working in the field. Over the past five years, the Programme has cleared a total of 54 square kilometres of high-priority area and destroyed over 110,000 mines and 215,000 unexploded devices. Approximately 2.5 million people received mine-awareness briefings.

972   Angola is probably the most mine-affected country in the world and, together with the implementation of the peace-keeping operation, a mine-action programme has been launched in cooperation between the United Nations, the parties to the Lusaka Protocol and non-governmental organizations. The Central Mine Action Office has been established as part of the Humanitarian Assistance Coordination Unit in Angola and is mandated to create an indigenous mine-clearance capacity. The Office is responsible for the implementation of the mine-action plan and coordinates all mine-related activities. UNAVEM III, in conjunction with the Office, is in the process of establishing a mine-clearance training school, which will form the core of the Angolan mine-action programme.

973   In Cambodia, the Cambodian Mine Action Centre (a governmental entity with technical advice provided through a UNDP project) has been coordinating all clearance activities. Over the past year, the Centre's 1,556 staff have continued to survey, mark and clear minefields, and teach mine awareness. Since the commencement of operations, 16,436,971 square

metres of land have been cleared, with 423,708 unexploded devices and 61,787 mines destroyed.

In June 1995, a United Nations demining expert undertook 974 a mission to Chad on behalf of the Department of Humanitarian Affairs to evaluate the land-mine problem in the Tibesti region.

Mine-clearance activities in Mozambique involve both the 975 United Nations own programme, the accelerated demining programme, and non-governmental organizations and companies funded by the United Nations or by donors. The accelerated demining programme consists of 500 Mozambican deminers who were trained, equipped and deployed by the United Nations.

The use of mines in the conflict in Abkhazia, Georgia, is 976 extensive. The Department of Humanitarian Affairs has sent an assessment mission to the area and has suggested activities to reduce the number of land-mine accidents. Approval from the Abkhaz authorities is required before a programme can be started.

The problem of land-mines and unexploded ordnance in 977 Rwanda has resulted in large numbers of accidents. Both the Department of Peace-keeping Operations and the Department of Humanitarian Affairs have assessed the situation and a plan has been developed. Action is of course dependent upon the approval of the Government.

In Somalia, a limited demining programme implemented 978 by local Somali entities worked well until the security situation prevented follow-up to clearance activities in the field.

In Yemen, the United Nations is providing expert technical 979 assistance to the Government on mine-clearance and mapping methods.

The continuing conflict in the former Yugoslavia has pre- 980 vented the development of a humanitarian demining programme. However, United Nations peace-keeping forces and other United Nations agencies have engaged in mine-clearance activities as part of their attempts to carry out their mandates.

981   At Headquarters, the Department of Humanitarian Affairs, pursuant to General Assembly resolution 49/215, established the Mine Clearance and Policy Unit to further strengthen support functions to demining operations. To facilitate the planning, implementation and support of mine-clearance programmes and policies, the Unit is developing a database containing information about the worldwide land-mine situation. Country-specific data, as well as general programme and financial data, are maintained in the database, which serves as a central repository of information for Member States, United Nations departments and agencies, and other interested parties.

982   On 30 November 1994, I established a voluntary trust fund for assistance in mine clearance. The fund's purpose is to provide special resources for mine-clearance programmes, including mine-awareness training and surveys, and to contract mine-clearance activities in situations where other funding is not immediately available. Some examples of the types of activities that could be funded from the trust fund include, but are not limited to, assessment missions, provision of seed money, emergency mine clearance, projects where other sources of funding are not readily available, consciousness-raising and enhancing Headquarters support for mine-clearance programmes in the field, including through the improvement of the central land-mine database.

983   In accordance with the recommendations contained in the Secretary-General's report on assistance in mine clearance (A/49/357 and Add.1), the Mine Clearance and Policy Unit began the process of creating a United Nations demining stand-by capacity in order to expedite the provision of expert personnel, specialized equipment and facilities to United Nations mine-action programmes. These in-kind contributions have been a

vital component of United Nations mine-action programmes. The establishment of a stand-by capacity is intended to institutionalize this support.

From 5 to 7 July 1995, I convened an international meeting *984* on mine clearance at the Palais des Nations at Geneva. The objective of the meeting was to enhance international awareness of the land-mine problem in all its dimensions, to seek further political and financial support for United Nations mine-action activities and to increase international cooperation in this field. It consisted of three elements: a high-level segment devoted to statements by Governments and organizations, which also provided the opportunity to announce pledges to the voluntary trust fund for assistance in mine clearance and the United Nations demining stand-by capacity; nine panels of experts that discussed various aspects of the land-mine problem; and an exhibition focusing on the impact of land-mines on affected populations and international efforts to address the problem.

The international meeting was attended by represen- *985* tatives of 97 Governments and more than 60 organizations, bringing together 800 participants. Contributions in the amount of $22 million were announced towards the voluntary trust fund and 23 countries indicated contributions to the United Nations stand-by capacity totalling $7 million.

All delegations referred to the magnitude of the global *986* land-mine crisis, which continues to deteriorate, and emphasized the need for urgent and effective measures to reverse the trend. Many delegations and organizations called for a total ban on land-mines; most delegations stressed the need to strengthen the provisions of the Convention on Prohibition or Restrictions on the Use of Certain Conventional Weapons Which May Be Deemed to Be Excessively Injurious or to Have Indiscriminate Effects.

There are still only 49 States parties to the Convention and *987* its protocols, which include the protocol placing prohibitions and restrictions on the use of land-mines. The Convention needs to be strengthened to make its provisions applicable to both internal and international conflicts. It is in internal conflicts that the indiscriminate use of mines has caused the most suffering and misery to civilian populations. The 1995 Review Conference provides an opportunity to strengthen the Convention and its land-mine protocol. Looking at the magnitude of the problem, States parties should seriously consider a total ban on anti-personnel land-mines.

988   A revitalized Advisory Board on Disarmament Matters is developing ideas for the better integration of disarmament-related security measures with development in countries emerging from inter- or intra-State conflict. The Board is preparing for the Secretary-General's review a study entitled "Some thoughts on the development of the disarmament agenda at the end of the century", which should be relevant to the proposed fourth special session of the General Assembly devoted to disarmament.

V. Conclusion

F ROM THE DEEP-ROOTED and far-reaching United Nations 989
work for economic, social and humanitarian progress to
the immediate and often urgent efforts to prevent, contain and resolve conflicts, what emerges from the pages of this
report is an image of a multifaceted and ever-evolving organization — an organization responding flexibly to global change
and to the changing needs of the international community.

There are signs that the massive educational effort under 990
way at all levels of national and international society in this
fiftieth anniversary year is helping to create a welcome realism
about the role of the United Nations in world affairs today, as
well as a renewed sense of commitment to fulfil the original
promise set down in the Charter 50 years ago.

Major aspects of this landmark year are still to come, in- 991
cluding the Special Commemorative Meeting of the General
Assembly, to be held at Headquarters from 22 to 24 October
1995, and the commemoration in London in January 1996 of
the first session of the General Assembly. None the less, it is
already evident that this anniversary has created a spirit and a
momentum that go well beyond the commemoration and cele-
bration expected at such a point in time. Virtually every dimension of the United Nations has been energized. New realities
are being used as the basis for reassessment and redesign. Successes are being built upon. A new spirit of cooperation at every
level and on virtually every issue is within the grasp of a wider
contingent of committed people than ever before.

It is vital, therefore, that the spirit of the fiftieth anniver- 992
sary be carried forward in all these respects. Most fundamentally, it will be important to continue the major efforts launched

this year with the objective of enabling the United Nations as an institution to become more intellectually creative, more financially stable, more managerially effective and more responsive to all sectors of society.

993   The fiftieth year has also generated criticism of the Organization, and this is serving to make the United Nations healthier and stronger. Shortcomings of the Organization itself, inadequate mandates, insufficient financial and material resources, the failure of Member States to fulfil their obligations or take on new responsibilities — all have, on occasion, been catalysts for criticism. However, the ultimate source of today's criticism can be found in the impact of globalization on the Organization and its Member States: as the United Nations is being asked to take on more duties and expand its activities, it is to be expected that the level of criticism should intensify. At the same time, globalization can work against the will to increase involvement, feeding fear and isolationism; criticisms born of these sentiments can create dangerous misperceptions.

994   Healthy criticism is an indispensable form of participation in and support for the United Nations in its effort to revitalize the international system. This report is itself an effort at transparency, revealing both the strengths and the weaknesses of the Organization to the widest possible audience. The continuing calls for reform, and the reforms already enacted and under way, testify to the recognition by far more people than ever before that the United Nations is a truly indispensable element in world affairs and that if it did not now exist, it would be impossible to create it under present conditions. Thus the legacy of 1945 must be cherished and carried forward. In parallel, techniques that have succeeded must be transformed to meet the challenges of a new era.

995   Reflection and reform are not new to this Organization. As envisioned by the founders, the United Nations has evolved

over time and adapted to new conditions, all the while in pursuit of a better life for all individuals and a better world for humanity as a whole. The fiftieth anniversary year, however, by arriving at such a critical juncture in the history of international relations, offers an unprecedented opportunity for change. As Secretary-General, I have from the outset been deeply committed to and concerned with reform. Looking back over the past three and a half years of effort for change and the substantial managerial steps taken during the period covered by this report, I believe that a continuing need exists for further, substantial reforms in the period ahead.

The communiqué issued by the Heads of State and Gov- *996* ernment of seven major industrialized nations and the President of the European Commission following their twenty-first annual economic summit meeting at Halifax provided suggestions for enhancing the effectiveness and coherence of the United Nations system in the economic, social and environmental fields and in the humanitarian area. The Halifax participants expressed their intention to utilize the gathering of Heads of State and Government in New York from 22 to 24 October 1995 for the observance of the fiftieth anniversary of the United Nations as an occasion to advance a consensus on ways to help the United Nations system to face the challenges of the next century.

Throughout this fiftieth anniversary year, serious consid- *997* eration has been given to the future role and responsibilities of the United Nations by conferences, workshops and study programmes held at every level and in every part of the world. Two independent commissions have issued reports: "The United Nations in Its Second Half-Century", produced by an independent working group under the co-chairmanship of Mr. Richard von Weizsäcker and Mr. Moeen Qureshi, sponsored at my request by the Ford Foundation and facilitated by Yale University; and "Our Global Neighbourhood", produced by the Commission on Global Governance under the co-chairmanship of Mr. Ingvar Carlsson and Mr. Shridath Ramphal. The South Center also has been active in reviewing various aspects of reform.

998   These projects and commitments deserve appreciation and serious consideration by the international community. Discussions have taken place regarding the establishment of an open-ended high-level working group of the General Assembly that would undertake a thorough review of all relevant United Nations materials, Member States' submissions and independent studies and reports relating to the revitalization, strengthening and reform of the United Nations system.

999   The days, weeks and months covered in this report have been filled with discouraging developments. But from a larger, longer-term point of view, there are many signs that progress is being made, giving cause for confidence that, over time, success is entirely possible. Never before have so many courageous and committed people been involved in world betterment. Never before have nations recognized so clearly that their fate is bound up with each other. And never before has it been so undeniable that mutually beneficial international institutions of co-operation — with the United Nations foremost among them — are a vital global necessity.

1000   It is therefore imperative to remain focused on the reality of movement towards long-term achievement and not to permit dismay over immediate difficulties to weaken the positive momentum that has been achieved.

1001   There are three immediate problems, however, that must concern us deeply, for if they are not effectively addressed they can irreparably damage the United Nations as a mechanism for progress.

1002   First, the safety and integrity of United Nations personnel in the field must be respected. When lightly armed peace-keepers or unarmed aid workers on a humanitarian mission are threatened, taken hostage, harmed or even killed, the world must act to prevent such intolerable behaviour. The credibility of all United Nations peace operations is at stake; to preserve it, personnel must be protected as they carry out the duties the international community has sent them to accomplish.

Secondly, the financial situation of the Organization must *1003* be placed on an adequate and sustainable footing. Calls for ever-greater United Nations effectiveness under conditions of financial penury make no sense. It is as though the town fire department were being dispatched to put out fires raging in several places at once while a collection was being taken to raise money for the fire-fighting equipment. The deterioration of the Organization's financial position must be reversed.

And, lastly, funds for development are drying up. This is a *1004* consequence of the end of the cold-war contest, of the competing demands of peace-keeping and development for scarce resources, and of donor fatigue over the time and difficulty of creating progress on the ground. The willingness to spend money to try to contain conflicts around the world, while necessary and admirable, is not enough. Unless development is funded as well, the world can expect only the continuation of cycles marked by the alternation of terrible strife, uneasy stand-off and strife once again. To break this downward spiral, sustainable human development must be instituted everywhere. A new vision of development, and a universal commitment to it, are indispensable for the world progress all peoples seek.

During the past year we have seen far too many innocent *1005* civilians, especially women and children, losing their lives or being condemned to carry on under appalling conditions. We continue to witness scenes of refugees deprived of their most basic rights and struggling desperately to survive. And hundreds of millions of people live in poverty so dire as to render them incapable of taking effective action to improve their own condition. Thus the existence of a true international community has yet to be demonstrated. Nothing could do more to bring such an instrument of human solidarity into being than a commitment undertaken now to ensure that all the poor countries of the world are set firmly on the path of development as we enter the next century. Such an achievement would bring an end to degradation and despair for a huge proportion of our fellow human beings and would represent one of history's most dramatic chapters of progress.

1006   We have before us an opportunity to combine the ongoing, incremental process of reform with a comprehensive vision of the future. The legacy of the founders at this half-century mark should be our inspiration as we step forward with pride to meet this challenge. Together we can bring the world of the Charter to the world of today.

United Nations publications
of related interest

The following UN publications may be obtained from the
addresses indicated below, or at your local distributor:

An Agenda for Peace
Second edition, 1995
By Boutros Boutros-Ghali,
Secretary-General of the United Nations
E.95.I.15 92-1-100555-8 155 pp. $7.50

An Agenda for Development
By Boutros Boutros-Ghali,
Secretary-General of the United Nations
E.95.I.16 92-1-100556-6 132 pp. $7.50

New Dimensions of Arms Regulation and Disarmament
in the Post–Cold War Era
By Boutros Boutros-Ghali,
Secretary-General of the United Nations
E.93.IX.8 92-1-142192-6 53 pp. $9.95

Basic Facts About the United Nations
E.95.I.31 92-1-100870-1 $7.50 forthcoming

World's Women 1995: Trends and Statistics
Second Edition
E.95.XVII.2 92-1-161372-8 $15.95

Women: Looking Beyond 2000
E.95.I.40 92-1-100592-2 180 pp. $14.95

Demographic Yearbook, Vol. 44
B.94.XIII.1 92-1-051083-6 1992 823 pp. $125.00

Statistical Yearbook, 39th Edition
B.94.XVII.1 H 92-1-061159-4 1992/93 1,174 pp. $110.00

World Economic and Social Survey 1995
E.95.II.C.1 92-1-109130-6 245 pp. $55.00

World Investment Report 1995—Transnational Corporations
and Competitiveness
E.95.II.A.9 92-1-104450-2 $45.00

Yearbook of the United Nations, Vol. 47
E.94.I.1 0-7923-3077-3 1993 1,428 pp. $150.00

(*continued*)

United Nations publications
of related interest
(*continued*)

The United Nations Blue Books Series

The United Nations and Apartheid, 1948-1994
E.95.I.7 92-1-100546-9 565 pp. $29.95

The United Nations and Cambodia, 1991-1995
E.95.I.9 92-1-100548-5 352 pp. $29.95

The United Nations and Nuclear Non-Proliferation
E.95.I.17 92-1-100557-4 199 pp. $29.95

The United Nations and El Salvador, 1990-1995
E.95.I.12 92-1-100552-3 611 pp. $29.95

The United Nations and Mozambique, 1992-1995
E.95.I.20 92-1-100559-0 321 pp. $29.95

The United Nations and the Advancement of Women, 1945-1995
E.95.I.29 92-1-100567-1 689 pp. $29.95

The United Nations and Human Rights, 1945-1995
E.95.I.21 92-1-100560-4 536 pp. $29.95

United Nations Publications
2 United Nations Plaza,
Room DC2-853
New York, NY 10017
United States of America
Tel.: (212) 963-8302;
      1 (800) 253-9646
Fax: (212) 963-3489

United Nations Publications
Sales Office and Bookshop
CH-1211 Geneva 10
Switzerland
Tel.: 41 (22) 917-26-13;
      41 (22) 917-26-14
Fax: 41 (22) 917-00-27

Printed on recycled paper
by the United Nations Reproduction Section, New York